y^{O}u^n g
Exceptional
children

Monograph Series No. 13

Gathering Information to Make Informed Decisions: Contemporary Perspectives About Assessment in Early Intervention and Early Childhood Special Education

**THE DIVISION FOR EARLY CHILDHOOD
OF THE COUNCIL FOR EXCEPTIONAL CHILDREN**

Mary E. McLean and **Patricia A. Snyder**
Co-Editors

Disclaimer

The opinions and information contained in the articles in this publication are those of the authors of the respective articles and not necessarily those of the editors or co-editors of the *Young Exceptional Children (YEC)* Monograph Series or the Division for Early Childhood (DEC). Accordingly, the Division for Early Childhood assumes no liability or risk that may be incurred as a consequence, directly or indirectly, or the use and application of any of the contents of this publication.

The DEC does not perform due diligence on advertisers, exhibitors, or their products or services, and cannot endorse or guarantee that their offerings are suitable or accurate.

Division for Early Childhood (DEC) Executive Board

ISSN 1096-2506 • ISBN- 978-0-9819327-6-7

Printed in the United States of America

Published and Distributed by:

27 Fort Missoula Road, Suite 2
Missoula, MT 59804
(406) 543-0872
FAX (406) 543-0887
www.dec-sped.org

features

A Message From the Editors

Ten years ago, the fourth issue of the *Young Exceptional Children* monograph series, edited by Michaelene Ostrosky and Eva Horn, was devoted to assessment practices. Articles appearing in that monograph were based on the Division for Early Childhood (DEC) recommended assessment practices available at that time (Neisworth & Bagnato, 2000). This 13th issue of the *Young Exceptional Children* monograph series revisits assessment with a focus on contemporary practices, current innovations, and promising approaches in assessment and assessment practices.

Much has happened in the past ten years. The DEC recommended practices in assessment were updated in 2005, providing an assessment glossary and resources related to the recommended assessment practices (Neisworth & Bagnato, 2005). The National Research Council convened a national committee to examine assessment practices in early childhood and to make recommendations on the why, what, and how of early childhood assessment (National Research Council, 2008). Assessment for the purpose of accountability or measuring the progress of children toward state or federal early learning standards, foundations, or outcomes has been mandated for some populations of young children and might be on the horizon for others. At the same time, the importance of assessment for informing decisions about the type and intensity of intervention provided for young children has been recognized as response-to-intervention frameworks are being applied in early childhood. Additionally, there has been growing emphasis on authentic and culturally responsive assessment practices as well as the use of contemporary measurement approaches to inform the development and validation of assessment instruments. The need is great for assessment instruments and processes that yield consistent and meaningful information useful for informing the decisions that practitioners, families, policymakers, and researchers need to make about child development, learning, and progress children are making toward desired outcomes.

In the midst of these and other changes, the traditional purposes of assessment in early intervention/early childhood special education are still relevant: child find, screening, eligibility determination, program planning, progress monitoring, and program evaluation. Innovations are occurring, however, in the ways we gather information to make decisions related to each of these purposes. As demand for high quality assessment data for each assessment purpose has increased, we have been challenged to ensure that recommended assessment practices, particularly those related to authenticity and ecological validity, remain the guideposts for development and innovation.

The authors of the articles in this monograph and others in our field are working diligently to ensure that contemporary assessment practices focus on gathering information about young children's development, behavior, and learning in familiar environments or activities with familiar adults or peers rather than in adult-directed, highly structured, and decontextualized situations. In the current accountability and outcome-focused climate, assessment and assessment practices must be carefully evaluated to avoid duplicative or "over" assessment of young children and unintended or negative consequences for children, practitioners, and programs. Moreover, given that practitioners are working with children and families who are increasingly diverse, culturally responsive assessment practices are essential.

Dunst, Trivette, and Hill describe an evidence-informed approach for improving Child Find practices through tailored outreach to primary referral sources. Tailoring involves methods and procedures for creating communication channels that are individualized to reach and influence specific audiences. The authors describe key elements of effective outreach, and they offer step-by-step guidelines for improving tailored outreach activities associated with each of the key elements. A checklist is included in the appendix for use by those responsible for planning and implementing tailored outreach to primary referral sources. The checklist specifies activities the literature has suggested are most likely to result in effective Child Find.

Clifford and colleagues consider historical and current recommended assessment practices related to developmental screening. They provide useful information for making decisions about the selection of developmental screening tools and examples of ways practitioners can incorporate screening into their existing programs or practices. Strategies for including parents meaningfully in screening activities in a culturally responsive manner are offered. The recommendations related to key components of effective screening are important for informing current and future screening practices.

McWilliam and colleagues describe interviewing as a method of assessment for the purpose of identifying IFSP outcomes or IEP goals through the use of the *Routines-Based Interview* (RBI). The authors provide guidance for professionals about how to implement a RBI and how to involve families in identifying and prioritizing functional child or family outcomes, goals, and strategies for the IFSP or IEP. The reader will find information relative to interviewing skills and strategies that will be helpful in gathering authentic assessment information with families.

Campbell describes the use of an interview for the purpose of gathering information to assist in embedding instruction in home or community activities or routines. The *Assessment of Family Activities and Routines* was developed for the purpose of gathering information about family activities or routines into which learning opportunities and strategies can be embedded. This assessment is focused on the development and implementation of outcomes for the IFSP, and includes processes that not only assist in identifying child outcomes, but also result in the design of embedded learning opportunities in which caregivers will be involved.

The rationale for using informed opinion (e.g., clinical judgment) and its importance in authentic assessment are highlighted by Neisworth and Bagnato. These authors provide a "pocket guide" to support using good judgment in assessment. They define informed opinion, describe the legislative and evidence base for its use, specify five essential features for the valid use of informed opinions, and provide information about instruments that can be used to structure and record informed opinions. Guidelines provided in this article related to the use of informed opinion should help advance its use as part of authentic assessment practices.

Edelman describes the use of digital video technology to enhance authentic assessment practices. Recent and continuing advancements in technology provide practitioners and families access to affordable and high quality equipment that can be used to capture, edit, store, and share images of young children in everyday learning activities. This documentation can be an important source of information for use in authentic assessment. Edelman describes two projects in California and Colorado that are using digital video as part of authentic assessment practices. He shares the perspectives of practitioners and administrators who have been involved in these projects about the utility and benefits associated with using digital video. Valuable lessons learned from these two projects are summarized and guidance is offered for how to capture, edit, and store digital video.

Santos and colleagues emphasize the importance of using evidence-based practices in the assessment of social-emotional development to inform quality teaching. The authors provide guidance for the selection of social-emotional assessment tools to be used in conjunction with strategies for gathering information from and sharing information with families. The authors assist the reader in bringing together the information needed to inform intentional instruction in social-emotional development.

Duran, Cheatham, and Santos provide guidance for the assessment of young children who are dual language learners. Through eight recommendations and accompanying vignettes, the authors provide guidance on evidence-based assessment strategies for this growing population of young children. The reader will find step-by-step guidance and resources for planning and implementing recommended assessment practices for children whose home language is not English.

The use of Goal Attainment Scaling (GAS) for the purpose of monitoring the progress of children toward their individualized priority learning goals or objectives is described by Dinnebeil, Spino, and McInerney. These authors define GAS and specify six steps that teams should use to apply this technique. They illustrate how the six steps are used by two teams to monitor the progress of two children who have individualized education programs and are served by an itinerant early childhood special educator. Worksheets are provided to help others use GAS as described in the article.

Hebbeler and colleagues describe key issues in assessment for accountability purposes. They identify special considerations for gathering and using assessment data to inform accountability decisions. Against this backdrop, they consider major decisions that stakeholders make when selecting assessment tools for use in accountability systems. They offer a vision for the next generation of assessment tools that might be used in accountability systems and suggest several important design features for the field to consider.

Readers of *Young Exceptional Children* know to expect a quality contribution from Camille Catlett as a culminating source of information for practitioners. The 13th YEC monograph continues this tradition. Camille has provided "Resources within Reason" devoted to assessment, which provides information about how to access position statements, books, videotapes and web resources that will support the gathering and use of information to improve assessment practices.

Each article included in the 13th *Young Exceptional Children* monograph highlights a practice or set of practices that align with the DEC recommended practices for assessment (Neisworth & Bagnato, 2005) and are consistent with recommendations from the National Research Council Committee on Developmental Outcomes and Assessments for Young Children (National Research Council, 2008). Information and recommendations included in each article are likely to be immediately useful for practitioners, families, and programs. The articles included in this monograph demonstrate the value of thoughtfully and systematically approaching assessment and assessment practices so that information gathered is useful for those who need to make informed decisions for the benefit of young children and their families.

Co-Editors: Mary E. McLean
               Patricia A. Snyder

References

National Research Council. (2008). *Early childhood assessment: Why, what and how.* Committee on Developmental Outcomes and Assessments for Young Children, C. E. Snow & S. B. Van Hemel (Eds.). Board on Children, Youth and Families, Board on Testing and Assessment, Division of Behavioral and Social Sciences and Education. Washington, DC: The National Academies Press.

Neisworth, J. T. & Bagnato, S. J. (2000). Recommended practices in assessment. In S. Sandall, M. McLean, & B. J. Smith (Eds.), *DEC recommended practices in early intervention/early childhood special education* (pp. 17-27). Longmont, CO: Sopris West.

Neisworth, J. T. & Bagnato, S. J. (2005). DEC recommended practices: Assessment. In S. Sandall, M. L. Hemmeter, B. J. Smith & M. McLean (Eds.), *DEC recommended practices: A comprehensive guide for practical application* (pp. 45-69). Missoula, MT: Division for Early Childhood.

Contributing Reviewers

David Allen, Portland State University
Kathleen Artman, Ohio State University
Lisa Backer, Minnesota State Department of Education
Rashida Banerjee, University of Northern Colorado
Kris Barnekow, University of Wisconsin–Milwaukee
Ann Bingham, University of Nevada-Reno
Patti Blasco, Oregon Health and Science University
Virginia Buysse, University of North Carolina at Chapel Hill
Judy Carta, University of Kansas
Lynette Chandler, Northern Illinois University
Deborah Chen, University of California Northridge
Robert Crow, Developmental Behavior Analysis
Sharon Darling, Florida Atlantic University
Laurie Dinnebeil, University of Toledo
Lise Fox, University of South Florida
Kristie Pretti Frontczak, Kent State University
Jennifer Grisham-Brown, University of Kentucky
Marci Hanson, San Francisco State University
Sharon Hennessy, North Central FL Early Steps
Robin Hojnoski, Lehigh University
Kere Hughes, Iowa State University
Kiersten Kinder, Vanderbilt University
Karen La Paro, University of North Carolina–Greensboro
David Lindeman, University of Kansas
Juin Liu, Northeastern University
Gayle Luyze, Iowa State University
Ellie Lynch, San Diego State University
Marisa Macy, Lycoming University
Chris Marvin, University of Nebraska–Lincoln
Rebecca McCathren, University of Missouri
Susan Maude, Iowa State University
Kristen Missal, University of Iowa
Tara McLaughlin, University of Florida
Katrina Moore, University of Florida
Cathy Pasia, University of Florida
Salih Rakap, University of Florida
Ruth Reinl, Early DLL Consultant, State of Wisconsin
Robyn Ridgley, Middle Tennessee State University
Beth Rous, University of Kentucky
Chris Salisbury, University of Illinois–Chicago
Tina Smith-Bonahue, University of Florida
Carol Trivette, Orlena Hawks Puckett Institute
Linda Tuchman, Waisman Center, University of Wisconsin
Amanda VanDerHeyden, Education Research and Consulting, Inc.
Susan Ward, Heartland Area Education Agency, Iowa
Juliann Woods, Florida State University
Yaoying Xu, Virginia Commonwealth University

Improving Child Find Through Tailored Outreach to Primary Referral Sources

Carl J. Dunst, Ph.D.,
Asheville, NC

Carol M. Trivette, Ph.D.,
Morganton, NC

Glinda Hill, M.Ed.,
U.S. Department of Education, Washington, DC

The purpose of child find is to *locate and identify* infants, toddlers, and preschoolers who are or might be eligible for early intervention or preschool special education (Dunst, Trivette, Appl, & Bagnato, 2004). Child find, in general, and outreach to primary referral sources, in particular, are typically part of a comprehensive system of child find, referral, early identification, and eligibility determination. Effective child find ensures that all children in need of early intervention or preschool special education are located, are identified, and receive the services, resources, and supports they need to promote learning and development (Dunst & Trivette, 2004; Dunst et al.).

As described in the Individuals With Disabilities Education Improvement Act of 2004, a comprehensive child-find system includes the methods and procedures for making referrals to early intervention or preschool special education to ensure timely identification of eligible children and the provision of services to those children. This includes, but is not limited to, outreach to primary referral sources to promote referrals to early intervention or preschool special education and to inform primary referral sources of the availability and benefits of early intervention and preschool special education. Child find as described in this paper is one component of a comprehensive approach to locating and identifying infants, toddlers, and preschoolers with developmental disabilities or delays eligible for early intervention or preschool special education and to providing these children individualized supports, resources, and services (Dunst et al., 2004).

This paper includes a description of an evidence-based approach to primary referral source outreach that can be used to increase referrals to early intervention or preschool special education. The approach is based on findings from research syntheses and systematic reviews completed by investigators at the Tracking, Referral, and Assessment Center for Excellence (TRACE) (Clow, Dunst, Trivette, & Hamby, 2005; Dunst & Gorman, 2006a, 2006b; Dunst & Hamby, 2006) and by others (e.g., Grimshaw et al., 2005; Hawkins, Kreuter, Resnicow, Fishbein, & Dijkstra, 2008; Maibach & Parrott, 1995; Paul & Redman, 1997; Paul, Redman, & Sanson-Fisher, 1997) interested in increasing referrals to specialty care (including early intervention and preschool special education) and improving the efficiency of outreach to primary referral sources. The approach is also informed by the collaborative efforts of TRACE and the American Academy of Pediatrics (Dunst, Trivette, Gramiak, & Hill, 2007; Gramiak, Trivette, Dunst, & Hill, 2006). These various sources of evidence and information were used to develop a research-informed approach to improving child find through outreach to primary referral sources. The practices were subsequently evaluated in a number of field-based studies (Dunst, Trivette, Shelden, & Rush, 2006; Trivette, Rush, Dunst, & Shelden, 2006).

The methods and procedures described herein can be implemented by early intervention and preschool special education personnel who have child-find responsibilities where those responsibilities include outreach to primary referral sources. These personnel include, but are not limited to, child-find specialists, outreach specialists, referral specialists, and other staff engaged in locating and identifying eligible or potentially eligible children for early intervention or preschool special education.

A Tailored Approach to Outreach to Primary Referral Sources

The outreach practice described in this paper is characterized by brief, repeated, face-to-face visits to primary referral sources so that tailored information and materials can be provided to promote referrals to early intervention or preschool special education. *Tailoring* refers to the methods and procedures for creating communicative channels that are individualized to reach and influence specific audiences (e.g., Kreuter, Strecher, & Glassman, 1999; Skinner, Campbell, Rimer, Curry, & Prochaska, 1999). Based on available research evidence, with a

Tailoring refers to the methods and procedures for creating communicative channels that are individualized to reach and influence specific audiences

focus on the characteristics of outreach practices that are associated with improving child find, the following five activities were found to be particularly important if outreach to primary referral sources was likely to be successful:

- *Building rapport and establishing credibility with primary referral sources.* The messenger matters a great deal in building rapport and establishing credibility. The person conducting outreach to primary referral sources needs to be assured, confident, and knowledgeable about his or her program and what the program has to offer both the primary referral source and the children and families being referred. It is worth the time and effort to plan what will be said, how it will be said, and how questions from the primary referral source will be answered.

- *Highlighting and repeating a tailored message about the benefits of making a referral to both the primary referral source and the child being referred.* Effective messages are highly focused and repeated a number of ways (e.g., orally and in a brochure) to be sure a primary referral source clearly understands the benefits of making referrals.

- *Using tailored written materials that describe the services the primary referral source and the child being referred will receive from a program.* Tailored materials are more effective than general descriptions of early intervention or preschool special education. Concise, graphic, written materials include descriptions of the children a program serves, the resources and supports that are available to eligible children, the benefits to both the referral source and the children referred, and the methods used to make referrals. Desktop publishing software makes it possible to easily tailor program brochures, referral forms, and other child-find materials for specific primary referral sources.

- *Using a referral procedure that is easy for primary referral sources to use to increase referrals.* Effective referral procedures easily fit into the way referrals are typically made by primary referral sources. Flexibility in how referrals are made is one key to increasing referrals to early intervention or preschool special education.

- *Making follow-up visits or contacts to reinforce primary referral source referrals, answer questions, and provide additional information as needed or requested.* Ongoing contact with primary referral sources keeps an early intervention or preschool special education program on the "radar screen" of referral sources. These contacts provide opportunities to accept new referrals and update primary referral sources about children who already have been referred.

Repeated follow-up visits or contacts are so important that if they are not done, the other activities do not matter much. What does this mean

Table 1

Key Elements of Effective Outreach to Primary Referral Sources

Planning
• Identify and know your referral sources
• Prepare a clear message about the benefits of making a referral
• Prepare a tailored brochure about the benefits of a referral
• Identify assured and credible messengers
Implementation
• Plan and schedule the visit carefully
• Make the visit and deliver the message
• Repeat and reinforce the message during the visit
• Clearly communicate who is eligible for your program services
• Keep the referral process flexible
• Provide the referral source with a tailored referral form (if requested)
• Ask how you can be of help
• Thank the primary referral source for his or her time
Follow-up
• Acknowledge all referrals
• Keep the primary referral source informed
• Personalize the feedback
• Provide timely feedback
• Make regularly scheduled follow-up visits or contacts

for improving child find? Establish and maintain ongoing contact with primary referral sources.

Guidelines for Improving Child-find Practices

Outreach to primary referral sources is more likely to be effective if certain activities are completed before, during, and after child find. Table 1 lists the key elements of planning, implementing, and following up contacts with primary referral sources. The

Improving child find is accomplished by establishing ongoing contact with primary referral sources.

Appendix includes a checklist to ensure the key elements of targeted outreach to primary referral sources are used as part of child find to promote referrals to early intervention and preschool special education.

Planning

Take time to prepare for face-to-face interactions with primary referral sources. Planning will go a long way toward making your child-find efforts successful. The key elements for planning outreach to referral sources include the following:

Identify and Know Your Referral Sources. The focus of outreach to primary referral sources should be those persons who have responsibility for making referrals. In small practices, for example, physicians are most likely to make referrals. In medium-size practices, nurses often make referrals for physicians. In large practices, referral specialists generally make referrals. Take the time to identify whom you should contact in physician practices, hospitals, child care programs, human services agencies, and other organizations serving children who might be eligible for early intervention or preschool special education.

Prepare a Clear Message. Primary referral sources need a reason to make a referral. You should prepare a concise, clear targeted message to build a case for referrals. The message should focus on what you offer and how it benefits the primary referral source and the children being referred. Less is more. The primary purpose of outreach is to locate children who are or might be eligible for early intervention or preschool special education. Keep your message tailored, targeted, focused and to the point.

Prepare a Tailored Brochure. Providing primary referral sources with written material about what you do and how it benefits the children being referred reinforces the orally delivered message. Your brochure should be tailored to the audience you are trying to reach. Generic brochures are not likely to be effective. The brochure should be concisely written. Information unrelated to whom you serve and what services you provide is distracting. Table 2 shows key characteristics for preparing tailored program materials. A more complete set of guidelines for developing tailored messages and materials is described in a *TRACE Practice Guide* (Dunst, 2006b).

A tailored brochure will more likely be read and understood.

The Messenger Matters. Your message is only as good as the person delivering the message. The messenger must be credible and must deliver

Table 2
Preparing Tailored Program Materials for Improving Child Find

Message Framing
• *Identify the target audience.* Be as specific as possible in terms of the audience you intend to reach. The more specific the target audience, the easier it is to tailor the message.
• *Identify the desired or expected benefit to the targeted audience.* What are the benefits both to the person making referrals and to the children being referred? Effective messages are relevant to the desired goals of the targeted audiences.
• *Prepare a positive, gain-framed message.* The message communicated to primary referral sources should focus on the positive consequences to the children being referred. What are the benefits of participating in your program?
Material Preparation
• *Personalize the written materials for the targeted audience.* This can be accomplished by specifically referring to the targeted audience by profession or group (e.g., "Pediatricians recognize the importance of early intervention"). The more personalized the tailored message, the more likely the recipient will read the materials and respond positively to the intent of the message.
• *Describe the reasons and benefits for making referrals.* Include a description of the specific kinds of resources and services available to children served by your program and the benefits of receiving these supports. Why would the primary referral source want to make a referral?
• *Include advice about and guidance for how to make referrals.* Describe the process or procedure the targeted referral source can use to refer a child. Keep the referral process as simple and straightforward as possible. Less is more when trying to improve referrals.
Intervention
• *Identify the ways the printed materials will be distributed and used to promote referrals.* Take the time to identify the different ways printed materials can be used to reach the targeted primary referral source. The same printed materials used in different ways will increase the effectiveness of child find.
• *Use the printed materials as part of outreach to primary referral sources.* The tailored printed materials will likely be more effective if used in conjunction with some type of face-to-face interactions with primary referral sources.
• *Provide tailored feedback to referral sources.* Provide immediate feedback to all referrals and personalize the feedback to the referral sources (e.g., "Dear Dr. Smith, thank you for referring your patient John Jones to the 'XYZ' program").

the message credibly. Messengers should take the time to practice and rehearse what will be said and how it will be said. Credible messengers dress and behave professionally. First impressions matter a great deal if primary referral sources are going to take your message seriously.

Implementation

Making contact with primary referral sources and promoting referrals is more likely to be effective if it is done in a thoughtful and systematic manner. The following activities are likely to lead to successful child find and to increased referrals.

Scheduling the Visit. Take the time to find out when primary referral sources are available to see you. You want to be able to make a visit without the need for an appointment. For example, physicians are often

Figure 1
**Referral Form to Tailor and Customize Outreach to Primary Referral
Sources (See www.tracecenter.info/practiceguides/practiceguides_
vol1_no2.pdf)**

Early Intervention Referral Form

Please complete this form for referring a child to early intervention if you prefer to do so in writing. Please indicate the feedback that you want to receive from the early intervention program in response to your referral.

CHILD CONTACT INFORMATION

Child Name:_____

Date of Birth:_____/_____/_____   Child Age (Months):_____   Gender: ☐ M   ☐ F

Home Address:_____

City:_____ State:_____ Zip:_____

Parent/Guardian:_____ Relationship to Child:_____

Primary Language:_____ Home Phone:_____ Other Phone:_____

Signature:_____ Date:_____

REASONS FOR REFERRAL

Reason(s) for referral to early intervention (Please check all that apply):

☐   Identified condition or diagnosis (e.g., spina bifida, Down syndrome): _____

☐   Suspected developmental delay or concern (Please circle areas of concern):

   Motor/Physical   Cognitive   Social/Emotional   Speech/Language   Behavior   Other_____

☐   At Risk (Please describe risk factors):_____

☐   Other (Please describe):_____

FEEDBACK REQUESTED BY THE REFERRAL SOURCE

☐   Status of Initial Family Contact   ☐   Developmental Evaluation Results
☐   Services Being Provided to Child/Family   ☐   Child Progress Report/Summary

☐   Other (Please describe):_____

REFERRAL SOURCE CONTACT INFORMATION

Person Making Referral: _____ Date of Referral: _____/_____/_____

Address: _____

Office Phone: ____/____-_____ Office Fax: ____/____-_____ E-mail: _____

Signature:_____ Date:_____

EARLY INTERVENTION PROGRAM

Program Name:_____

Address:_____City:_____State:____ Zip:_____

Telephone Number:_____ Fax Number:_____ E-mail Address:_____

available first thing in the morning and during hours that patients are not scheduled. A simple strategy is to call before the visit and ask when is a good time to drop off some materials about your program and also is a good time to talk with the primary referral source.

Making the Visit. Ask to see the person(s) you have identified who make referrals. Introduce yourself, tell the person(s) the name of your program, explain the purpose of the visit, and deliver the message you developed during the planning phase. Keep the message short and to the point (less than 5 minutes). Brief, focused, and tailored visits are more likely to be effective than visits that try to cover too many aspects of your program.

Repeat and Reinforce the Message. Immediately after delivering the message, provide the person who makes referrals with copies of your brochure and explain what the brochure includes. Repeat your message in a manner that reinforces the reasons for making a referral. Repeating the same message in a number of different ways increases the likelihood that the message is heard and, more important, understood and remembered.

Clearly Communicate Eligibility Criteria. It is important to describe explicitly which children are eligible for early intervention or preschool special education. This should also be included on your tailored brochure. Having a checklist that includes the conditions that makes a child eligible for enrollment in your program can facilitate appropriate referrals (see Dunst, Trivette, & Hill, 2007). This type of checklist can lessen referrals that do not meet the eligibility criteria for your program.

Keep the Referral Process Flexible. If a primary referral source already has a referral process in place, do not ask the referral source to change his or her procedures. If the referral source prefers to call, use e-mail, or write a referral prescription, accept whatever procedure with which they are comfortable. Offer to provide referral forms if they do not already use some type of referral procedure.

Tailored referral forms make it easier for a referral source to refer children.

Tailor Your Referral Form. It will be easier for a primary referral source to make a referral if you customize your referral form. Figure 1 shows an example of a referral form for a program that serves infants and toddlers with developmental delays, identifiable conditions, and children at-risk for medical, environmental or other reasons. The referral form is available from TRACE and can be customized for your program so that it includes only those eligibility categories applicable to your state, the name and contact information for your program, and the referral source contact information if known. The American Academy of Pediatrics adopted a version of the referral form as part of their Medical Home policy (American Academy of Pediatrics, 2007a, 2007b).

Ask How You Can Be Helpful. After delivering the message and providing the person with copies of your tailored brochure and referral forms (if requested), ask if there is any other information he or she needs or may find helpful. Ask if there is anything you can do for the primary referral source or any of the children he or she sees. This will create opportunities for a mutually beneficial exchange of information.

Thank the Primary Referral Source. Thank the primary referral source for taking the time to talk to you. Explain how he or she can contact you (business card) or your program (phone number on brochure). Establish as many opportunities as you can to establish and maintain contact between the primary referral source and you and your program.

Follow-up

The key to maintaining referrals to early intervention or preschool special education is to be responsive to any and all referrals. Follow-up is so important that if it is not done, the likelihood of continued referrals is

Table 3
Improving Primary Referral Source Referrals Through Follow-up and Feedback

Feedback
• *Acknowledge all referrals.* All referrals should be acknowledged immediately and include information about what steps will be taken by you or your program.
• *Provide feedback in a desired manner.* Take the time to learn the manner in which feedback is desired. Does the primary referral source want you to call, e-mail, write, or fax the acknowledgment?
• *Provide regular feedback, especially when a child's status changes.* Put into place a system where "status reports" are provided on a regular basis. Physicians, for example, often want to be informed about what services a child is receiving and what progress is being made.
• *Provide ongoing feedback in a desired format.* Too little information is not helpful and too much information is likely not to be read. Take the time to learn the format, amount, and mechanism that primary referral sources find most helpful.
Follow-up
• *Make contact with primary referral sources as appropriate.* If a primary referral source requests specific information that he or she needs for his or her own purposes, provide the requested information to be sure you provided what was wanted or needed.
• *Establish ongoing lines of communication with primary referral sources.* Take the time and find ways to ensure feedback continues to be useful. Ask if there is anything you can do to better inform a primary referral source about children referred to your program.

diminished. Table 3 lists a number of considerations for providing feedback to primary referral services (see especially Dunst, 2006a).

Acknowledge All Referrals. All referrals should be immediately acknowledged and should include the steps that will be taken to respond to requests from primary referral sources. The acknowledgment can be a simple thank-you note with an indication of when and how the referral will be processed. For example, "Thank you for referring Johnny Blake to the 'XYZ' early intervention program. The assessment you requested is scheduled for next week. You can expect the results about 2 weeks after the evaluation."

Keep the Primary Referral Source Informed. Send the primary referral source a short note telling him or her when an action is about to be taken for the child who was referred. Inform him or her of what will be done. Most primary referral sources want to be kept informed about the status of a referral. A simple rule of thumb is to provide feedback about any significant decision or action that is taken on behalf of a child.

Personalize the Feedback. Personalize any material you provide to primary referral sources, both in terms of the person being provided feedback and about the child for whom feedback is being provided. Primary referral sources are more likely to read and respond to concise, tailored feedback. Most primary referral sources only want a summary of evaluation results and the status of service provision to a child referred to early intervention or preschool special education.

Provide Timely Feedback. As soon as you know, inform the primary referral source about the findings or results of an evaluation or requested service(s) and the actions that will or have been taken. The more timely the feedback, the more likely primary referral sources will continue to make referrals.

Make Regularly Scheduled Follow-up Visits or Contacts. Primary referral sources are busy professionals. You need to plan and make brief, regularly scheduled follow-up visits or contacts in order to keep the primary referral source informed about individual children and to encourage new referrals. The more contact you have with primary referral sources, the more likely referrals will be made to your program. It is a good idea, for example, to provide timely feedback about the status of individual children, as appropriate. This will give you additional opportunities to talk to primary referral sources about your program.

Plan and make brief, regularly scheduled follow-up visits to primary referral sources.

Conclusion

This paper provided a description of a tailored approach to outreach that includes activities that are important to conduct before, during, and after child find. Hawkins et al. (2008), in a review of more than 100 studies of tailoring practices, found three aspects of tailoring increased the effectiveness of communication to intended audiences. The first was *personalization*. This included, but was not limited to, preparing and delivering a message that communicated "this was designed specifically for you." The second was *feedback*. This included, but was not limited to, providing a primary referral source information about any previous referrals and their outcomes and describing other professionals with similar backgrounds who also make referrals to your program. The third was *content matching*. This included, but was not limited to, direct messages to those aspects of the referral process that a primary referral source considers most important. All three aspects of tailoring are part of the child-find procedures described in this paper.

The approach to outreach described herein constitutes an evidence-based approach for locating and identifying eligible or potentially eligible children for early intervention or preschool special education. The approach, together with other child-find methods and procedures, can be used as part of a comprehensive approach to child find, referral, early identification, and eligibility determination (see especially Dunst & Trivette, 2004). The key to success is to personalize outreach to primary referral sources by tailoring the outreach procedures, materials, and processes to increase referrals to early intervention or preschool special education.

The benefits of tailored outreach to primary referral sources can be expected to be realized in a number of ways. One is an increase in the number of children located through child find. Another is the identification of eligible children at earlier ages. A third is the development of a broader-based cadre of primary referral sources. Yet another benefit is improved primary referral source understanding of the worth of early intervention and preschool special education. These benefits taken together should result in stronger practitioner-primary referral source relationships and the timely provision of supports, resources, and services to infants, toddlers, and preschoolers with developmental disabilities or delays and their families.

Notes

Carl J. Dunst, Ph.D., cdunst@puckett.org (Corresponding Author)

Carol M. Trivette, Ph.D., ctrivette@puckett.org

Glinda Hill, M.Ed., glinda.hill@ed.gov

The preparation of this paper was supported in part by the U.S. Department of Education, Office of Special Education Programs (H324G020002). The opinions expressed, however, are those of the authors and do not necessarily reflect the official position of either the Department or Office.

References

American Academy of Pediatrics. (2007a). *Early intervention program referral form*. Elk Grove Village, IL: Author. Retrieved May 23, 2007, from http://medicalhomeinfo.org/downloads/pdfs/EIReferralform_1.pdf

American Academy of Pediatrics, Council on Children With Disabilities. (2007b). Role of the medical home in family-centered early intervention services: Policy statement. *Pediatrics, 120*, 1153-1158.

Clow, P., Dunst, C. J., Trivette, C. M., & Hamby, D. W. (2005). Educational outreach (academic detailing) and physician prescribing practices. *Cornerstones, 1*(1), 1-9. Retrieved from http://tracecenter.info/cornerstones/cornerstones_vol1_no1.pdf

Dunst, C. J. (2006a). Providing feedback to primary referral sources. *TRACE Practice Guide: Referral, 1*(4). Retrieved from http://www.tracecenter.info/practiceguides/practiceguides_vol1_no4.pdf

Dunst, C. J. (2006b). Tailoring printed materials can help improve child find and increase referrals from primary referral sources. *Endpoints, 2*(4), 1-2. Retrieved from http://tracecenter.info/endpoints/endpoints_vol2_no4.pdf

Dunst, C. J. & Gorman, E. (2006a). Physician referrals of young children with disabilities: Implications for improving child find. *Cornerstones, 2*(1), 1-9. Retrieved from http://tracecenter.info/cornerstones/cornerstones_vol2_no1.pdf

Dunst, C. J. & Gorman, E. (2006b). Practices for increasing referrals from primary care physicians. *Cornerstones, 2*(5), 1-10. Retrieved from http://tracecenter.info/cornerstones/cornerstones_vol2_no5.pdf

Dunst, C. J. & Hamby, D. W. (2006). Tailoring printed materials for improving child find. *Cornerstones, 2*(4), 1-11. Retrieved from http://tracecenter.info/cornerstones/cornerstones_vol2_no4.pdf

Dunst, C. J. & Trivette, C. M. (2004). Toward a categorization scheme of child find, referral, early iden-tification and eligibility determination practices. *Tracelines, 1*(2), 1-18. Retrieved from http://www.tracecenter.info/tracelines/tracelines_vol1_no2.pdf

Dunst, C. J., Trivette, C. M., Appl, D. J., & Bagnato, S. J. (2004). Framework for investigating child find, referral, early identification, and eligibility determination practices. *Tracelines, 1*(1), 1-11. Retrieved from http://www.tracecenter.info/tracelines/tracelines_vol1_no1.pdf

Dunst, C. J., Trivette, C. M., Gramiak, A., & Hill, G. (2007). Pediatricians' appraisals of a universal checklist for making early intervention referrals. *Snapshots, 3*(1), 1-5. Retrieved from http://www.tracecenter.info/snapshots/snapshots_vol3_no1.pdf

Dunst, C. J., Trivette, C. M., & Hill, G. (2007). A universal checklist for identifying infants and toddlers eligible for early intervention. *TRACE Practice Guide: Referral, 2*(1), 1-5. Retrieved from http://www.tracecenter.info/practiceguides/practiceguides_vol2_no1.pdf

Dunst, C. J., Trivette, C. M., Shelden, M., & Rush, D. (2006). Academic detailing as an outreach strategy for increasing referrals to early intervention. *Snapshots, 2*(3), 1-9. Retrieved from http://www.tracecenter.info/snapshots/snapshots_vol2_no3.pdf.

Gramiak, A., Trivette, C. M., Dunst, C. J., & Hill, G. (2006). Pediatricians' judgments of the applicability of a universal early intervention referral form. *Snapshots, 2*(1), 1-5. Retrieved from http://www.tracecenter.info/snapshots/snapshots_vol2_no1.pdf

Grimshaw, J. M., Winkens, R. A. G., Shirran, L., Cunningham, C., Mayhew, A., Thomas, R., & Fraser, C. (2005). Interventions to improve outpatient referrals from primary care to secondary care (Review). *Cochrane Database of Systematic Reviews, 4.*

Hawkins, R. P., Kreuter, M., Resnicow, K., Fishbein, M., & Dijkstra, A. (2008). Understanding tailoring in communicating about health. *Health Education Research, 23*, 454-466.

Individuals With Disabilities Education Improvement Act of 2004, Pub. L. No. 108-446, 118 Stat. 2647 (2004).

Kreuter, M. W., Strecher, V. J., & Glassman, B. (1999). One size does not fit all: The case for tailoring print materials. *Annals of Behavioral Medicine, 21*, 276-283.

Maibach, E. & Parrott, R. L. (Eds.). (1995). *Designing health messages: Approaches from communication theory and public health practice.* Thousand Oaks, CA: Sage.

Paul, C. L. & Redman, S. (1997). A review of the effectiveness of print material in changing health-related knowledge, attitudes and behaviour. *Health Promotion Journal of Australia, 7,* 91-99.

Paul, C. L., Redman, S., & Sanson-Fisher, R. W. (1997). The development of a checklist of content and design characteristics in printed health education materials. *Health Promotion Journal of Australia, 7,* 153-159.

Skinner, C. S., Campbell, M. K., Rimer, B. K., Curry, S., & Prochaska, J. O. (1999). How effective is tailored print communication? *Annals of Behavioral Medicine, 21*, 290-298.

Trivette, C. M., Rush, D., Dunst, C. J., & Shelden, M. (2006). Direct mailings to parents and self-referrals to early intervention. *Snapshots, 2*(2), 1-7. Retrieved from http://www.tracecenter.info/snapshots/snapshots_vol2_no2.pdf

Appendix
Checklist for Conducting Outreach to Primary Referral Sources

This checklist is used to ensure that outreach to primary referral sources includes those activities that are most likely to result in effective child find. The majority of questions should be answered Yes to ensure successful outreach.		Was the practice used?	
		Yes	No
Planning	Have the most appropriate referral sources for the children served by your program been identified?		
	Has a clear message tailored to each primary referral source been prepared?		
	Does the message include the benefits of early childhood intervention?		
	Has a tailored brochure that communicates the message been prepared?		
	Have the practitioners who are likely to be the most credible messengers been identified?		
	Have the messengers been trained to conduct outreach?		
Implementation	Has the visit to the referral source been carefully planned?		
	Has the appropriate person(s) been identified to visit during the outreach?		
	Was the visit arranged at a convenient and appropriate time?		
	Was the tailored message delivered during the visit?		
	Was the message repeated and reinforced during the visit?		
	Was the primary referral source provided with a tailored brochure?		
	Was your program's eligibility criteria clearly explained?		
	Was the preferred referral process used?		
	Was input elicited regarding referral source needs?		
	Was the referral source thanked for his or her time?		
Follow-up	Have all referrals been acknowledged in a timely manner?		
	Has the referral source been informed about the status of referrals?		
	Has feedback been provided to the referral sources on a regular basis?		
	Have regularly scheduled follow-up visits or contacts been made?		
	Have referral sources been asked how you can be helpful?		

Developmental Screening in Early Childhood

Potential Roadmaps for Those Considering the Journey

Jantina Clifford,
University of Oregon, Early Intervention Program

Jane Squires,
University of Oregon, Early Intervention Program

Suzanne Yockelson,
Brandman University, California

Elizabeth Twombly,
University of Oregon, Early Intervention Program

Diane Bricker,
University of Oregon, Early Intervention Program

Practitioners, parents, and scientists increasingly have come to appreciate the importance of early development and learning and its implications for later life successes. A growing body of evidence (e.g., Hart & Risley 1995; Sameroff & Chandler, 1975; Sameroff & Fiese, 2000; Shonkoff & Phillips, 2000; Shonkoff & Meisels, 2000; Zeanah, 2009) emphasizes the significance of providing young children with a succession of responsive and stimulating environmental conditions that are essential to nurturing optimal physical, cognitive, social, and emotional growth. Since the landmark enactment of Public Law 94-142 (later known as the Individuals with Disabilities Education Act, or IDEA) in 1975, much has been learned about the effectiveness of early intervention services (birth to age 5) for children at risk for developmental delays, as well as for those who evidence a delay or an established condition (Dunst & Trivette, 2009; Guralnick, 2005). In addition, recent advances in brain research have highlighted the importance of the early years in setting the stage for successful development *throughout* the life span (Blackman, 2002; Kirp, 2007; National Scientific Council on the Developing Child, 2007).

The premise that it is essential to identify developmental delays early in order to provide intervention that leads to desired outcomes for children, families, and, ultimately, communities, is widely accepted (e.g., Hemmeter et al., 2005; Meisels & Shonkoff, 2000; Shonkoff & Phillips, 2000). Early identification of developmental delays has been recognized as a national priority (American Academy of Pediatrics, 2006; Kirp, 2007). Fundamental to early intervention is the timely identification of developmental delays or disabilities, and fundamental to early detection is periodic developmental screening.

Developmental Screening Defined

Developmental screening refers to ongoing, brief formal assessment of a child to determine whether further and more comprehensive assessment

is required (McLean, 2004; Meisels & Provence, 1989). Developmental screening is considered a recommended practice by educational professionals (Copple & Bredekamp, 2009, Head Start Performance Standards, 2008; Sandall, Hemmeter, Smith, & McLean, 2005) and is a required component of preventive health care under the Patient Protection and Affordable Care Act (2010). Early and periodic developmental screening is recommended because it helps identify young children who may be at risk for developmental delays or disabilities, and assists families and providers in deciding whether or not further evaluation might be warranted to determine eligibility for intervention.

Fundamental to early intervention is the timely identification of developmental delays or disabilities, and fundamental to early detection is periodic developmental screening.

In addition, conducting developmental screening can often promote conversations between parents and providers that assist in increasing parental knowledge about what to expect developmentally, provide information on how to promote their child's growth across developmental areas, and deepen or strengthen relationships between parents and the providers who take an interest in their child's development (McLean & Crais, 2004; Trivette & Dunst, 2005).

Screening is particularly important for young children whose development is at risk due to environmental factors such as poverty or medical issues (e.g., prematurity, prenatal substance exposure). Research has clearly and consistently indicated that children who experience multiple risk factors have a higher incidence of developmental delays than children with no or very few risk conditions in their lives (Sameroff, 2010; Sameroff & Chandler, 1975; Sameroff & Fiese, 2000; Sameroff, Seifer, Baldwin, & Baldwin, 1993; Werner & Smith, 2001). Programs that serve young children from families with known risk factors (e.g., Head Start, subsidized child care, and home visiting programs) typically are required by their funders to offer developmental screening at regular intervals during the child's enrollment in the program. Such requirements, although justified and appropriate in relation to recommended practices, might place additional burdens on programs. Programs with modest or limited funding have to determine how to provide developmental screening that is low cost but accurate. Program administrators and practitioners who are launching a screening system must make many decisions, including (1) which screening tool(s) to select, (2) how to implement a screening system, (3) how to administer the screening tool(s), (4) how and when to provide follow-up referral or services to participating families, and (5) how to evaluate the effectiveness of their screening efforts.

The purpose of this article is to provide a brief history of developmental screening and to discuss current recommended screening practices. We present information useful for informing decisions about the selection of developmental screening tools. Examples of ways that practitioners responsible for early detection have incorporated screening into their programs or practices are illustrated. In addition, the importance of and strategies for including parents in the screening process in a culturally responsive manner are reviewed. Finally, we offer general recommendations related to key components of effective screening systems and considerations for ongoing development and improvement of current screening practices.

Brief History of Developmental Screening in the United States and Current Recommended Practices

In the 1940s, influential work by developmental psychologist Arnold Gesell and other child development specialists focused on the creation of comprehensive assessment measures with the purpose of establishing developmental expectations for children at specific ages (Neisworth & Bagnato, 1992), while an increasing accumulation of evidence about the effectiveness of early intervention, and availability of early intervention services suggested a need for effective methods to identify early children whose development was not following "typical" developmental sequences and who might be at risk for developmental delays or disabilities. The costly administration of comprehensive assessment measures and interpretation of their results, however, argued against their use for broadscale screening efforts and suggested a need for affordable alternatives (Squires, Nickel, & Eisert, 1996).

In 1968, this need was acknowledged when the Early and Periodic Screening, Diagnosis, and Treatment program (EPSDT) was enacted. Primary care providers were charged with the responsibility of conducting development screening "to discover, as early as possible, the ills that handicap our children" and to provide "continuing follow-up and treatment so that handicaps do not go neglected" (U.S. Department of Health and Human Services, Health Resources and Services Administration, Maternal and Child Health, n.d.). Nearly 10 years later, in 1975, screening and efforts to identify children with special needs (i.e., Child Find) were also mandated in education with the passage of Public Law 94-142, now known as the Individuals with Disabilities Education Act (IDEA, 2004).

In addition to the need for low-cost, accurate, and alternative methods of early identification to satisfy legislation, two lines of research also highlighted the need for developmental screening: investigations focusing on children experiencing multiple-risk factors and investigations examining early brain development.

Children at Risk. Beginning in the 1980s, many projects were initiated to monitor groups of infants identified as being at risk for medical reasons such as prematurity. Data from these projects revealed that while most of these children appeared typical in all respects during yearly follow-ups, eventually up to 30% of them manifested a delay that required some form of intervention (Widerstrom & Nickel, 1997). Procedures were needed for the "timely" identification of infants at risk because of medical factors who might benefit from early intervention services.

Conducting evaluations using comprehensive assessment measures for large groups of infants was economically unfeasible and geographically challenging for rural families; therefore, a demand arose for less expensive, easily implemented "shortcuts" that would be useful for informing accurate screening decisions. The need for these low-cost shortcuts also paved the way for the onset of large-scale developmental screening programs in the United States in order to monitor the development of infants at medical risk. Over time, data analyses revealed that many chil-

dren who were exposed to adverse environmental conditions were also at increased risk for developmental problems and disabilities (Ramey & Ramey, 1998; Sameroff & Chandler, 1975; Werner, 1993); consequently, screening programs were expanded to include infants and young children at environmental risk.

Historically, the screening tool used most frequently in early risk monitoring projects was the Denver Developmental Screening Test (DDST; Frankenburg & Dodds, 1967). This measure was individually administered, but offered information on the development of large groups of young children (e.g., children born prematurely) at a cost considerably lower than the cost of administering a comprehensive evaluation. In many hospitals, educational programs, and research projects, the DDST was adopted to assess and monitor the development of infants and young children—many of whom were identified as at-risk based on medical or environmental factors.

Although the DDST somewhat met a need, the method for administering the tool raised questions about accuracy of screening decisions when these decisions were informed, in whole or in part, by findings from an assessment conducted in an unfamiliar setting (e.g., physician's office), by an individual relatively unfamiliar with the child. Research was conducted beginning in the mid-1970s to address these concerns (Bricker & Littman, 1985; Nickel & Squires, 2000).

In the latter part of the 1970s and early 1980s, an alternative strategy for screening young children was developed that involved having parents provide information about the developmental status of their child (Bricker & Squires, 1989; Glascoe, Altemeier, & Maclean, 1989; Knobloch, Stevens, Malone, Ellison, & Risemburg, 1979). Initial concerns identified in the literature about the reliability and validity of parental report lessened as accumulating empirical evidence suggested the majority of parents were able to assess accurately whether their children had achieved or mastered developmental milestones or skills when given high quality measures that asked questions about the child's current behaviors using language and examples familiar to parents (Glascoe, 2000; Squires, Twombly, Bricker, & Potter, 2009). Involving parents in the screening process by using a parent-completed tool was also considered ecologically valid in that the child's behavior was being observed while in a familiar context, with familiar people and materials, often while engaged in play or routine care giving activities.

Brain Development and Early Experiences. The second line of research that supported the development of screening in the United States entails the growing evidence related to the importance of the early

years for healthy brain development together with research that supports the effectiveness of early intervention (Guralnick, 1997; Shonkoff
& Phillips 2000; Zigler & Styfco, 2004). Findings from research suggested
that to maximize the impact of intervention efforts, early and timely identification was important.

As noted previously, early developmental screening efforts were ham-
pered by a lack of empirically validated measures. In the 1990s, however,
a variety of technically adequate developmental screening tools and procedures became available (Glascoe, 1991). The increasing evidence that
early intervention is effective, coupled with the development of new
screening measures and procedures, served to emphasize the need and
bolster support for universal developmental screening and monitoring as
a national priority. In 2001 and 2006, the American Academy of Pediatrics
(AAP) stated that the early identification of developmental delays is critical to the wellbeing of children and their families and that pediatricians
are responsible for conducting periodic developmental screening during well-child visits to ensure the early identification of young children.
Despite this guidance, as of 2009, fewer than 48% of pediatricians in
the United States reported they were conducting routine developmental screening in their offices (Radecki, Sand-Loud, O'Connor, Sharp, &
Olson, 2011). The fact that fewer than half of all children are screened for
risk of developmental delay by their pediatricians might help to explain
why young children are not receiving timely early intervention and early
childhood special education services under IDEA. As noted in a report
from the Centers for Disease Control and Prevention, fewer than 50% of
children needing services are identified as having a problem before entering school (U.S. Department of Health and Human Services, Centers for
Disease Control and Prevention, 2005).

Consensus currently exists that all children should receive periodic
developmental screening with technically adequate measures including
appropriate follow up and referral as necessary (American Academy of
Pediatrics, 2001, 2007; Copple & Bredekamp, 2009; Neisworth & Bagnato,
2005; Snow & Van Hemel, 2008). Federal programs serving families of
young children who are at risk for developmental delays or disabilities,
such as Head Start, include mandates for screening with valid and reliable screening tools (Head Start Performance Standards, 2008). Federal
laws such as EPSDT (1989) and the IDEA (2004) require states to screen
and identify children early who might benefit from intervention services
and encourage states that do not serve at-risk populations to track and
monitor these children's development. Both IDEA and the Child Abuse
and Prevention Treatment Act (CAPTA, 2003) require that states receiving CAPTA funds develop provisions and procedures for the referral of a

child under the age of 3 years who is involved in a substantiated case of abuse or neglect to the early intervention program funded under Part C of IDEA (2004). Several entities that advocate early and periodic developmental screening of young children have created resources to support recommended practices, including the AAP, Early Head Start, the National Academy for State Health Policy, the National Research Council, and the TRACE Center (e.g., Dunst, Trivette, Appl, & Bagnato, 2004). Interested readers can access up-to-date online resources from these sources by conducting a computer search using the term "developmental screening" in conjunction with the name of the program. While children receiving high quality health care, or those who are at risk and involved in federal programs are, in most cases, receiving periodic screening and referral, the current challenge lies in making timely and periodic developmental screening a reality for all children.

Developmental Screening Tools and Methods of Administration

Two major types of developmental screening tools are used in early childhood, social welfare, and pediatric settings: professionally administered and parent-completed. Professionally administered tools require the provider to either observe the child performing specific skills or

to provide an opportunity to assess directly the presence of target behaviors. These tools can be administered individually (e.g., Brigance Screens; Brigance, 2005) or to groups of children (e.g., Developmental Indicators for the Assessment of Learning–Third Edition, DIAL–3; Mardell-Czudnowski & Goldenberg, 1998). Different tools require varying levels of training to administer, although the majority of multidomain screening tools can be administered by well-trained paraprofessionals, teachers, and allied health professionals. Other professionally administered tools such as the Bayley Infant Neurodevelopmental Screen (BINS; Aylward, 1995) and the latest edition of the Denver Developmental Screening Test, the Denver II (DDST–II, Frankenburg, Dodds, Archer, Shapiro, & Bresnick, 1992) require trained professionals with advanced training, degrees, or licensure to administer.

While children receiving high quality health care, or those who are at-risk and involved in federal programs are, in most cases, receiving periodic screening and referral, the current challenge lies in making timely and periodic developmental screening a reality for all children.

Parent-completed tools are those in which the parent is asked to respond to questions related to their child's skills (e.g., Ages and Stages Questionnaires, Edition, [ASQ–3; Squires & Bricker, 2009]; Child Development Inventory [CDI; Ireton, 1990]), or to rate their level of concern related to developmental domains or behavior [e.g., Parental Evaluation of Developmental Status (PEDS; Glascoe, 2006)]. Parent-completed tools are typically written between the third- to fifth-grade reading levels and are scored and interpreted by paraprofessionals or professionals in early childhood education, special education, social work, health care, and allied health fields.

While both professional- and parent-completed tools can be used effectively in developmental screening efforts, the added advantages of including parents and caregivers in developmental screening processes are widely understood and accepted (e.g., Bagnato, Neisworth, & Pretti-Frontczak, 2010; McLean & Crais, 2004). Research has shown that parents generally can provide valid and reliable reports on their children's developmental skills and behaviors when given tools designed for parent/caregiver use (Bodnarchuk & Eaton, 2004; Dinnebeil & Rule, 1994; Glascoe, 1999; Ring & Fenson, 2000), thus providing the assessment team with valuable information that might not be easily obtained from a professional with whom a child is unfamiliar. In addition, parent-completed tools can be a cost-effective way for programs to gather information on a child's current repertoire of skills that may also fit within the time constraints of busy programs such as a pediatric practice, community program, or classroom (Glascoe, Foster, & Wolraich, 1997).

Involving parents in assessment, including screening, is a recommended practice in early intervention/early childhood special education (Neisworth & Bagnato, 2005) and in early childhood education (Copple & Bredekamp, 2009). Parents have much to gain from involvement in assessment processes, including a sense of empowerment, learning about child development, partnership in their child's development, and confirmation of the influential role they play in supporting their child's development. When delays do occur and a child qualifies for early intervention, parents are already "on the team," and positioned to have an influential role in the development and implementation of their child's early intervention services and supports (McLean & Crais, 2004; Squires et al., 2009).

Selecting Developmental Screening Tools

Several factors should be considered when selecting a screening tool. Among the factors to consider are technical adequacy, age range, and targeted area(s) (e.g., communication, social-emotional, autism), as well as practical issues such as recommended administration methods, including respondent and mode. A brief synopsis of several developmental screening tools, and information about age range, administration time, respondent, completion mode, and technical adequacy is shown in Table 1.

Technical adequacy refers to the ability of screening tool to do the "job" for which it was designed with accuracy and consistency. There are many ways to evaluate the technical adequacy of a screening tool, which are covered in depth elsewhere (e.g., McLean, Wolery, & Bailey, 2004; Salvia, Ysseldyke, & Bolt, 2009). Typically, studies designed to evaluate technical adequacy address aspects such as the normative population (e.g., Was the test normed on a representative sample of the population? How does the normative sample compare to the targeted population in a program?), reliability or consistency of scores (e.g., Are test scores consistent across short periods of time such as 1 to 2 weeks? Are test scores consistent across raters? Are test items related to each other such that they appear to be measuring different aspects of one particular construct, such as fine motor or adaptive skills?), and validity of scores or accuracy of test results (e.g., Do test scores accurately identify children known to be typically developing [specificity] as well as those known to have a delay [sensitivity] in order to minimize both over-

Table 1
Characteristics of Select Developmental Screening Tools

Name	Author(s) and Copyright Year	Publisher	Age Range	Administration Time	Respondent	Completion Mode	Technical Adequacy
Ages and Stages Questionnaires, 3rd Edition (ASQ–3™)	Jane Squires & Diane Bricker (2009)	Paul H. Brookes Publishing Company	1–66 months	10–15 minutes	Parent	Paper/pencil or online	Sensitivity = .86 Specificity = .86
Battelle Developmental Inventory Screening Test–II (BDIST–2)	Jean Newborg (2006)	Riverside Publishing Company	0–95 months	10–30 minutes	Professional	Direct assessment, observation, parental interview	Sensitivity = .72–.93 Specificity = .79–.88
Bayley Infant Neurodevelopmental Screener (BINS)	Glen P. Aylward (1995)	Psychological Corporation	3–24 months	10 minutes/set	Professional	Structured tasks	Sensitivity = .75–.86 Specificity = .75–.86
Bayley–3 Screen	Nancy Bayley (2005)	Pearson/ American Guidance Service	1–42 months	15–25 minutes	Professional	Direct elicitation	Specificity = .77–1.00

Table 1 (*continued*)

Name	Author(s) and Copyright Year	Publisher	Age Range	Administration Time	Respondent	Completion Mode	Technical Adequacy
Brigance Screens–II	Albert H. Brigance (2005)	Curriculum Associates, Inc.	Birth–1st Grade	10–15 minutes	Professional	Direct elicitation and observation, interview	Sensitivity = .81–1.00 Specificity = .72–.94
Child Development Inventories (CDI)	Harold Ireton (1990)	Behavior Science Systems Inc.	3–72 months; IDI[1] for 3–18 months; ECDI[2] for 18–36 months; PDI[3] for 36–60 months	10 minutes, less if parents complete independently	Parent	Paper/pencil or interview	Sensitivity = 50–76 Specificity = .76
Denver Developmental Screening Test II (Denver II)	William K. Frankenburg et al. (1992)	Denver Developmental Materials	0–72 months	10–20 minutes	Professional	Structured tasks and paper/pencil	Sensitivity = .83 Specificity = .40
Developmental Indicators for the Assessment of Learning-3rd Edition (DIAL–3)	Carol Mardell & Dorothea S. Goldenberg (1998)	Pearson/American Guidance Service	30 months through 6–11 years	20–30 minutes; Speed DIAL: 15–20 minutes	Professional	Direct elicitation and observation	Sensitivity and specificity not available

Table 1 (continued)

Name	Author(s) and Copyright Year	Publisher	Age Range	Administration Time	Respondent	Completion Mode	Technical Adequacy
Kent Inventory of Developmental Skills–3rd Edition (KIDS)	Jeanette Reuter, Lewis Katoff, & Chris Gruber (1996)	Western Psychological Services	Infancy to 15 months (or up to 6 years when a severe developmental delay is present)	45 minutes	Parent	Paper/pencil	Sensitivity = .44–59 Specificity = .91–97
Parents' Evaluations of Developmental Status (PEDS)	Frances P. Glascoe (2006)	Ellsworth & Vandemeer Press	0–96 months	2–10 minutes, less if parents complete independently	Parent	Paper/pencil or interview	Sensitivity = .70–94 Specificity = .77–93

Note. [1] = Infant Development Inventories, [2] = Early Childhood Development Inventories, and [3] = Preschool Development Inventories.

and under-referral rates?). In this article, only sensitivity and specificity rates are shown in Table 1. Readers considering the adoption of specific screening tools are encouraged to examine other aspects of technical adequacy, including those mentioned above. Technical adequacy information is often available from various sources, including reviews of specific tools (e.g., Buros Mental Measurements Yearbooks; http://buros.unl.edu/buros/jsp/search.jsp) or compendiums of developmental screening tools (e.g., American Academy of Pediatrics, 2006; Glascoe, 2009, Ringwalt, 2008; Snow & Van Hemel, 2008) and the examiner's manuals or user's guides for specific tools.

The goals, resources, and population served by a program are additional factors to consider when selecting a screening tool. For example, if a screening program targets children from birth to 5 years, then it is essential that the screening tool also cover that developmental range or that more than one measure is selected. The ASQ–3 (Squires & Bricker, 2009), Brigance–II screens (Brigance, 2005), CDI (Ireton, 1992), and PEDS (Glascoe, 2006) can be used from infancy through school entry or later (see Table 1). Other screening tools are geared specifically to either infants and toddlers (e.g., BINS; Aylward, 1995) or preschool age children (e.g., DIAL–3 [Mardell-Czudnowski & Goldenberg, 1998] and Early Screening Inventory–Revised [ESI-R; Meisels, Marsden, Wiske, &

Henderson, 2008]) and would need to be supplemented with other tools if the screening program targets children from birth to 5 years.

Administration method and mode are also important considerations when selecting a tool. For example, professionally administered screening tools might be preferred by programs that serve children of parents with cognitive impairments or when the child is in temporary care due to abuse or neglect, whereas parent-completed tools might be selected when program goals include parent participation and education. Recommended practices in both early intervention and early childhood education endorse parent-completed questionnaires (Copple & Bredekamp, 2009; Neisworth & Bagnato, 2005), with both financial as well as parent involvement benefits. For example, a program with limited resources might select a screening tool that can be completed independently by parents (i.e., mailed home and returned). Conversely, a program that has the resources to provide home visits might choose a screening tool that could be completed together by a parent and professional in the home environment. Regardless of the program's goals, resources, or population served, the level and extent to which a screening program promotes parent involvement is an important factor to take into consideration as the way screening activities are undertaken can have an influential effect on the relationship between parents and professionals.

In addition to the considerations involved in selecting a screening tool, programs must also make decisions regarding the mode of administration (i.e., *who* will complete the tool and *how, when,* and *where* it will be administered). While professionally administered screening tools are typically completed by a trained professional in a clinic or in a structured evaluation or assessment setting, many parent-completed tools can be completed by a parent or other caregiver (e.g., a teacher or daycare provider who knows the child well) and have the flexibility to be completed in a variety of contexts and settings. Different administration modes for developmental screening tools include mailing or sending the screening tool home with a parent, assisting the parent to complete the tool during a home visit, administering questions over the phone as an interview, completing the tool in a clinic or early childhood setting, and completing the tool online.

Table 2 shows examples of different screening approaches and illustrates how different programs serving young children and their families have created developmental screening systems that meet program needs while including parents in the process. Potential advantages and issues to consider are offered along with descriptions of the settings in which each administration approach might be used.

Table 2
Examples of Screening Approaches with Illustrations and Advantages, Considerations, and Settings

Approach	Illustration	Advantages	Considerations	Settings
Mail out	Parent-completed screening tool is mailed to parents at 6-month intervals to monitor child's development. Questionnaires are sent back to a professional to review. Reports are sent to the parents and copied to the child's physician (with permission). Parents who express concerns, or screenings that indicate "red flags" receive personalized follow-up.	• Parent participation ensured • Low-cost • Can be used to screen populations not served in community-based programs or those programs that serve children at risk • Parents anticipate results as they self-select to participate	• Parents need skills to complete screening tool independently • Return rates might be low • No professional "eyes" on the child • Home environments might not have materials needed to practice or observe certain developmental skills	• Large-scale child find programs • Infant follow-along programs • NICU partners • Public health programs
Telephone interview	Parents are mailed a parent-completed screening tool in advance of a scheduled phone interview to begin considering the response or observing their child's skills. During the interview, the parent provides the requested information to a paraprofessional or professional who records the information provided by the parent. Following the interview screening results are reviewed, questions and concerns are addressed, and if necessary, follow-up referrals or evaluations are scheduled.	• Parent participation ensured • Less costly than face-to-face contact. • Allows for item clarification, concerns addressed immediately	• Professional time involved in going through questionnaire • No professional "eyes" on the child • Home environments might not have materials needed to practice or observe certain developmental skills	• Large-scale child find programs • Health care agencies • Nursing programs (e.g., Ask-A-Nurse) • Pediatric offices

Table 2 (continued)

Approach	Illustration	Advantages	Considerations	Settings
Home visit	Parents are provided a parent-completed screening tool a week or two prior to the scheduled screening. Parents are asked to observe their child or provide opportunities for their child to practice skills. At the next parent/professional visit, the screening tool is reviewed together (or completed together, if necessary). The professional answers questions, addresses concerns, and discusses follow-up referrals, if indicated.	• Parent participation ensured • Face-to-face contact provides opportunity for culturally appropriate processes • Provides opportunity for professional to observe child and support parents	• Parents might require support to complete tool (e.g., reading assistance) • Home environments might not have materials needed to practice or observe certain developmental skills • Home visitation is a costly service • There may be distractions in the environment that add to the time it takes to complete the tool	• Nurse home visiting programs • Social welfare home visiting programs • Public health home visiting programs • Early childhood home visiting programs • Early literacy home-based programs • Community health nursing home-based programs
Parent Conference	When a child is enrolled in an early care or educational setting, the parent is given a parent-completed screening tool to complete at home. At the same time, the classroom teacher completes the screening tool based on classroom observations. Results of the parent- and teacher-completed screenings are compared during a parent–teacher conference, scores are discussed, concerns are addressed, and appropriate referrals are made, as indicated.	• Parent participation encouraged • Face-to-face contact provides opportunity for culturally appropriate processes • Provides opportunity for professional to observe child and support parents • Can strengthen the parent–teacher relationship	• Increases possibility of professional dominating screening process, decreasing potential involvement of parent • Teachers need to be trained how to communicate and collaborate with parents when differences in observations occur • Differences in perspectives between parents and teachers should be approached with curiosity and respect	• Early care and education settings • Preschool settings

Table 2 (continued)

Approach	Illustration	Advantages	Considerations	Settings
Online	Parents are provided a way to access an online version of a parent-completed screening tool. Parents either print out the screening tool and enter answers at a later time, or complete the screening tool online. Results are either scored by a professional, or can be automatically scored. Reports are sent to parents and any concerns expressed by parents or "red flags" receive personalized follow-up.	• Parent participation ensured • Low-cost • Can be used to screen populations not served in programs for children at risk	• Parents must have access to computer • Parents must have skills necessary to complete screening forms independently • If questionnaires completed online, parent might have had limited opportunity to observe child or provide opportunities for child to practice skills • No professional "eyes" on the child	• Medical offices • Programs with developmental screening initiatives • Health care agencies • Child find agencies such as public health
On-site	Professionals administer screening tools in a clinic-based or community setting. Professionals directly assess children's skills across domains. Parents might be present, and might be asked to complete specific domains of the screening tools. Results are discussed with the parents, concerns addressed, and recommendations for referrals are made as indicated by screening tool.	• Provides opportunity for professional to observe child and support parents • Can be used to screen populations not served in programs for children at risk • One or many children can be screened quickly and efficiently	• Parent participation can be limited • Parents less likely to feel part of process, or to learn much in process • May result in over-referral of children due to unfamiliarity of children with environment or with stimulus materials	• Kindergarten or preschool "round-ups" • Physician's offices • Walk-in clinics • Health fairs

Cross-Cultural Issues in Developmental Screening

While parent report has become widely accepted as a reliable and valid way to gather information about a child's development, concerns have been expressed about the use of parent-completed developmental screening tools with high risk and ethnically diverse families (Pizur-Barnekow et al., 2010). Inclusion of parents in developmental screening processes requires the use of tools and approaches that are effective with a broad range of parents, across a diverse spectrum of cultural, economic, and individual characteristics (Lynch & Hanson, 2004a). Language is a major determinant of score validity, as a parent or family member must be able to speak or read the language in which the tool is administered in order to gather accurate information. Several screening tools (e.g., ASQ and PEDS) have been adapted (i.e., items translated and in some instances revised in order to reflect linguistic or cultural differences) for speakers of different languages. In many instances, however, programs must rely on interpreters to translate items for parents who do not speak English. Extensive guidelines about language translation and adaptation can be found for test developers (e.g., Hambleton, Merenda, & Spielberger, 2005) in cases where programs serving non-English-speaking families must adapt screening tools on their own. In addition, guidelines are available regarding the sensitive use of translators and interpreters by service providers, although programs serving significant proportions of linguistically diverse families should consider hiring bilingual or bicultural staff (Ohtake, Santos, & Fowler, 2005).

Cultural appropriateness can also affect score validity and reliability. For instance, items on a screening tool related to pretend play with dolls might not measure play skills in children whose parents do not let them play with toys having likenesses to people. Children whose parents do not give them scissors for cutting or crayons for writing might not demonstrate age-appropriate fine motor skills as defined on a specific screening tool. In these and other circumstances, delays evidenced on a screening tool might be attributed to lack of experience rather than "true" delays in development.

Assessment instruments, including screening tools, should contribute to collaborative and culturally sensitive work with families (Lyman, Njoroge, & Willis, 2007). Parents from different cultural communities might have different expectations about what types of activities young children can or should engage in, and what skills are considered to represent "developmentally on track" at a given age (Lynch & Hanson, 2004b). While it is likely that an assessment instrument developed in a particular culture will view development through that cultural lens (Lyman et al., 2007), gathering developmental information and concerns from families about their child provides a foundation for shared learning between parents and providers and can help clarify developmental expectations and cultural "norms" for both parties.

Gathering developmental information and concerns from families about their child provides a foundation for shared learning between parents and providers and can help clarify developmental expectations and cultural "norms" for both parties.

Whenever possible, screening tools should be used that have been developed (or appropriately adapted) and normed with a "representative" sample of a population (Bailey, 2004; Salvia et al., 2009). Because of the variability in the types of activities or experiences families might provide to their very young children, regardless of their cultural group, selecting screening tools and processes that have a parent component as well as flexible administration procedures offers the most potential for a culturally sensitive approach to developmental screening. A screening tool should facilitate measurement of a child's typical or optimal behavior in natural settings, not a child's ability to take a test. As Bagnato noted, "Testing of infants, toddlers, and preschoolers by strange adults, in unnatural places, at tables with flip cards and small, unmotivating toys does not make much sense" (2005, p. 17).

Screening tools should offer flexibility in the types of activities, materials, responses, or settings in which a child can demonstrate a specific skill. Flexibility in administration procedures provides additional assurance that developmental screening information represents typical or optimal behaviors for children from a variety of geographic, economic, or cultural backgrounds. Finally, screening tools should offer scoring procedures that allow for the omission of items in situations where these items represent skills or activities that have been identified as culturally inappropriate for the child or family.

The need for training and ongoing reflective supervision is critical for providers who are conducting developmental screenings with children and families, and especially true for providers working with children and families from diverse backgrounds. Training needs to be provided not only on the "nuts and bolts" of administering developmental screening tools, but also on the entire *process* of screening and how to ensure the process is conducted in a culturally sensitive manner. Providers should receive training on cultural self-awareness, including their own assumptions about cultures, development, and appropriate parenting practices (Lynch & Hanson, 2004b). When possible, programs should strive to use "cultural brokers" in screening processes (Lyman et al., 2007). Activities such as describing the purpose of screening; interpreting scores with consideration to a wide variety of factors, including cultural factors that may impact a child's performance; sensitively communicating results; and negotiating with families about what, if any, referrals should be made are critical training and procedural issues. If providers do not consider cultural factors such as communication style, nonverbal communication, and values regarding developmental delays or disabilities, a variety of negative outcomes could result. These negative outcomes might include the over- or underidentification of children, unnecessary follow-up assessment, and parents who are reluctant (or refuse) to take the "next steps" to access services for their children when developmental concerns are indicated.

Considerations for Ongoing Development and Improvement of Screening Practices

Over the last four decades, developmental screening tools and processes have changed substantially. What began primarily as a professionally centered, infrequently administered, and resource-intensive approach to early identification has evolved through research and recommended practice into more flexible, potentially less costly, family-centered approaches (Glascoe et al., 1997). Three major developments have significantly altered the developmental screening landscape: (1) availability of technically adequate screening tools appropriate for young children; (2) growing awareness of the importance of early development and evidence that early childhood interventions yield significant short- and long-term benefits; and (3) recommended practices and professional standards disseminated by organizations such as the Division for Early Childhood (Sandall, Hemmeter, Smith, & McLean, 2005), the National Association for the Education of Young Children (Copple & Bredekamp, 2009), National Research Council (Snow & Van Hemel, 2008), and the American Academy of Pediatrics (AAP, 2001, 2006).

Despite these advances, significant numbers of children still do not receive developmental screening in their early years and enter school with cognitive, motor, or communication delays that have not been identified. These delays could likely have been lessened, and general social and academic outcomes improved, had recommended screening practices (i.e., the periodic use of high-quality screening tools) and early identification of delays occurred (Radecki et al., 2011; Squires et al., 2009; U.S. Department of Health and Human Services, Centers for Disease Control and Prevention, 2005). For children from minority and other underserved groups, problems are magnified in that these groups are not receiving developmental screening services with the same frequency as children from white, majority groups (Delgado & Scott, 2006); plus, they are entering early intervention programs in lower numbers (Johnson & Theberge, 2007). Children who do not regularly see physicians or who do not attend childcare centers might not be part of screening initiatives, such as those described in the present article. Universal screening efforts that involve establishing systems and procedures that ensure at least all young children receive one or more developmental assessments in their first 5 years remains an important goal for the future.

To improve the accuracy and efficiency of developmental screening systems and processes, the following enhancements and alterations can be made to existing programs and are strongly encouraged to be considered and included in the development of new screening programs.

1. **Evaluation of screening efforts**. To assure accuracy and efficiency, evaluation procedures need to be part of the screening system. The numbers of children who (1) are being referred for follow-up evaluations, (2) are qualifying for early intervention, and (3) did not immediately qualify but did after a period of time are among the data that need to be gathered to evaluate screening programs and to promote equal access for minority children and those children living in rural and underserved areas.

2. **Involvement of parents and family members**. A cornerstone of effective screening assessment practices is parent involvement. Emphasis on culturally sensitive practices that promote parent involvement can increase the accuracy of the screening processes and enhance future intervention efforts. Language barriers, cultural sensitivity, and determination of the appropriateness of screening tools for their intended purpose should be addressed to support the involvement of family members in all aspects of screening.

3. **Ongoing training of practitioners**. An accurate and effective screening system depends upon well-trained practitioners who understand screening processes, can skillfully assist parents as they participate in the system, and administer screening tools as intended, with sensitivity to cultural and individual variations. Quality personnel are the key to a successful system.

Developmental screening practices have come a long way and continued advancements in the coming decades are anticipated in terms of the development of universal systems, technically adequate tools, and culturally relevant practices. Through universal screening and accurate early identification of delays, children in need of early interventions will receive them in a timely manner. Universal systems will help to assure that children with delays or disabilities are identified and receive early inter-

Figure 1
Factors to Consider When Developing a Screening System

DEVELOPMENTAL SCREENING IN EARLY CHILDHOOD

Factors to Consider when Developing a Screening System

- Population to be screened (e.g., age of children served, characteristics of parents such as language and cultural diversity, literacy levels)
    - ✓ Which tools are age-appropriate?
    - ✓ Which tools are available in the languages our parents speak?
    - ✓ Which tools provide flexibility in terms of administration methods and test materials?
- Community partners and health care providers (e.g., WIC, YMCA, Resource and referral services, United Way, pediatric groups)
    - ✓ What other programs are serving children and families?
    - ✓ What other programs are providing screening?
    - ✓ What tools are pediatricians and other health care providers already familiar with?
- Technical adequacy of the selected tool (e.g., validity, or level of under- and over-referral rates, reliability, or consistency of scores across raters and administration times, normative population)
    - ✓ How many children might be over-referred based on sensitivity and specificity studies?
    - ✓ How does the normative sample on which the cut-offs are based compare to the population of families that our program serves?
    - ✓ What are reliability rates between parents and professionals?
- Cost and available resources
    - ✓ How much will it cost to purchase and use the tool?
    - ✓ Are the forms reproducible or will we need to purchase a form for each child we screen?
    - ✓ Will existing staff need to be trained and/or will new staff need to be hired?
- Systems issues such as referral sources
    - ✓ What types of resources are available to assist families when concerns are identified?
    - ✓ What are eligibility requirements for referral sources?
    - ✓ Are potential referral sources ready to receive referrals?
- Training on how to administer the tool as designed
    - ✓ What type of training is needed to support administration of tool, interpretation of results, communication of results, and supporting parents in decision making when concerns are identified?

vention services prior to school entry. Practitioners working in many different capacities including early intervention, early childhood education environments, family daycare, home visiting, and community support programs (e.g., Women, Infants, and Children, Family Resource Centers) can be valuable participants in universal screening efforts. Establishing effective screening systems can be a challenging endeavor, and there are many decisions that must be made along the way. Figure 1 shows factors to consider as screening systems are established or enhanced.

Practitioners working in many different capacities including early intervention, early childhood education environments, family daycare, home visiting, and community support programs (e.g., Women Infants and Children, Family Resource Centers) can be valuable participants in universal screening efforts

The purpose of this article has been to provide guidance to practitioners and program administrators who are considering creating or expanding screening efforts. When implementing screening programs, those involved will have to balance recommended practices with real-life application. There is no definitive roadmap for creating screening programs, and there are likely many alternate routes that might be taken, some possibly more effective than others. In the present article, we offered insights and resources for those who decide to take the journey. It is a trip worth taking and we encourage and applaud your efforts.

Note
You may reach Jantina Clifford by e-mail at jantinac@uoregon.edu

References
American Academy of Pediatrics (AAP). (2001). Developmental surveillance and screening of infants and young children. *Pediatrics, 108*, 192-196.
American Academy of Pediatrics (AAP). (2006). Identifying infants and young children with developmental disorders in the medical home: An algorithm for developmental surveillance and screening. *Pediatrics 118*, 405-420.
American Academy of Pediatrics (AAP). (2007). Recommendations for preventive pediatric health care. *Pediatrics, 120*, 1376.
Aylward, G. (1995). *Bayley Infant Neurodevelopmental Screener.* San Antonio, TX: Pearson.
Bagnato, S. (2005). The authentic alternative for assessment in early intervention: An emerging evidence-based practice. *Journal of Early Intervention, 28*, 17-22.
Bagnato, S. J., Neisworth, J. T., & Pretti-Frontczak, K. (2010). *Linking authentic assessment and early childhood intervention* (2nd ed.). Baltimore: Brookes.
Bailey, D. (2004). Tests and test development. In M. McLean, M. Wolery, & D. Bailey (Eds.), *Assessing infants and preschoolers with special needs* (3rd ed., pp. 22-44), San Antonio, TX: Pearson.
Blackman, J. (2002). Early intervention: A global perspective. *Infants & Young Children, 15*(2), 11-19.
Bodnarchuk, J. & Eaton, W. (2004). Can parent reports be trusted? Validity of daily checklists of gross motor milestone attainment. *Applied Developmental Psychology, 25*, 481-490.

Bricker, D. & Littman, D. (1985). Parental monitoring of infant development. In R. McMahon & R. Peters (Eds.). *Childhood disorders: Behavioral-developmental approaches* (pp. 90-115). New York: Brunner/Mazel.

Bricker, D. & Squires, J. (1989). Low cost system using parents to monitor the development of at-risk infants. *Journal of Early Intervention, 13,* 50-60.

Brigance, A. (2005). *Brigance–II Infant & Toddler Screen.* North Billerica, MA: Curriculum Associates.

Child Abuse Prevention and Treatment Act, 42 U.S.C.A. § 5106g (2003).

Copple, C. & Bredekamp, S. (2009). *Developmentally appropriate practice in early childhood programs: Serving children from birth through age 8.* Washington, DC: National Association for the Education of Young Children.

Delgado, C. & Scott, K. (2006). Comparison of referral rates for preschool children at risk for disabilities using information obtained from birth certificate records. *Journal of Special Education, 40,* 28-35.

Dinnebeil, L. & Rule, S. (1994). Congruence between parents' and professionals' judgments about the development of young children with disabilities: A review of the literature. *Topics in Early Childhood Special Education. 14,* 1-25.

Dunst, C. & Trivette, C. (2009). Let's be PALS: An evidence-based approach to professional development. *Infants & Young Children, 22*(3), 164-176.

Dunst, C. J., Trivette, C. M., Appl, D. J., & Bagnato, S. J. (2004). Framework for investigating child find, referral, early identification, and eligibility determination practices. *Tracelines, 1,* 1-11. Retrieved September 15, 2011, from http://www.tracecenter.info/tracelines/tracelines_vol1_no1.pdf

Early and Periodic Screening, Diagnosis, and Treatment, 42 U.S.C. § 1396 (1989).

Frankenburg, W. & Dodds, J. (1967). The Denver Developmental Screening Test. *Journal of Pediatrics, 71*(2), 181-191.

Frankenburg, W., Dodds, J., Archer, P., Shapiro, H., & Bresnick, B. (1992). The Denver II: A major revision and restandardization of the Denver Developmental Screening Test. *Pediatrics, 89,* 91-97.

Glascoe, F. P. (1991). Developmental screening: Rationale, methods, and application. *Infants & Young Children, 4,* 1-10.

Glascoe, F. P. (1999). Using parents' concerns to detect and address developmental and behavioral problems. *Journal of the Society of Pediatric Nurses, 4,* 24-35.

Glascoe, F. (2000). Evidence-based approach to developmental and behavioral surveillance using parents' concerns. *Child: Care, Health & Development, 26,* 137-149.

Glascoe, F. (2006). PEDS: *Parent's Evaluation of Developmental Status.* Nashville, TN: Ellsworth & Vandermeer.

Glascoe, F. P. (2009). *Developmental, mental health/behavioral and academic screens.* Retrieved September 15, 2011, from http://www.first5ecmh.org/docManager/1000000058/screening%20tools.pdf

Glascoe, F., Altemeier, W., & Maclean, E. (1989). The importance of parents' concerns about their children's development. *American Journal of Diseases of Children, 143,* 855-858.

Glascoe, F., Foster, M., & Wolraich, M. (1997). An economic analysis of developmental detection. *Pediatrics, 99,* 830-837.

Guralnick, M. (1997). *The effectiveness of early intervention.* Baltimore: Brookes.

Guralnick, M. (2005). *The developmental systems approach to early intervention.* Baltimore: Brookes.

Hambleton, R., Merenda, P., & Spielberger, C. (2005). *Adapting educational and psychological tests for cross-cultural assessment.* Hillsdale, NJ: Erlbaum.

Hart, B. & Risley, T. (1995). *Meaningful differences in the everyday experience of young American children.* Baltimore: Brookes.

Head Start Performance Standards, 45 C.F.R. § 1304 (2008).

Hemmeter, M., Santos, R., Snyder, P., Hyson, M., Harris-Solomon, A., Bailey, D., et al. (2005). Young children with, or at risk for, developmental disabilities. In K. C. Lakin & A. Turnbull (Eds.), *National goals & research for people with intellectual and developmental disabilities* (pp. 15-37). Washington, DC: American Association on Mental Retardation.

Individuals with Disabilities Education Act, 20 U.S.C. § 1400 (2004).

Ireton, H. (1990). *Child Development Review Parent Questionnaire.* Minneapolis, MN: Behavior Science Systems.

Ireton, H. (1992). *Child Development Inventory.* Minneapolis, MN: Behavior Science Systems.

Johnson, K. & Theberge, S. (2007). *Reducing disparities beginning in early childhood.* New York: National Center for Children in Poverty.

Kirp, D. (2007). *The sandbox investment: The preschool movement and kids-first politics.* Cambridge, MA: Harvard University Press.

Knobloch, H., Stevens, F., Malone, A., Ellison, P., & Risemburg, H. (1979). The validity of parental reporting of infant development. *Pediatrics, 63,* 872-878.

Lynch, E. & Hanson, M. (2004a). Family diversity, assessment, and cultural competence. In M. McLean, M. Wolery, & D. Bailey (Eds.), *Assessing infants and preschoolers with special needs* (3rd ed., pp. 71-99). San Antonio, TX: Pearson.

Lynch E. & Hanson, M. (2004b). *Developing cross-cultural competence: A guide for working with children and their families* (3rd ed.). Baltimore: Brookes.

Lyman, D., Njoroge, W., & Willis, D. (2007). Early childhood psychosocial screening in culturally diverse populations: A survey of clinical experience with the Ages and Stages Questionnaires: Social-Emotional. *Zero to Three, 27*(5), 46-54.

Mardell-Czudnowski, C. & Goldenberg, D. S. (1998). *Developmental Indicators for the Assessment of Learning* (3rd ed.) Circle Pines, MN: American Guidance Service.

McLean, M. (2004). Identification and referral. In M. McLean, M. Wolery, & D. Bailey (Eds.), *Assessing infants and preschoolers with special needs* (3rd ed., pp. 100-122). San Antonio, TX: Pearson.

McLean, M. & Crais, E. (2004). Procedural considerations in assessing infants and preschoolers with disabilities. In M. McLean, M. Wolery, & D. Bailey (Eds.), *Assessing infants and preschoolers with special needs* (3rd ed., pp. 45-70). San Antonio, TX: Pearson.

McLean, M., Wolery, M., & Bailey, D. B. (2004). *Assessing infants and preschoolers with special needs* (3rd ed.). Upper Saddle River, NJ: Merrill/Prentice Hall.

Meisels, S., Marsden, D., Wiske, M., & Henderson, L. (2008). *Early Screening Inventory–Revised*. San Antonio, TX: Pearson.

Meisels, S. & Provence, S. (1989). *Screening and assessment: Guidelines for identifying young disabled and developmentally vulnerable children and families*. Washington, DC: National Center for Clinical Infant Programs.

Meisels, S. & Shonkoff, J. (2000). Early childhood intervention: A continuing evolution. In J. P. Shonkoff & S. J. Meisels (Eds.), *Handbook of early childhood intervention* (2nd ed., pp. 3-31). New York: Cambridge University Press.

National Scientific Council on the Developing Child. (2007). *The science of early childhood development*. Cambridge, MA: Harvard University.

Neisworth, J. T. & Bagnato, S. (1992). The case against intelligence testing in early intervention. *Topics in Early Childhood Special Education, 12*, 1-20.

Neisworth, J. T., & Bagnato, S. J. (2005). DEC recommended practices: Assessment. In S. Sandall, M. L. Hemmeter, B. J. Smith, & M. E. McLean (Eds.), *DEC recommended practices: A comprehensive guide for practical application in early intervention/early childhood special education* (pp. 45-69). Missoula, MT: Division for Early Childhood.

Nickel, R. & Squires, J. (2000). Developmental screening in young children. In R. Nickel & L. Desch (Eds.), *Physician's guide to caring for children with disabilities and chronic conditions* (pp. 16-29). Baltimore: Brookes.

Ohtake, Y., Santos, R., & Fowler, S. (2005). It's a three-way conversation: Families, service providers, and interpreters working together. *Young Exceptional Children Monograph, 6*, 33-43.

Patient Protection and Affordable Care Act, 42 U.S.C. § 18001 (2010).

Pizur-Barnekow, K., Erickson, S., Johnston, M., Bass, T., Lucinski, L., & Bleuel, D. (2010). Early identification of developmental delays through surveillance, screening, and diagnostic evaluation. *Infants & Young Children, 23*, 323-330.

Radecki, L., Sand-Loud, N., O'Connor, K. G., Sharp, S., & Olson, L. M. (2011). Trends in the use of standardized tools for developmental screening in early childhood: 2002-2009. *Pediatrics, 128*, 14-19.

Ramey, C. T. & Ramey, S. L. (1998). Early intervention and early experience. *American Psychologist, 53*, 109-120.

Ring, E. & Fenson, L. (2000). The correspondence between parent report and child performance for receptive and expressive vocabulary beyond infancy. *First Language, 20*, 141-159.

Ringwalt, S. (2008). *Developmental screening and assessment instruments with an emphasis on social and emotional development for young children ages birth through five*. Chapel Hill: The University of North Carolina, Frank Porter Graham Child Development Institute, National Early Childhood Technical Assistance Center.

Salvia, J., Ysseldyke, J., & Bolt, S. (2009). *Assessment in special and inclusive education* (11th ed.). Boston: Houghton-Mifflin.

Sameroff, A. (2010). A unified theory of development: A dialectic integration of nature and nurture. *Child Development, 81*, 6-22.

Sameroff, A. & Chandler, M. (1975). Reproductive risk and the continuum of caretaking casualty. In F. Horowitz, et al. (Eds.), *Review of child development research* (Vol. 4, pp. 187-244). Chicago: University of Chicago Press.

Sameroff, A. & Fiese, B. (2000). Transactional regulation: The development ecology of early intervention. In J. P. Shonkoff and S. J. Meisels (Eds.), *Handbook of early childhood intervention* (2nd ed., pp. 135-159). New York: Cambridge University Press.

Sameroff, A. J., Seifer, R., Baldwin, A., & Baldwin, C. (1993). Stability of intelligence from preschool to adolescence: The influence of social and family risk factors. *Child Development, 64*, 80-97.

Sandall, S., Hemmeter, M. L., Smith B. J., & McLean, M. E. (Eds.). (2005). *DEC recommended practices: A comprehensive guide for practical application in early intervention/early childhood special education*. Missoula, MT: Division for Early Childhood.

Shonkoff, J. P. & Meisels, S. J. (Eds.). (2000). *Handbook of early childhood intervention* (2nd ed.). New York: Cambridge University Press.

Shonkoff, J. & Phillips, D. (2000). *From neurons to neighborhoods: The science of early childhood development*. Washington, DC: National Academy Press.

Snow, C. & Van Hemel, S., (Eds.). (2008). *Early childhood assessment: Why, what, and how*. Washington, DC: National Research Academies Press.

Squires, J. & Bricker, D. (2009). *Ages and Stages Questionnaires: A parent-completed child-monitoring system,* (3rd ed.). Baltimore: Brookes.

Squires, J., Nickel, R., & Eisert, E. (1996). Early detection of developmental problems: Strategies for monitoring young children in the practice setting. *Journal of Developmental and Behavioral Pediatrics, 17*, 410-427.

Squires, J., Twombly, E., Bricker, D., & Potter, L. (2009). *ASQ–3 User's Guide*. Baltimore: Brookes.

Trivette, C. & Dunst, C. (2005). DEC recommended practices: Family-based practices. In S. Sandall, M. L. Hemmeter, B. Smith, & M. McLean (Eds.), *DEC recommended practices: A comprehensive guide for practical application in early intervention/early childhood special education* (pp. 107-126). Missoula, MT: Division for Early Childhood.

U.S. Department of Health and Human Services, Centers for Disease Control and Prevention. (2005). *Child development: Developmental screening.* Retrieved September 15, 2011, from http://www.cdc.gov/ncbddd/child/devtool.htm

U.S. Department of Health and Human Services, Health Resources and Services Administration, Maternal and Child Health. (n.d.). *EPDST Overview.* Retrieved September 15, 2011, from http://www.hrsa.gov/epsdt/overview.htm

Werner, E.E. (1993). Risk, resilience and recovery: Perspectives from the Kauai longitudinal study. *Development and Psychopathology, 5*, 503-515.

Werner, E. E. & Smith. R. S. (2001). *Journeys from childhood to midlife: Risk, resilience, and recovery*. Ithaca, NY: Cornell University Press.

Widerstrom, A. & Nickel, R. (1997). Determinants of risk in infancy. In A. H. Widerstrom, B. A. Mowder, & S. R. Sandall (Eds.), *Infant development and risk: An introduction* (2nd ed., pp. 61-88). Baltimore: Brookes.

Zeanah, C. Z. (2009). *Handbook of infant mental health* (3rd ed.). New York: Guilford Press.

Zigler, E. & Styfco, S. (2004). *The Head Start debates.* Baltimore: Brookes.

Assessment of Family-Identified Needs Through the *Routines-Based Interview*

R. A. McWilliam,

Amy M. Casey,
Siskin Children's Institute, Chattanooga, TN

Debbie Ashley,
Hamilton County (OH) Developmental Disabilities Services

Jeanne Fielder,

Peg Rowley,
Gretna Public Schools, Gretna, NE

Kelly DeJong,

Julie Mickel,
Siskin Children's Institute, Chattanooga, TN

Sarintha B. Stricklin,
New Orleans, LA

Kristen Votava,
University of North Dakota

The Routines-Based Interview (RBI) is a method for families to identify their needs, including those of the eligible child (McWilliam, 1992, 2010c). This identification of individualized needs is essential for individualized family service plans (IFSPs) and individual education programs (IEPs) to be meaningful. IFSP outcomes and IEP goals are supposed to be based on the results of assessment. In this article, we discuss (a) interviewing as a valid method of assessment in early intervention/early childhood special education (EI/ECSE), (b) helping families select outcomes/goals, (c) interviewing across cultures and languages, and (d) training to conduct the RBI.

Interviewing for Assessment

Krista looked over the test results for the newest child on her case-load, EJ, a 14-month-old living with his mother, a child care worker, and father, a factory worker. The test scores showed that he was eligible for early intervention services because of his delays in communication, social, and adaptive skills. His cognitive and motor skills were within normal limits. As Krista considered the upcoming individualized family service plan (IFSP) development process, usually involving a couple of meetings, she wondered what kinds of needs she would be trying to help this family address. She had conducted an "ecomap" (described below in the section Family Needs Emerging From the RBI), so she knew they had only a few family members in the area, but those were very supportive, and she knew that EJ was enrolled in the child care center where his mother worked. But Krista needed to conduct a routines-based interview (RBI) even to begin to know what functional needs had to be addressed—child and family needs.

Authentic assessment should capture a child's ability to function in meaningful contexts (Neisworth & Bagnato, 2005). One method for assessing child and family needs is interviewing at least one adult member of the family with whom the child lives. If we add *needs* to our traditional focus on developmental status in assessment, the fundamentals of a clinical interview can be used in our field to derive authentic assessment information. Clinical interviews can be used to obtain parent report, which allows IFSP/IEP teams to learn about the actual needs of children and families (McWilliam, 2010a).

> *One method for assessing child and family needs is interviewing at least one adult member of the family with whom the child lives.*

Clinical Interviews

The RBI is a "clinical" interview in the sense that it is used to obtain a rich and thick description of child and family functioning, has beneficial effects on the interviewee, and leads to a treatment plan (McWilliam, 2005, 2010a, 2010b). It is conducted as a step in the development of the IFSP/IEP, asking families to describe their naturally occurring routines (i.e., events, times of day). Within each routine, the interviewer asks about the role of all people in the home; the child's engagement, independence, and social relationships; and the interviewee's rating of satisfaction with the routine. The interview proceeds from the beginning of the parents' day to the end of their day, and, if the child is cared for by somebody else for 15 hours a week or more, that person is interviewed too. At the end of the interview, the interviewer recaps concerns the interviewees mentioned or concerns the interviewer had, and the parents choose their priorities. The team later converts these priorities into outcomes/goals. The interview lasts approximately 2 hours and results in 6–12 outcomes/goals. The steps for conducting the RBI are listed in Appendix 1.

In the RBI, the transition from one routine to another occurs with the interviewer asking, "What happens next?" He or she asks an open-ended question, such as "What does breakfast time look like?" about the next routine. After that, the interviewer asks follow-up questions to arrive at the predetermined type of information (what everyone else is doing, engagement, independence, social relationships, satisfaction with the routine). This combination of open and follow-up questions is what makes the RBI a semistructured interview (Barriball & While, 1994). Such interviews have been used successfully in qualitative or "grounded" research to gather data about families' experiences with their children and with early intervention services (Bailey et al., 1998; McWilliam et al., 1995). Semistructured interviews allow the interviewee to speak freely and elaborate on issues, yet the information is bounded by the interviewers' questions, both leading and follow-up.

> *The result of this conversation is that families are comfortable with the professional and the professional has information that would be very useful for helping the family*

The RBI provides a safe context for families to talk about their everyday experiences. It is safe because the stated and actual purpose is to let the family decide what they want to change about their routines or what they think the child will do in the future that he or she is not currently doing. Interviewers are trained to withhold judgment, to refrain from becoming the expert by giving advice, and to speak plainly and without jargon. The result of this conversation is that families are comfortable with the professional and the professional has information that would be very useful for helping the family (Dunst, Trivette, & Hamby, 1996; Dunst, Trivette, Boyd, & Brookfield, 1994). Parents provide multiple exemplars (Stokes & Baer, 1977), the perspective of the person who will actually be intervening with the child, and knowledge about the demands of the environment. The RBI differs from other interviews, such as "creating conversations" (Turnbull, Erwin, Turnbull, Soodak, & Shogren, 2010), in its routines-by-engagement/independence/social relationships structure. It is perhaps closest to Bernheimer and Weisner's (2007) "family story," being a description of what occurs through the day; the firm rooting of the RBI in engagement theory, however, makes it unique.

Role of Needs Assessment in IFSP and IEP Processes

Child assessment information is required on the IFSP and the IEP. In addition, assessment of the family's concerns, priorities, and resources is needed on the IFSP. In practice, many professionals separate the family's concerns and priorities from the child's. They have child assessment information, usually related to eligibility determination, and they have family-level priorities on the concerns, priorities, and resources (CPR) section of the IFSP. Family-level priorities can include housing, financial, or parent-education needs, among many others. When these needs are listed on the CPR page of the IFSP, they can lie fallow: there is no obligation actually to address them. If, instead, they were treated with the same seriousness as child outcomes (e.g., sitting independently), professionals might provide as much help as they do to address child outcomes. Family-level needs do not even show up on IEPs, where there is no requirement to list such needs.

Part C of the Individuals With Disabilities Education Improvement Act (IDEA; § 322), which is the part pertaining to infants and toddlers and their families, requires assessment of the child's strengths and needs (in this sense, *needs* is often considered a euphemism for *weaknesses*) and the concerns, priorities, and resources of the family. The law says the family assessment must "be conducted by personnel trained to utilize appropriate methods and procedures" ((3)(i)), which highlights the fact that it should not be done haphazardly or amateurishly (Cox, Keltner, & Hogan, 2003). Unfortunately, in practice, this assessment is usually carried out without any particular methods or procedures or with the use of a home-grown questionnaire. Furthermore, the early intervention professionals conducting the assessments are usually not trained to do so. Why should they be? The methods they are using require no training. The law indicates that the assessment must be conducted through a personal interview. In practice, a short conversation as part of the intake or the IFSP meeting might be considered a personal interview, but that stretches the definition of such.

The language in the law regarding child assessment repeats the admonishment to have trained personnel use appropriate methods. It also states that the evaluation and assessment must be based on informed clinical opinion—a requirement often neglected in practice. Many states have had informed clinical opinion as a third eligibility criterion, in addition to an established condition and developmental delay, but most if not all have ignored the requirement that it be used for all assessments. Although all states report the child's level of development in the five required domains, in practice a needs assessment is not usually conducted beyond identifying weaknesses.

In IEPs, under IDEA 2004, "a statement of the child's present levels of academic achievement and functional performance," rather than simply "levels of educational achievement," as IDEA 1997 said, must be included. In developing the IEP, the team is supposed to consider the child's strengths, the parents' concerns for enhancing the child's education, the result of an evaluation, and the child's academic, developmental, and functional needs (§ 1414(d)(3)(A)). In addition to the strengths statement, these requirements are important for including parents' concerns and "functional needs." In practice, both are often overlooked. Parents' concerns might be politely asked about, but they carry no weight in the pragmatic hurly-burly of churning out IEPs. Most educators and administrators are still oriented to the traditional focus of the IEP, which is academics (Pretti-Frontczak & Bricker, 2000).

Both Part C and Section 619 of Part B (the section of IDEA dealing with preschoolers) state that children need to be evaluated for eligibility, if they are not eligible automatically as a function of their disability. Their needs also must be assessed, as a careful reading of the law shows.

Helping Families Select Outcomes/Goals

One late afternoon, Krista and her colleague Claudia met EJ's mother, Janice, at her small house in a neighborhood of very similar houses. Janice had been allowed to go home from work early for this meeting, so she had EJ with her. Claudia's role during the interview was going to be that of note taker, but now she was going to have to be a babysitter too. From the beginning, Janice was open and friendly, but Krista could tell that having a linear discussion, such as going through the day, was going to be challenging. Krista asked Janice what her main concerns were (EJ's talking) and, with questions about waking-up time, diaper change, and breakfast, she began to form a picture of EJ's abilities and interests as well as of Janice's parenting and self-efficacy. After a few more routines (hanging out, going out to the car, the car ride to work and child care) were discussed, Krista saw that she and Claudia, who had actually been able to take notes, had plenty of starred items. These were the needs or concerns that had emerged during the conversation. She knew that they would not necessarily become outcomes on the IFSP, but she was relieved to see that there would be a lot for Janice to think about when it came time to select outcomes.

Janice described the family's activities in a rambling way, but Krista kept track. As Janice wandered off into tangents, Krista gently brought her back to the time of day in question. It might not have been a well-structured report, but, like a gifted painter, Janice made dabs and strokes all over the canvas, gradually forming a coherent picture. The picture was a combination of EJ's interests and abilities and Janice's and her husband's own needs as parents and a couple. EJ's deficits in communication skills, which had been Janice's main concern, did come up, but so did many other things that Janice said she wanted to see him doing in the next 6 months. During the conversation about each routine, Krista found out what Janice would like EJ to be doing. Sometimes, he wasn't showing a particular skill because he was delayed and sometimes because he simply had not matured enough. It didn't really matter. Krista knew the RBI was about solutions, helping parents identify their dreams, and planning to make those dreams come true. It was not just about failure.

Part C and preschool services differ in the nature of family participation in the development of the IFSP or IEP, respectively. In Part C, it is generally assumed that families' priorities are central to the selection of outcomes. Furthermore, family-level outcomes are allowed, even though many IFSP teams are still concentrating exclusively on child-level needs. In preschool services, families must be given the opportunity to participate in IEP development, but usually the goals are recommended by professionals, and family-level needs are not allowed as goals (Gallagher & Desimone, 1995). Therefore, IFSPs provide a structure for making the plan family centered, but professionals do not generally take advantage of the opportunity, whereas IEPs do not provide any structure for making the plan family centered.

We should not let the first question, "What are your main concerns?" be the last question.

Assuming that professionals developing the IFSP or IEP are interested in families' being able to have their priorities result in outcomes or goals, the RBI provides a structure for that to happen. In this section, we discuss why asking parents for their priorities should not be the only question, why test performance as a source of outcomes is problematic, how to steer families toward functionality, and how family needs emerge from the RBI.

Why the First Question Should Not Be the Last Question

When professionals ask families what their main concerns are, those concerns become the IFSP outcomes. We know this because, in providing training and technical assistance across the United States, we have seen that the average number of outcomes is between two and three and that many of them are walking/movement or talking/communication outcomes. On IEPs, it appears that families' priorities are either not sought or they are ignored, because most IEPs have goals looking suspiciously like professionals' concerns, including skills on tests or curricula (Westby, 1990).

We should not let the first question, "What are your main concerns?" be the last question. In other words, we should not take families' answers to this question to develop IFSP/IEP outcomes/goals. The first reason is because families are likely to answer without knowing the implications of their answer. Even if they did know that professionals were asking this to develop outcomes/goals, families going through the IFSP/IEP process for the first time would not know the implications this might have on service decisions and service delivery.

The second reason is that main concerns differ from the list of priorities delivered at the end of an intensive discussion about child and family functioning throughout the day—that is, an RBI. For example, one family of a toddler said their main concerns were the child's talking and crawling, so the IFSP had those two outcomes and only those two outcomes. After an RBI, the list of priorities, in order of importance, was as follows:

1. Communicate *mama*, *dada*, *more*, *done*
2. Move independently, shifting weight
3. Finger-feeding
4. Be more vocal
5. Throw things
6. Swallow liquid from cup
7. Clap by himself
8. Melissa and Halli get along
9. Halli not scream at dinner prep time

The main concerns were reflected in the top two priorities, but another seven priorities were also identified. In the routines-based early intervention model (McWilliam, 2010b), all nine priorities would be converted to measurable outcomes, even though not all would be addressed on any one visit. The last two outcomes refer to the sister, Halli, of the target child, Melissa. These are, therefore, family-level outcomes. The reader is referred to McWilliam (2005) for a transcript of a typical interview.

The third reason for not making the first question (What are your main concerns?) the last question (What outcomes/goals will we work on?) is that families have no framework for determining outcomes/goals (Zhang & Bennett, 2003). The RBI gives them a way to think about their child's engagement, independence, and social relationships in everyday routines, thereby helping them construct a functional list of outcomes/goals.

Professionals, therefore, need to conduct a much more in-depth assessment of needs than simply asking families about main concerns. They also should avoid simply using test performance results to determine IFSP/IEP goals.

Why Test Performance Is Problematic

Test performance is often used as a source of outcomes/goals, which is problematic. First, on tests, individual items are generally not considered to be important; credible scores using the test come from aggregating item scores into subscale or scale scores. So picking skills represented by individual items is a misuse of the test. Second, individual test items might have good "item response" in that they contribute to the validity of the tool, but the skill might not be at all important in an individual's life. Even if subscale or domain scores are used, they do not necessarily provide a good basis for outcome/goal selection. The area of deficit might not be a priority for the family.

Functional behavior can be defined as actions the child can use to participate in his or her routines.

A tenet of assessment is that instruments should be restricted to the use for which they were intended. Eligibility determination instruments, therefore, are questionable sources for intervention planning, including outcome/goal selection. There is a way, though, of steering families toward functionality when planning interventions.

Steering Families Toward Functionality

Functional behavior can be defined as actions the child can use to participate in his or her routines. It therefore excludes prerequisite skills that do not have an immediate impact on participation or engagement (e.g., maintaining kneeling for 20 seconds) and practice of a behavior if each instance of the behavior does not result in meaningful engagement (e.g., drill activities) (McWilliam, 1995). It can include actions that are fun for the child, because having fun is an ingredient of early childhood.

Because professionals and advocates have been so focused on whether children receive the services they need, as though *need* were an absolutely determined construct, the functionality of outcomes/ goals has been viewed as less important than whether the outcomes/ goals will justify the services desired even before outcomes/goals were considered. In other words, professionals and parents looked first at the diagnosis or deficit, picked the therapies they thought would address them, and then picked outcomes/goals to justify the services. This, of course, is backward and not how IDEA requires service decisions to be made.

Due to federal requirements to report children's progress in child outcomes (http://www.fpg.unc.edu/~eco/pages/fed_req.cfm), teams are forced to think about how their interventions might affect children's taking action to meet their needs, acquiring knowledge and skills, and engaging in social relationships (the three federal child outcomes). These outcomes were designed to represent functional skills. The requirement to report progress in these areas has the potential to shift professionals' orientation to results rather than services. The RBI is all about function, in that the interviews are about engagement or participation in routines, independence, and social relationships, which are similar to acquiring knowledge and skills, taking action to meet one's needs, and engaging in social relationships.

The RBI, therefore, orients the team—family and professionals— toward functional outcomes, using natural resources whenever possible to attain those outcomes. This functionality orientation stands in contrast to a service orientation (Dunst, Trivette, & Deal, 1994). Because functionality in early childhood is embedded within the child's primary ecology, the family, the needs of the adults in the family emerge from the RBI.

Family Needs Emerging From the RBI

Family needs include basic needs such as shelter, clothing, and food; parenting needs such as information on feeding and behavior management; self-actualization such as spending time the way the adults want to (including time alone); and self-improvement such as higher education and living in a better neighborhood. Because the RBI examines what everyone in the family is doing during each routine and because RBI implementers are maneuvered into adopting a family-centered orientation, family-level needs emerge.

It is important to assess family-level needs, in part, because child outcomes are more likely to be better when family needs are met, although the National Institute of Child Health and Human Development (NICHD) Early Child Care Research Network found that this relationship between family needs and child outcomes was weaker for children in child care than for children not in child care (NICHD Early Child Care Research Network, 2005). A parent's bucket has to be filled before he or she can fill the child's. The RBI has both immediate and longer term impacts on bucket filling, in that families report feeling truly listened to by a caring person when they participate in an RBI, and the identification of family needs sets up the early interventionist to address those needs with the family.

The RBI helps families understand that early intervention/early childhood special education (EI/ECSE) has a broad scope, especially early intervention. Once a family has been interviewed with this process, it is no surprise to them that professionals are willing to help with parenting, siblings, using community resources, and more.

The emergence of family needs from the RBI is especially important when working with families with particular parent-level vulnerabilities such as poverty, mental-health or intellectual-disability problems, and intra-familial conflicts.

The emergence of family needs from the RBI is especially important when working with families with particular parent-level vulnerabilities such as poverty, mental-health or intellectual-disability problems, and intrafamilial conflicts. If professionals are not aware of these needs, they will be less effective in working with the family. Similarly, the RBI manages to secure information about the child's and family's strengths, assets, and support systems, although the "ecomap" is more ideally suited to capturing informal and formal supports. The ecomap, a depiction of the family's friends, family, neighbors, faith-based connections, work connections, health- and development-related professionals, and other resources (Cox et al., 2003), is typically developed before the RBI. Therefore, this is the first place where supports are identified. They then are further identified during the RBI.

Assessing family needs is a requirement in Part C and, developmentally, should be in Section 619 (preschool). The RBI is a tool professionals can use to conduct such an assessment. By giving families a method for them to identify their own needs, steering them toward functionality, providing an alternative to test performance, and going beyond the main-concerns question, the RBI helps families select outcomes/goals. A logical question might be how well it works for all kinds of families.

Interviewing Across Cultures and Languages

Many of Krista's families were African American, as was this one. She was aware that she looked every bit the well-educated, White professional she was. Her life and Janice's were worlds apart. Yet, in the context of talking about helping Janice and her husband with EJ, the gap between them narrowed quickly. During the RBI, Krista tried not to come across as the educated agency representative interrogating the client family, but rather as a friendly neighbor who was very interested in EJ. She used an informal approach, with no professional jargon, but also not condescending by trying to emulate the family. Krista had a good sense of who she was—a pretty straightforward, unassuming, young woman with an easy laugh. She matched Janice's affect, so that when Janice told a funny story, Krista laughed heartily. When Janice spoke about her frustrations, Krista looked concerned and asked more questions. The cultural gulf between these two people seemed small when talking about Janice's family life and what she wanted for her little boy.

Families participating in EI/ECSE are even more diverse than the population at large (Scarborough et al., 2004; Workgroup on Principles and Practices in Natural Environments, 2007). The RBI is for everyone. In the spirit of the mission of early intervention (Workgroup on Principles and Practices in Natural Environments), it should not be denied to certain families just because professionals assume it is unsuitable for them. The way the RBI is done should be molded to different families, rather than excluding families from the opportunity to participate. Issues related to cultures and languages include intrusiveness, interviewing style, and interpreters.

Intrusiveness and Interest

One of the most common concerns about the RBI among professionals is that it might be intrusive, and yet this has never been identified as a concern among families (McWilliam, Tocci, & Harbin, 1998). Families have expressed appreciation for interviewers' wanting to understand the details of their lives as parents and, in our experience, have said that, compared with people coming into their homes, this interview is hardly intrusive. At the beginning of the interview, families are told not to say anything they do not want to say. The RBI captures only what families want to tell us about family functioning. Professionals concerned about intrusiveness also mistake the product for the process. That is, just because the family revealed seemingly private information does not mean the interviewer sought it.

Some professionals feel awkward about the difference between them and the families they are interviewing. For example, White professionals might state that, when they are interviewing Native Americans, the family might be more reserved than if the interviewer were also Native American. Unfortunately, we do not have the luxury in the United States of making these matches; in fact, most professionals in our field are university-educated White women, and of course, huge numbers of families in EI/ECSE are not. Some professionals go to considerable lengths to join families, by dressing informally, speaking in slang, and so on. This could backfire. Families can see who we are, and our approach is more important than our dress and language patterns. In fact, the more honest interviewers are about who they are as people, the more likely families will be comfortable.

So few problems have been reported in the actual, as opposed to the anticipated, use of the RBI with families from different backgrounds that we believe our assumption to be true—that most families like professionals to be interested in them. They know the interviewer is of a different background, but they know this person is genuinely interested in what happens with the child and family and is going to help. Intrusiveness is, therefore, largely a nonissue when families can tell the interviewer is truly interested.

Style in Interviewing

The interviewer's approach or style affects the likely success of an interview across cultures and language (Banks, Santos, & Roof, 2003). Interviewers need to pay attention to how they come across. Professionals' demeanor is an underappreciated skill set. We use *skill set* deliberately because interview behaviors can be shaped, although the interviewer's existing interpersonal traits make a difference. In conducting RBIs, interviewers should be respectfully informal, curious, empathetic, and nonjudgmental. The RBI Implementation Checklist (see Appendix 2), which is used for training, includes a number of items related to the person's style.

The nonverbal communication the interviewer uses is powerful (Knapp & Hall, 2009). RBI interviewers are trained to sit at right angles to the parent who is likely to do most of the talking, to hold papers flat so parents can see them, and to nod and smile in affirmation frequently throughout the interview.

In studies on teaching styles, the aggregate of the affect items predicted child engagement more than the teaching behaviors did (McWilliam, Scarborough, & Kim, 2003). Although the impact was on children, it was another example of the importance of positive affect. In a study of 550 return visits to 127 different doctors at 11 sites across the country, doctors' asking questions about biomedical topics was negatively associated with patient satisfaction, but doctors' questions about psychosocial topics were positively related (Bertakis, Roter, & Putnam, 1991). This showed the relationship of doctor interview style to patient satisfaction. The interviewer's style or affect is, therefore, a key to building trust, which helps obviate feelings of intrusiveness, and genuineness, which helps the flow of information the family provides.

Awkwardness of Interpreted Interviews

The most awkward aspect of conducting the RBI across languages is the interpreted interview. In the best of situations, a certified interpreter would be used. This person interprets exactly what each person says, both English to the other language and the other language to English. In the second-best situation, a professional but uncertified interpreter does the same thing. In the third-best situation, an informal interpreter, such as a neighbor or a family member interprets. Of course, the worst situation is when no interpreters are available. Because the interview is an entirely verbal activity, the inability to communicate in the same language renders the interview impossible. Interviewing across cultures and languages, therefore, is a challenge due to professionals' assumptions because they have to find the right style and because interpretation is awkward.

Training to Conduct the RBI

On the surface, the RBI is a straightforward, semistructured interview. Beneath the surface, however, conducting it requires the interviewer to display a plethora of knowledge and skills, including knowledge of child development and family functioning, people skills, following the protocol, taking the right amount of notes (which can be done by a second interviewer), eliciting information without implying correct and incorrect parenting, and managing the time. The field now has the experience of some states mandating that RBIs be conducted but failing to provide adequate training to service coordinators. As observed by the first author in many technical-assistance visits, these states have seen debased versions of the RBI resulting in inadequate IFSPs. On the other hand, some states have provided excellent training in the RBI, resulting in high-quality IFSPs.

Generally, we recommend that training consist of the following steps:

1. Introductory workshop to explain the purpose of the RBI and demonstrate the RBI, followed by a reflective session.

2. Practice with vignettes in a workshop, with at least four people per group: a simulated parent, a primary interviewer, a second interviewer, and a feedback giver (using the RBI Implementation Checklist).

3. If possible, accompany an experienced interviewer, perhaps serving as the second interviewer and feedback giver, using the RBI Implementation Checklist.

4. Practice with two families already in early intervention, unobserved, to gain confidence; use the RBI Implementation Checklist as a self-check.

5. Interview families, observed (the observer can also function as the second interviewer), until achieving more than 90% correct on the RBI Implementation Checklist.

6. Periodically, return for follow-up workshops to solve problems and gather ideas from other interviewers.

This training relies heavily on checklist-based performance feedback (Casey & McWilliam, 2011; Lattimore, Stephens, Favell, & Risley, 1984). Workshops are valuable but only for inspiration (through demonstration), information, and problem solving. The actual training happens through feedback and, to some extent, observing experienced interviewers.

A cadre of certified RBI trainers has been developed through the annual RBI Certification Institute, held at the Siskin Children's Institute in Chattanooga, TN. This week-long institute provides much opportunity for real practice interviews with families in early intervention and feedback from certified RBI coaches. At the time of writing, 65 people have participated in these institutes, but only 39 have met the rigorous certification requirements so far. Of these, 37 trainers are distributed across 14 states. In the interest of self-disclosure, we should state that the authors are all graduates of or involved in the running of the Certification Institute.

The RBI, therefore, has potential for directing early intervention toward functional activities, for increasing children's engagement in home and community routines, and for empowering families by giving them a meaningful role in planning.

Conclusion

We used to teach children skills out of a box (Shearer & Shearer, 1976), so the early interventionist and the family simply chose the next skill the child could not perform. Meanwhile, therapists were using a similar approach, assessing children's function in their area of development and teaching the skills the child could not perform. The functionality of these predetermined skills for an individual child and family were really not of major importance. With the advent of the IFSP and superficial understanding of the concept of family centeredness, early interventionists painted themselves into a corner by asking families what they wanted to work on, resulting in only two or three ill-defined outcomes (Jung & McWilliam, 2005). Three influential factors emerging in the field are (a) in the United States, attention to functional child outcomes (as well as family outcomes) to demonstrate the effectiveness of early intervention (Hebbeler, Barton, & Mallik, 2008); (b) internationally, the implementation of the International Classification of Functioning–Children and Youth, which emphasizes the child's participation in home, school, and community (Simeonsson et al., 2003); and (c) a new appreciation for the contexts or routines in which children live as a basis for determining functional interventions (Dunst, Bruder, Trivette, Raab, & McLean, 2001; McWilliam, 2010b; Weisner, Matheson, Coots, & Bernheimer, 2005). The RBI, therefore, has potential for directing early intervention toward functional activities, for increasing children's engagement in home and community routines, and for empowering families by giving them a meaningful role in planning.

Note

You may reach Robin McWilliam by e-mail at robin.mcwilliam@siskin.org

References

Bailey, D. B., Jr., McWilliam, R. A., Darkes, L. A., Hebbeler, K., Simeonsson, R. J., Spiker, D., & Wagner, M. (1998). Family outcomes in early intervention: A framework for program evaluation and efficacy research. *Exceptional Children, 64*, 313-328.

Banks, R. A., Santos, R. M., & Roof, V. (2003). Discovering family concerns, priorities, and resources: Sensitive family information gathering. *Young Exceptional Children, 6*(2), 11-19.

Barriball, K. & While, A. (1994). Collecting data using a semi-structured interview: A discussion paper. *Journal of Advanced Nursing, 19*, 328-335.

Bernheimer, L. P. & Weisner, T. S. (2007). "Let me just tell you what I do all day . . .": The family story at the center of intervention research and practice. *Infants and Young Children, 20*, 192-201.

Bertakis, K. D., Roter, D., & Putnam, S. M. (1991). The relationship of physician medical interview style to patient satisfaction. *The Journal of Family Practice, 32*, 175.

Casey, A. M. & McWilliam, R. A. (2011). The impact of checklist-based feedback on teachers' use of the zone defense schedule. *Journal of Applied Behavior Analysis, 44*, 397-401.

Cox, R. P., Keltner, N., & Hogan, B. (2003). Family assessment tools. In R. P. Cox (Ed.), *Health related counseling with families of diverse cultures: Family, health, and cultural competencies* (pp. 145-167). Westport, CT: Greenwood Press/Greenwood Publishing.

Dunst, C. J., Bruder, M. B., Trivette, C. M., Raab, M., & McLean, M. (2001). Natural learning opportunities for infants, toddlers, and preschoolers. *Young Exceptional Children, 4*(3), 18-25.

Dunst, C. J., Trivette, C. M., Boyd, K., & Brookfield, J. (1994). Help-giving practices and the self-efficacy appraisals of parents. In C. J. Dunst, C. M. Trivette, & A. G. Deal (Eds.), *Supporting and strengthening families: Methods, strategies, and practices* (Vol. 1, pp. 212-220). Cambridge, MA: Brookline Books.

Dunst, C. J., Trivette, C. M., & Deal, A. G. (1994). Resource-based family-centered intervention practices. In C. J. Dunst, C. M. Trivette, & A. G. Deal (Eds.), *Supporting and strengthening families: Methods, strategies, and practices* (Vol. 1, pp. 140-151). Cambridge, MA: Brookline Books.

Dunst, C. J., Trivette, C. M., & Hamby, D. W. (1996). Measuring the helpgiving practices of human services program practitioners. *Human Relations, 49*, 815-835.

Gallagher, J. & Desimone, L. (1995). Lessons learned from implementation of the IEP: Applications to the IFSP. *Topics in Early Childhood Special Education, 15*, 353-378.

Hebbeler, K., Barton, L., & Mallik, S. (2008). Assessment and accountability for programs serving young children with disabilities. *Exceptionality, 16*, 48-63.

Jung, L. A. & McWilliam, R. A. (2005). Reliability and validity of scores on the IFSP Rating Scale. *Journal of Early Intervention, 27*, 125-136.

Knapp, M. L. & Hall, J. A. (2009). *Nonverbal communication in human interaction.* Florence, KY: Wadsworth.

Lattimore, J., Stephens, T. E., Favell, J. E., & Risley, T. R. (1984). Increasing direct care staff compliance to individualized physical therapy body positioning prescriptions: Prescriptive checklists. *Mental Retardation, 22*, 79-84.

McWilliam, R. A. (1992). *Family-centered intervention planning: A routines-based approach.* Tucson, AZ: Communication Skill Builders.

McWilliam, R. A. (1995). Integration of therapy and consultative special education: A continuum in early intervention. *Infants & Young Children, 7*, 29.

McWilliam, R. A. (2005). Assessing the resource needs of families in the context of early intervention. In M. J. Guralnick (Ed.), *A developmental systems approach to early intervention* (pp. 215-234). Baltimore: Brookes Publishing.

McWilliam, R. A. (2010a). Assessing families' needs with the routines-based interview. In R. A. McWilliam (Ed.), *Working with families of young children with special needs* (pp. 27-59). New York: Guilford Press.

McWilliam, R. A. (2010b). *Routines-based early intervention: Supporting young children with special needs and their families.* Baltimore, MD: Brookes Publishing.

McWilliam, R. A. (Ed.). (2010c). *Working with families of young children with special needs.* New York: Guilford.

McWilliam, R. A., Ferguson, A., Harbin, G. L., Porter, P., Munn, D., & Vandiviere, P. (1998). The family-centeredness of individualized family service plans. *Topics in Early Childhood Special Education, 18*, 69-82.

McWilliam, R. A., Lang, L., Vandiviere, P., Angell, R., Collins, L., & Underdown, G. (1995). Satisfaction and struggles: Family perceptions of early intervention services. *Journal of Early Intervention, 19*, 43-60.

McWilliam, R. A., Scarborough, A. A., & Kim, H. (2003). Adult interactions and child engagement. *Early Education and Development, 14*, 7-27.

McWilliam, R. A., Tocci, L., & Harbin, G. L. (1998). Family-centered services: Service providers' discourse and behavior. *Topics in Early Childhood Special Education, 18*, 206-221.

National Institute for Child Health and Human Development (NICHD) Early Child Care Research Network. (2005). Relations between family predictors and child outcomes: Are they weaker for children in child care? [Abridged] *Child care and child development: Results from the NICHD Study of Early Child Care and Youth Development* (pp. 407-417). New York: Guilford Press.

Neisworth, J. T. & Bagnato, S. J. (2005). DEC recommended practices: Assessment. In S. Sandall, M. L. Hemmeter, B. J. Smith, & M. McLean, *DEC recommended practices: A comprehensive guide for practical application,* (pp. 45-69). Longmont, CO: Sopris West.

Pretti-Frontczak, K. & Bricker, D. (2000). Enhancing the quality of individualized education plan (IEP) goals and objectives. *Journal of Early Intervention, 23*, 92-105.

Scarborough, A. A., Spiker, D., Mallik, S., Hebbeler, K. M., Bailey, D. B., & Simeonsson, R. J. (2004). A national look at children and families entering early intervention. *Exceptional Children, 70*, 469-484.

Shearer, D. E. & Shearer, M. S. (1976). The Portage Project: A model for early childhood intervention. In T. Tjossem (Ed.), *Intervention strategies for high risk infants and young children* (pp. 335-350). Austin, TX: PRO-ED.

Simeonsson, R. J., Leonardi, M., Lollar, D., Bjorck-Akesson, E., Hollenweger, J., & Marinuzzi, A. (2003). Applying the international classification of functioning, disability and health (ICF) to measure childhood disability. *Disability & Rehabilitation, 25*, 602-610.

Stokes, T. F. & Baer, D. M. (1977). An implicit technology of generalization. *Journal of Applied Behavior Analysis, 10*, 349-367.

Turnbull, A., Erwin, E. J., Turnbull, R., Soodak, L. C., & Shogren, K. A. (2010). *Families, professionals, and exceptionality: Positive outcomes through partnerships and trust* (6th ed.). Saddle River, NJ: Prentice Hall.

Weisner, T. S., Matheson, C., Coots, J., & Bernheimer, L. P. (2005). Sustainability of daily routines as a family outcome. In M. I. Martini & A. E. Maynard (Eds.), *Learning in cultural context: Family, peers, and school* (pp. 41-73). New York: Kluwer Academic/Plenum Publishers.

Westby, C. E. (1990). Ethnographic interviewing: Asking the right questions to the right people in the right ways. *Communication Disorders Quarterly, 13*, 101.

Workgroup on Principles and Practices in Natural Environments. (2007). Agreed-upon practices for providing early intervention services in natural environments Retrieved July 6, 2008, from http://www.nectac.org/~pdfs/topics/families/AgreedUponPractices_FinalDraft2_01_08.pdf

Zhang, C., & Bennett, T. (2003). Facilitating the meaningful participation of culturally and linguistically diverse families in the IFSP and IEP process. *Focus on Autism and Other Developmental Disabilities, 18*, 51-60.

Appendix 1

Key Steps in the Routines-Based Interview

1. Find out who lives in the home(s) with the child and possibly conduct an ecomap (a depiction of the family's supports).
2. Ask the family for their main concerns.
3. Ask the family to describe how their day starts—the adults' day.
4. Keep the agenda to specific routines (i.e., times of day, events, activities, places).
5. During the description of each routine, determine
   a. What everyone in the family is doing during the routine;
   b. What the child's engagement is like;
   c. How independent the child is;
   d. What the child's social relationships are like;
   e. The parents' satisfaction with the routine, on a scale of 1–5.
6. Ask the child care provider or teacher about child care or "school" routines, including engagement, independence, and social relationships.
7. Throughout the interview, mark areas of concern for the parent, the teacher, or the interviewer(s).
8. Ask the family
   a. What they worry about (this question is asked in a very specific way; see the RBI Implementation Checklist) and
   b. What they would like to change in their life (also asked in a very specific way).
9. Recap the marked areas of concern.
10. Drawing out a blank sheet of paper (i.e., not reviewing the marked concerns yet), list the things the family says they want to work on: These are outcomes/goals. If helpful, the interviewer can show the family the starred items as a reminder of their concerns.
11. Ask the family to put outcomes/goals into priority order.

Appendix 2

RBI Implementation Checklist
R. A. McWilliam, 2008

Interviewer_____ Date_____

Observer _____ Items Correct:_____

Scored: _____ %: _____

Scoring.

+ Observed as described.

+/− Partially observed.

− Not observed or observed to be incorrect.

	+	+/−	−	Comments
Beginning				
1. Did the interviewer prepare the family, at least the day before the interview, by telling them (a) that they will be asked to describe their daily routines, (b) they can choose a location, and (c) they can choose who participates (including whether it's one or both parents)?				
2. Did the interviewer greet the family then review the purpose for the meeting (e.g., to get to know the family and to determine how best to provide support to their child and family)?				
3. Did the interviewer ask the parents if they have any major questions or concerns before starting the interview?				
Routines				
4. Did the interview stay focused on routines rather than developmental domains?				
5. Were open-ended questions used initially to gain an understanding of the routine and functioning (followed by closed-ended questions if necessary)?				

	+	+/−	−	Comments
6. Did the interviewer find out what people in the family other than the child are doing in each routine?				
7. Were there follow-up questions related to engagement?				
8. Were there follow-up questions related to independence?				
9. Were there follow-up questions related to social relationships?				
10. Did the interviewer ask follow-up questions to gain an understanding of functioning?				
11. Were follow-up questions developmentally appropriate?				
12. Did the interviewer ask for a rating of each routine?				
13. To transition between routines, was the question *What happens next?* or something similar used?				
14. Did the interviewer attempt to get the parent's perspective on behaviors (why he/she thinks the child does what he/she does)?				
15. If there were no problems in the routine, did the interviewer ask what the parent would like to see next?				
16. Did the interviewer avoid unnecessary questions, such as the specific time something occurs?				
17. Did the interviewer use "time of day" instead of "routine"?				
18. Did the interviewer put a star next to the notes where a family has indicated a desire for change in routine or has said something they would like for their child or family to be able to do?				

	+	+/−	−	Comments
Style				
19. Did the interviewer use good affect (e.g. facial expressions, tone of voice, responsiveness)?				
20. Did the interview have a good flow (conversational, not a lot of time spent writing)				
21. Did the interviewer maintain focus without attending too much to distractions?				
22. Did the interviewer use affirming behaviors (nodding, positive comments or gestures)?				
23. Did the interviewer use active listening techniques (rephrasing, clarifying, summarizing)?				
24. Did the interviewer avoid giving advice?				
25. Did the interviewer act in a nonjudgmental way?				
26. Did the interviewer return easily to the interview after an interruption?				
27. Did the interviewer allow the family to state their own opinions, concerns, etc. (not leading the family towards what the interviewer thinks is important)?				
Family Issues				
28. Did the interviewer get information on the parent's down time (any time for him/herself)?				
29. Ask the family, "When you lie awake at night worrying, what is it you worry about?"				
30. Ask the family, "If you could change anything about your life, what would it be?"				

	+	+/−	−	Comments
Outcome/Goal Selection				
31. Did the person taking notes recap (i.e., summarize) the starred concerns?				
32. Did the recap take no more than 5 minutes?				
33. Was it clear that these concerns (i.e., starred items) were not outcomes/goals?				
34. After the interviewer has summarized concerns, was the family asked if anything should be added?				
35. After summarizing concerns (starred items) did the interviewer take out a clean sheet of paper and ask the family what they wanted to work on (a new list)?				
36. Did the interviewer ask the family to put the outcomes into a priority order of importance?				
37. Did the interviewer say what will happen next with this information (e.g., outcomes/goals written in behavioral, measurable terms; services decided upon)?				

Goal: 90% items scored as +

Using the *Assessment* of *Family Activities and Routines* to Develop Embedded Programming

Philippa H. Campbell
Thomas Jefferson University

Established early intervention practices recommend that professionals gain information about different aspects of family life, including family strengths, priorities, concerns, and resources (Sandall, Hemmeter, Smith, & McLean, 2005). Different strategies are suggested to gain this information, including formal protocols such as the Routines-Based Interview (McWilliam, Casey, & Sims, 2009) or more informal strategies such as written checklists or community map drawings (Sexton, Snyder, Rheams, Barron-Sharp, & Perez, 1991; Woods & Lindeman, 2008). Information gathered from families is the foundation of family-centered practices including professional-parent collaboration (Mott et al., 1986; Trivette & Dunst, 2005). Service coordinators frequently collect information from the family and incorporate priorities into the Individual Family Service Plan (IFSP) document. The information provides a picture of current life including what matters to a family and what they would like to have happen. Optimally, early intervention services are infused into family life in ways that support each family's ability to promote their child's development and learning.

At the heart of early intervention are the services provided to families and children via various philosophies (e.g., family centered), models (e.g., routines based), and approaches (e.g., transdisciplinary, interdisciplinary, single service provider; Stremel & Campbell, 2007). Service providers design and use teaching strategies to enable children to learn and develop. These strategies may be delivered mainly by the service provider, as is the case in traditional service models (e.g., Campbell & Sawyer, 2007; Dunst, Trivette, Humphries, Raab, & Roper, 2001) or via parents, siblings, child care providers, or other caregivers as is a recommended component of many early intervention approaches (e.g., Bruder & Dunst,

2000; Campbell, 2004; Cripe, Hanline, & Dailey, 1997; Rush & Shelden, 2011; McWilliam, 2000, 2010; Stremel & Campbell, 2007). In traditional models, service providers are both the designers and implementers of the intervention strategies, which means that service providers determine an activity (e.g., play), the materials needed (e.g., toys), and the strategies (e.g., hand-over-hand guidance) that will be used to promote child learning. In routines-based models, adults who spend time with the child (e.g., parents, family members, child care staff) identify family activities or routines into which learning opportunities and strategies are embedded. In this approach, service providers design embedded learning opportunities and strategies and teach other adults how to use them; other adults are the primary implementers. Embedding learning opportunities and strategies is a widely accepted approach with preschoolers although not explicitly discussed in the infant-toddler early intervention literature. Opportunities to use identified skills naturally or with the support of teaching strategies, are embedded into the daily schedule of activities and routines in preschool classrooms as a way to promote children's skill acquisition (e.g., Bruder, 1993; Buysee & Wesley, 2007; Campbell, Cooper, & McInerney, 1984; Pretti-Fronczak & Bricker, 2004; Sandall & Swartz, 2008; Wilcox, Bacon, & Greer, 2005).

Assessing Family Activities and Routines

In contrast to the fairly predictable schedules, activities, and routines in child care and preschool settings, when children's services are provided at home, an assessment of a family's schedule of activities/routines helps identify situations in which learning opportunities and strategies may be embedded. Learning opportunities include either natural or adult-created opportunities for children to perform skills generally identified as learning outcomes on the IFSP. For example, a child may need to learn a skill of reaching. Opportunities to reach may occur naturally because a child wishes to obtain a particular object or communicate a message such as "pick me up," or these opportunities may be adult created within the context of activities or routines. During mealtimes, for example, the caregiver may position a spoon far enough away from the child that reaching is necessary to get the spoon or may wait for a child to reach toward the adult before automatically picking the

Learning opportunities include either natural or adult-created opportunities for children to perform skills generally identified as learning outcomes on the IFSP.

Table 1
**Categories of Activities/Routines on the Assessment of Family Activities/
Routines**

Routines	Bath time Morning routine (getting up, getting dressed, bathing/washing) Bedtime (getting ready for bed, going to bed, sleeping) Mealtimes (appetite, level of assistance) Leaving the house Travel time (riding in a car, bus; walking, etc.)
Activities	Play time (indoor play) Story time Outdoor play (riding a bike, playing outside, playing on playground equipment, swimming) At home chores (cleaning, preparing meals, watching TV, caring for pets, etc.) Running errands (grocery store, mall/store shopping, banking, wash/cleaners) Outings (visit a friend/relative, eat at a restaurant/fast food, go to museums, amusement parks, zoo, etc.)

child up. In many situations, natural or created learning opportunities may be sufficient, but in other circumstances, additional teaching strategies may be needed. Guidance or cues may be added to help a child reach the spoon. Both learning opportunities and strategies may be embedded within activities and routines.

The *Assessment of Family Activities and Routines* (Campbell, 2009) was designed for use by service providers during or after completion of the IFSP but as a first step in developing embedded programming. The purpose is to provide a vehicle for provider-caregiver collaboration to identify activities/routines as contexts for programming. The form is available at http://jeffline.jefferson.edu/cfsrp/pdfs/Assessment%20of%20Caregiver%20Activities%20and%20Routines.pdf). The form consists of three parts: (1) six activity and six routine categories listed in Table 1, (2) five functional skill areas (i.e., communication, socialization, getting around, use of arms/hands, and problem solving), and (3) summary matrices used to target activities or routines for programming. Broad-ranging categories of both routines and activities are intentionally sampled. The two categories separate caregiving routines (e.g., bath time, mealtimes) from family activities

> *The Assessment of Family Activities and Routines (Campbell, 2009) was designed for use by service providers during or after completion of the IFSP but as a first step in developing embedded programming.*

(e.g., outings, errands) on the basis of frequency of occurrence and family lifestyle, a distinction that is primarily important for later programming decisions. Most families engage in caregiving routines regularly with infants and toddlers but may neither engage in all listed activities nor do so at high frequencies. The occurrence of family activities is dependent on a family's priorities, choices, time constraints, or other factors. The *Assessment* includes spaces in which additional activities/routines may be added or divided into smaller components. For example, going to the zoo or a community toddler music group or the library might be individually listed to subdivide activities within the outings category.

General Guidelines for Using the Assessment Form

The format (see Figure 1) is designed as a flexible framework to structure an interview or conversation with children's caregivers to identify the contexts in which future programming will occur.

Figure 1
The *Assessment of Family Activities and Routines* Is Designed to Guide Conversation Between the Provider and Child's Caregiver(s) to Identify Activities/Routines as Contexts for Embedded Instruction

PARTICIPATION-BASED SERVICES

Assessment of Family Activities & Routines

Date: _____ Child's name: _____ Completed As Guided Interview with _____ by Provider Name: _____

DIRECTIONS FOR USING THE ASSESSMENT AS AN INTERVIEW/CONVERSATION WITH CAREGIVERS

1. Ask the caregiver open ended questions about each activity/routine. For example, start by saying "tell me about bathtime and what you and your child do during bathtime." Follow-up by asking additional questions so that you gain an understanding, a picture, of what the routine or activity looks like. Then ask the caregiver to rate the child's participation in terms of the caregiver's expectations (e.g., exceeds, meets, occasionally meets, does not meet). Then, ask the caregiver about satisfaction with how the activity/routine is going.
2. Ask the caregiver to rate the child's use of functional skills (e.g., socializing, communicating) within activities and routines and satisfaction with the child's abilities. You are not trying to find out about the child's deficit or delay (e.g., speech) but rather about the extent to which problems or limitations interfere with a child's participation.
3. Identify any routines which may not be going well (so that you can help families make them go better); Identify routines that are positive for families/children as these will provide a context in which to show families how to teach developmental skills to their children.

	EXPECTATIONS					SATISFACTION				
ROUTINE/ACTIVITY	Exceeds	Meets	Occasionally Meets	Does not meet	**COMMENTS**	Very	Is OK	Somewhat	Not	Did Not Ask
BATHTIME										
MORNING ROUTINE (getting up, getting dressed, bathing/washing)										
BEDTIME (getting ready for bed, going to bed, sleeping)										
MEALTIMES (appetite, level of assistance)										

Assessment of Activities/Routines   Available from Child & Family Studies Research Programs, Thomas Jefferson University, Philadelphia, PA   Campbell/6-2009REV/page 1 of 4

Service providers may use the form to speak with a group of family members (e.g., mother, father, grandparents) together or may interview only the adult identified as the child's primary caregiver. The conversa-

tion may be completed in about 30 to 45 minutes with most families and may occur in one or more sessions, depending on the preferences of the family and provider. Tables 2 and 3 provide examples of two ways of structuring conversations to discuss activities/routines. One approach begins the conversation with talk about the family's day. A second approach starts with discussing one activity/routine and then moving to others. In either case, a framework is provided so that all activities/routines are ultimately discussed although not necessarily in the order listed on the assessment form.

Steps for Conducting the Provider-Caregiver Interview Using the Assessment Form

The first step in using the *Assessment* is to plan a time when the service provider and the family may have a conversation about family activities/routines. The *Assessment* allows providers to learn information from caregivers about particular activities or routines, some of which providers may be unable to observe directly (e.g., bedtime). The most likely time to schedule the interview is during the initial home visit(s) made by providers because the primary purpose of the interview is to aid in the design of child programming.

The Assessment allows providers to learn information from caregivers about particular activities or routines, some of which providers may be unable to observe directly (e.g., bedtime).

The second step is to actually have a conversation with the caregiver. The depth of information obtained is dependent on (1) available time, (2) how the assessment is administered, and (3) interviewer skills. The *Assessment* is designed to accomplish three goals: (1) to learn about the activity or routine (e.g., "tell me about bath time"), (2) to elicit the caregiver's perspective of the extent to which the child's performance in the activity or routine meets caregiver expectations, and (3) to learn about

Table 2
Typical Day Conversational Structure for Using the Assessment of Family Activities/Routines

What Provider Says	What Provider Writes
Ask the caregiver to tell you about a typical day – what happens from when everyone gets up in the morning until they go to bed.	As the caregiver discusses each routine on the questionnaire, write notes in the middle space on the form, then follow up by asking the caregiver to rate the child's performance.
Using the form as a guideline, ask the caregiver about activities/routines that were not mentioned. For example, "You talked about putting ____ to bed at night but you didn't mention bath time. When does ___ usually get a bath and how does this work?"	By using probing questions, the provider makes sure that descriptions of activities/routines are noted in the comments section and that caregivers have rated the child's performance.
Ask caregivers if there are other activities/routines they would like to talk about and find out caregiver ratings of child performance.	List these activities/routines in the blank boxes and indicate the caregiver's rating of the child's performance; write any information under the comments section.
In addition to knowing about child performance, knowledge about the caregiver's satisfaction with the child's performance can also be helpful. The caregiver can be asked about satisfaction as a follow-up.	Indicate the satisfaction rating on the form.
Summarize and end the interview by reviewing information and indicating any activities/routines that are not going well (i.e., do not meet expectations).	List activities/routines where caregivers are not satisfied and child performance does not meet expectations and write descriptions of what the caregiver would like to see happen.
	Some caregivers may not have activities/routines where the child's performance does not meet expectations. Leave the form blank in these instances.
Follow-up questions may be used to probe what has been tried, how well it worked or did not work, etc.	This information is written on the form.

Table 2 (*continued*)

What Provider Says	What Provider Writes
Summarize those activities/routines that are successful or enjoyable for the caregiver/child. Ask any needed follow-up questions to understand why these go well (e.g., child enjoys riding in the car; loves music that caregiver plays during breakfast). This information will be used to help select one or more activities/routines in which to embed learning opportunities.	Add in any notations about why the activity/routine is enjoyable. Plans for embedding learning opportunities and intervention strategies will be made using intervention planning formats.

Table 3

Conversational Structure for Using the Assessment of Family Activities/ Routines by Starting With One Routine/Activity

What Provider Says	What Provider Writes
Begin by asking the caregiver to tell you about what happens during one activity/ routine (e.g., bath time). The goal is to understand what this activity/routine looks like. Ask any needed follow-up or probe questions to get a full understanding – "You talked about _____ sitting in the bathtub in a bath seat, but tell me how he helps with washing?" "When bath time is going on, do you use this as a time for playing in the tub?" "What kinds of toys does ___ like to play with?" "What happens when you wash his hair?" When the caregiver has discussed the routine, ask him or her to rate the child's performance.	As the caregiver discusses bath time, write notes in the middle space on the form, then follow up by asking for ratings of the child's performance and mark the correct box.
Using the form as a guideline, ask the caregiver about each activity and routine listed on the form. You may ask in the order the items appear on the form or vary the order, making sure that all areas are discussed. Use follow-up questions or probes so that you understand what each routine looks like for this caregiver/child; summarize/ end the discussion of each activity/routine by asking for the caregiver's rating of the child's performance.	Written descriptions of activities/ routines are completed for each category, and the form is marked to indicate caregiver ratings of child performance.
Ask caregivers if there are other activities/ routines they would like to talk about and find out about the caregiver's expectations of the child's performance.	List these activities/routines in the blank boxes and indicate caregiver's rating of the child's performance; write any information under the comments.

Table 3 (*continued*)

What Provider Says	What Provider Writes
It may be helpful to know how satisfied the caregiver is with the child's performance in order to determine the importance of this activity/routine for the caregiver. All activities/routines may be reviewed – "You talked about mealtimes and said that ____'s performance sometimes met your expectations. How satisfied are you with how this routine is going?" Or, ask about satisfaction ratings at the end of the discussion about each activity or routine.	Indicate the satisfaction rating on the form.
Summarize and end the interview by reviewing information and indicating any activities/routines that are not going well. These will be those where the child's performance does not meet expectations. List all of the activities/routines identified in this way and ask the caregiver to describe what each would look like if it were going well. Follow-up questions may probe what has been tried, how well it worked or did not work, etc.	List activities/routines and write descriptions of what the caregiver would like to see happen. Some caregivers may not have activities/routines where the child's performance does not meet expectations. Leave the form blank in these instances.
Summarize those activities/routines that are successful and enjoyable for the caregiver/child. Ask any needed follow-up questions to understand why these go well (e.g., child enjoys riding in the car; loves music that caregiver plays during breakfast). This information will be used to help select one or more activities/routines in which to embed learning opportunities.	Add in any notations about why the activity/routine is enjoyable. Plans for embedding learning opportunities and intervention strategies will be made using intervention planning formats.

the caregiver's satisfaction with the activity or routine. If the form is used as a checklist whereby the provider asks questions and records the caregiver's answers to each item, the information will be obtained quickly (i.e., will not require a lot of time) and is likely to be so superficial as to be ineffective as a source of information for programming. The point of the provider-caregiver interview is to gain an understanding of how activities/routines are experienced by the caregiver and child. Using follow-up questions and probes within each activity/routine category promotes conversation about how the activities/routines work, children's participation, and caregiver expectations and satisfaction. Table 4 provides examples of probes that may be used to elicit more information from the caregiver.

Table 4
Examples of Probe Question Areas to Provide More Depth About Family Activities/Routines

The ease with which the activity/routine is conducted
What the caregiver expects from the child
How the caregiver helps the child during the activity/routine
How much the child and caregiver enjoy the routine
Any strategies the caregiver has used to enable the child's participation or to make the activity/routine enjoyable or manageable
How often the activity/routine is done
How much time the caregiver spends daily doing the activity/routine or how much time is spent when the activity/routine is done

In Step 3, the provider discusses children's functional skills. This conversation is designed to explore the impact of any limitations in functional skills on children's participation in family activities and routines. Caregivers' perspectives of children's functional skill performance and its impact on activity/routine participation are rated in terms of caregiver expectation. Caregivers also rate their satisfaction with what children are able to do. Functional skill ratings measure children's functional competence in terms of participation in activities/routines and are not ratings about developmental delay or disability. For example, a caregiver may rate a child's functional communication as meeting expectations even when the child is unable to speak and may do so because the child uses a communication device. Similarly, a child may be unable to walk independently but may meet caregiver expectations in the functional skill of getting around because the child crawls well enough to get around the house or may use a power chair competently. As with discussions about participation in activities/routines, the interviewer attempts to understand the specific ways in which any functional skill limitations alter a child's participation and uses probe questions to find out how limitations have been addressed, what has been tried before, or what a situation would "look like" to the caregiver if this functional skill limitation were reduced.

Functional skill ratings measure children's functional competence in terms of participation in activities/routines and are not ratings about developmental delay or disability.

In Step 4, activities/routines that fit into one of two categories are summarized. First, activities/routines that are not going well are identified. Many families manage activities/routines well and no challenging activities/routines are identified. But for other families, participating in simple routines such as being positioned in a car seat and riding in a car or going to the grocery store or on errands may be challenges for caregivers and children. Second, activities/routines that go well for families and children are identified. These activities/routines become possible contexts for embedding both skill-learning opportunities and the strategies for teaching those skills. For example, a nighttime book-reading activity may allow a child to acquire or practice skills such as receptive vocabulary by hearing pictures labeled, expressive vocabulary by imitating or initiating words, motor skills by pointing to pictures or turning book pages, and so forth.

How Information From the Assessment Is Used

The end of the provider-caregiver activities/routines interview provides a transition to a discussion about programming. This final *Assessment* step results in lists of potentially challenging and/or enjoyable activities/ routines from which caregivers select those on which to focus in early intervention programming. If the assessment has taken place as part of

developing the IFSP, the information may be used to write the outcome statements on the IFSP. When the assessment has been completed by a service provider during an initial home visit (and after the completion of the IFSP), information about activities/routines is combined with any skill-focused IFSP outcomes to design early intervention programming.

Writing IFSP outcome statements. One use of information about activities/routines is to develop participation-based or functional outcome statements (McWilliam, 2010). These state-

ments combine targeted developmental skills with information about caregiver-selected activities/routines to emphasize children's participation. "Rayel will partici-pate in mealtimes by using utensils to feed herself and drinking independently from a cup," is an example of an outcome state-ment in which the developmental skills that a child needs to learn are incorpo-rated into the activity or routine in which the skills will be both learned and used. The identified activity/routine provides an initial context for where and when planned opportunities for learning and practicing the identified skill will take place. In addition to opportu-

nity or practice, many children with dis-abilities or delayed development require planned teaching strategies that will also be embedded into designated activities/routines so that children receive needed intervention strategies (Campbell, 2009). Further expansion of an outcome state-ment for Rayel to specify opportunities and strategies might be written as, "Rayel

will participate in mealtimes by using utensils when prompted for a mini-mum of 20 opportunities and by drinking independently from a cup 10 times during the meal."

Families or other caregivers are more likely to understand both par-ticipation-based or functional outcome statements and their roles in implementing plans with their children. When parents, caregivers, and child care teachers see an outcome statement that targets a particular skill (e.g., "Susan will use a pincher grasp to pick up small objects"), their role in providing learning opportunities and specific interventions may not be as clear as in a statement that targets participation (e.g., "Susan will par-ticipate at restaurants by picking up Cheerios or Fruit Loops between her thumb and the tip of her first finger (pincher grasp)"). Although neither outcome statement specifies the implementer, the implication is that the person with the child in the restaurant will be the implementer.

Designing early intervention programming. Early intervention programming takes place within both challenging and going-well activities/routines and in particular within those identified for focus by the caregiver (Jung, 2003). Providers can enable families to carry out any problematic activities/routines in more efficient, educational, or pleasant ways (Bernheimer & Weisner, 2007; Campbell, Sawyer, & Muhlenhaupt, 2009; Kling, Campbell, & Wilcox, 2010). One important aspect of the

Providers can enable families to carry out any problematic activities/routines in more efficient, educational, or pleasant ways.

Assessment of Family Activities and Routines is the structured discussion about and identification of any challenging activities/routines. This discussion may not come up in typical caregiver-provider interactions, and therefore, providers may not know about situations in which their expertise may be helpful. The purpose of caregiver identification of any activities/routines that may not be going well is so that providers may assist in designing interventions that will improve child participation and lessen caregiving demands (Campbell, Milbourne, & Wilcox, 2008; Milbourne & Campbell, 2007).

Developmental assessments, child observations, and caregiver reports about children's functional skill use are combined to design embedded learning opportunities and teaching strategies.

For example, a first-then picture board might be used to prepare a child for leaving the house, thus decreasing a child's challenging behavior by increasing participation. Figure 2 illustrates a simple first-then picture board used by a toddler's parents to help her understand the sequence of events in the going-to-bed routine. Alternatively, toys might be adapted so that a child can participate in play without needing an adult to be present to position or move the toys.

Caregivers also identify specific activities/routines in which opportunities for children's learning may be embedded (Woods, Kashinath, & Goldstein, 2004). Providers then collaborate with caregivers to design learning opportunities and strategies to enable children to perform desired behavior. This process is not dependent solely on information from the *Assessment of Family Activities and Routines* but requires

Figure 2
An Illustration of a First-Then Board Used to Help a Toddler Learn the Sequence of Events During Bedtime

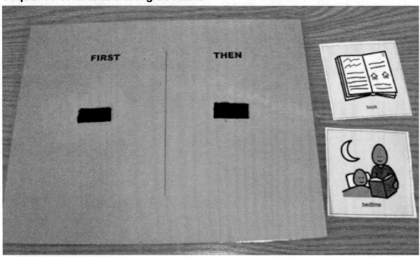

assessment data about activities/routines to be merged with other sources of information. Developmental assessments, child observations, and caregiver reports about children's functional skill use are combined to design embedded learning opportunities and teaching strategies.

Implications

Many different types of assessment measures and instruments are used in the early intervention field. Some measure child performance or developmental competence, whereas others provide various ways of assessing family resources, strengths, needs, or priorities. The *Assessment of Family Activities and Routines* is an interview format and recording form to elicit information about children's participation in daily life situations. The structure of this assessment form and its relationship to child programming within activities/routines makes it easier for families to provide needed information and for service providers to successfully obtain the information. In the absence of this type of format, service providers are required to sort out caregivers' perspectives about their children's participation from other family information such as interaction patterns, needs, strengths, resources, concerns, priorities, or other aspects of family life. Family assessments yield information that is the foundation of family-cen-

tered early intervention service models (e.g., Sandall, Hemmeter, Smith, & McLean, 2005; Stremel & Campbell, 2007). Use of the *Assessment of Family Activities and Routines* builds on this family-centered base to obtain specific information needed for developing and providing effective child intervention within an activity/routine context.

References

Bernheimer, L. P. & Weisner, T. S. (2007). "Let me just tell you what I do all day...": The family story at the center of intervention research and practice. *Infants and Young Children, 20*, 192–201.

Bruder, M. B. (1993). The provision of early intervention and early childhood special education within community early childhood programs: Characteristics of effective service delivery. *Topics in Early Childhood Special Education, 13*(1), 19–37.

Bruder, M. B. & Dunst, C. J. (2000). Expanding learning opportunities for infants and toddlers in natural environments: A chance to reconceptualize early intervention. *Zero to Three*, December 1999/January 2000, 34–36.

Buysse, V. & Wesley, P. W. (2007). *Consultation in early childhood settings*. Baltimore: Paul H Brookes.

Campbell, P. H. (2004). Participation-based services: Promoting children's participation in natural settings. *Young Exceptional Child, 8*(1), 20–29.

Campbell, P. H. (2009). *Assessment of family activities and routines; revised*. Philadelphia: Child & Family Studies Research Programs, Thomas Jefferson University. Retrieved August 16, 2011, from http://jeffline.jefferson.edu/cfsrp/pbs.html

Campbell, P. H., Cooper, M. A., & McInerney, W. F. (1984). Therapeutic programming for students with severe handicaps. *American Journal of Occupational Therapy, 38*, 594–602.

Campbell, P. H., Milbourne, S., & Wilcox, M. J. (2008). Adaptation interventions to promote participation in natural settings. *Infants and Young Children, 21*, 94–106.

Campbell, P. H. & Sawyer, L. B. (2007). Supporting learning opportunities in natural settings through participation-based services. *Journal of Early Intervention, 29*, 287–305.

Campbell, P. H., Sawyer, L. B., & Muhlenhaupt, M. (2009). Parent and professional views of natural environment services. *Infants and Young Children, 22*, 264–278.

Cripe, J. W., Hanline, M. F., & Dailey, S. E. (1997). Family-guided routines for early intervention services. *Young Exceptional Children, 1*(1), 18–26.

Dunst, C. J., Trivette, C. M., Humphries, T., Raab, M., & Roper, N. (2001). Contrasting approaches to natural learning environment interventions. *Infants and Young Children, 14*(2), 48–63.

Jung, L. A. (2003). More is better: Maximizing natural learning opportunities. *Young Exceptional Children, 6*(3), 21–27.

Kling, A., Campbell, P. H., & Wilcox, M. J. (2010). Young children with physical disabilities: Caregiver perspectives about assistive technology. *Infants and Young Children, 23*, 169–183.

McWilliam, R. A. (2000). Its only natural—To have early intervention in the environments where it is needed. *Young Exceptional Children Monograph Series, 2*, 17–26.

McWilliam, R. A. (2010). *Routines-based early intervention: Supporting young children and their families*. Baltimore: Paul H. Brookes.

McWilliam, R. A., Casey, A. M., & Sims, J. (2009). The routines-based interview: A method for gathering information and assessing needs. *Infants and Young Children, 22*, 224–233.

Milbourne, S. A. & Campbell, P. H. (2007). *CARA's kit: Creating adaptations for routines and activities*. Distributed by the Division for Early Childhood (DEC), Missoula, MT.

Mott, S. E., Fewell, R. R., Lewis, M., Meisels, S. J., Shonkoff, J. P., & Simeonsson, R. J. (1986). Methods for assessing child and family outcomes in early childhood special education programs: Some views from the field. *Topics in Early Childhood Special Education, 6*(2), 1–15.

Pretti-Frontczak, K. & Bricker, D. (2004). *An activity-based approach to early intervention* (3rd ed.). Baltimore: Paul H Brookes.

Rush, D. & Shelden, M. (2011). *The early childhood coaching handbook*. Baltimore: Paul H Brookes.

Sandall, S., Hemmeter, M. L., Smith, B., & McLean, M. (2005). *DEC recommended practices: A comprehensive guide for practical application in early intervention/early childhood special education*. Longmont, CO: Sopris West.

Sandall, S. & Swartz, I. (2008). *Building blocks for teaching preschoolers with special needs* (2nd ed.). Baltimore: Paul H Brookes.

Sexton, D., Snyder, P., Rheams, T., Barron-Sharp, B., & Perez, J. (1991). Considerations in using written surveys to identify family strengths and needs during the IFSP process. *Topics in Early Childhood Special Education, 11*(3), 81–91.

Stremel, K. & Campbell, P. H. (2007). Implementation of early intervention within natural environments. *Early Childhood Services, 1*(2), 83–105.

Trivette, C. M. & Dunst, C. J. (2005). Recommended practices: Family-based practices. In S. Sandall, M. L. Hemmeter, B. Smith, & M. McLean (Eds.), *DEC recommended practices: A comprehensive guide for practical application in early intervention/early childhood special education.* Longmont, CO: Sopris West.

Wilcox, M. J., Bacon, C. K., & Greer, D. C. (2005). *Evidence-based early language intervention: Caregiver verbal responsivity training.* Tempe, AZ: Infant Child Research Programs, Arizona State University.

Woods, J., Kashinath, S., & Goldstein, H. (2004). Effects of embedding caregiver-implemented teaching strategies in daily routines on children's communication outcomes. *Journal of Early Intervention, 26,* 195–193.

Woods, J. A. & Lindeman, D. (2008). Gathering and giving information with families. *Infants and Young Children, 21,* 272–284.

Using Your Good Judgment

Informed Opinion for Early Intervention

John T. Neisworth
Penn State University

Stephen J. Bagnato
University of Pittsburgh, Office of Child Development

An Informed Opinion Vignette

Jordan was 28 months old, and his mother was very concerned about his development and behavior. He was not talking, did not play with peers, showed positive emotions only with his mother, and played with toys like a much younger infant. Jordan was not doing nearly as many things as his cousin. Jordan's mother took him to be evaluated at the local early childhood center so that he could be involved in a good preschool. The team from the local early intervention program evaluated Jordan in the center using conventional developmental tests mandated by their state department of education, which required him to sit still at a table and to play only with toys from the test kit. No matter what the professionals on the team used, Jordan was upset, failed to play with toys, seemed not to understand the test tasks, and did not complete any of the items on the tests. At the end of one hour, they and Jordan were exhausted, and Jordan's mother was anxious. The team could not determine whether to enroll him in their program without the testing being completed.

At the request of Jordan's mother, a representative from the team came to the home and watched while Jordan's mother and sister played with him using toys with which he was familiar in natural play activities. They observed that he could do several things that were not apparent before. After they were finished, Jordan's mother and the team representative completed a judgment-based rating scale which enabled them to identify and rate some of things that Jordan could do in playing, moving about, communicating, and getting along with *others. A team meeting was held, and Jordan's mother attended to contribute her observations and reports about Jordan's usual behavior at home, and the team representative did the same. It was clear when using these judgment-based measures, instead of the conventional tests, that Jordan did qualify for services. Moreover, the team had better information to make decisions with his mother about the type of supports or services that would promote his development and behavior.*

Introduction

Informed opinion (e.g., clinical judgment) is a recommended practice, authorized in the Individuals with Disabilities Education Act (IDEA), to (1) document the often unrecognized capabilities and subtle dimensions of the development and behavior of infants and toddlers with special needs; (2) guide parent and professional team decision-making about eligibility for early intervention services and supports; and (3) plan individualized programs for young children in early intervention.

> *Informed opinion (e.g., clinical judgment) is a recommended practice, authorized in the Individuals with Disabilities Education Act (IDEA), to (1) document the often unrecognized capabilities and subtle dimensions of the development and behavior of infants and toddlers with special needs; (2) guide parent and professional team decision-making about eligibility for early intervention services and supports; and (3) plan individualized programs for young children in early intervention.*

Despite its recommended use, both state and federal regulations neither define informed opinion, nor provide clear guidance on its use. The purpose of this article is to provide a "pocket guide" for early intervention practitioners by defining informed opinion, introducing its promising evidence base, detailing guidelines to ensure its reliable and valid use, and recommending structured informed opinion scales that have been field-validated for use in early intervention assessment.

What's Wrong with Using Tests?

If you are responsible for evaluating children's development that is not "typical" or "standard," you likely recognize that conventional tests and testing practices rarely provide information useful for teachers, other practitioners, and families who are responsible for making important decisions about eligibility, intervention, or progress. Conventional tests and testing practices routinely fail to capture the unique strengths and needs of young children, especially those with special needs. By "conventional," we refer to materials developed for and with "typical" children, often "administered" at a table by a stranger, and involving scripted examiner procedures and "examinee" expected or scorable responses. Conventional tests were rated in a national survey of over 1,100 consumers (interdisciplinary practitioners) as failing to meet developmentally appropriate standards for use in the early childhood intervention fields, while authentic assessment methods were highly rated (Bagnato, Neisworth, & Pretti-Frontczak, 2010).

Authentic assessment includes the use of informed-opinion measures that are developmentally appropriate and meet recommended practice standards in the early childhood intervention fields. Authentic assessment is defined as the use of observational materials and methods that sample naturally occurring behaviors in everyday settings and routines by knowledgeable caregivers in the child's life. Authentic assessment has been embraced by professional fields associated with early childhood intervention as "best practice." In addition, authentic assessment practices meet professional standards for developmentally appropriate assessment (Bagnato et al., 2010).

What Is Informed Opinion and Why Use It?

The difficulties of conventional testing most often involves the (1) invalid force-fitting of tools designed, standardized, and normed using only samples of children with typical development; (2) after-the-fact "validation" studies on some children with special needs; and (3) inflexible procedures which disallow the use of sensible accommodations for children with functional limitations such as visual, hearing, and neuromotor impairments. These limitations have been recognized by professionals from various disciplines and in government policy and regulations, which created the opportunity to use more realistic and natural assessment approaches based on observations and judgments, or *informed opinions* (IO), of people who know the child best. Informed opinions are provided by various caregivers who are knowledgeable about and familiar with the child in everyday settings and routines (Bagnato, McKeating, Fevola, & Bartolamasi, 2008).

IO is widely recognized as accepted practice and used regularly in disciplines such as nursing, neonatology, and physical and occupational therapy to appraise subtle aspects of neurodevelopment and behavior in infants and young children (Bagnato et al., 2008). In addition, there often are difficult-to-quantify, qualitative differences that characterize a child's capabilities and needs that are best appraised by IO of practitioners with particular expertise (Neisworth, 1990). Physical therapists, for example, routinely use their judgment to describe and evaluate muscle tone and motor-planning skills; speech and language therapists must judge qualities of speech and reciprocal communication. Parents are among the most important judges of their child's temperament, daily living skills, and social skills with adults and peers.

IO is recognized by federal regulations as well as most state's policies as legitimate and necessary, especially in IDEA Part C (birth-to-3) early intervention programs. Part C mandates that clinical opinion be included in eligibility determination in IDEA, 20 U.S.C. §1432(5), 1435(a)(1), 1997. The current legislation states that the use of informed clinical opinion is particularly warranted "when standardized instruments are unavailable, unreliable, or inappropriate for use in measuring developmental delay or evaluating a diagnosed condition such as autism spectrum disorder or pervasive developmental delay" (IDEA, 20 U.S.C. §303.300, 2004).

What are the Cautions in Using Informed Opinion?

An increasing number of concerns have been expressed within and across states about the use/misuse of IO. Many states have posted restrictions and qualifications for employing IO to inform eligibility determination decisions. Clearly, using your informed opinion—good judgment—is important. The confidence we place, however, on people's opinions depends on several important factors, including the person's knowledge and familiarity with a child, knowledge of developmental expectancies, and agreement among parents and professionals about a child's skills and needs. It is not acceptable to have IO be based merely on intuition or a guess about a child's competencies. Informed opinions must be based on direct experience with the child and his or her behavior across time, in various daily routines, and activities in home and community contexts. Opinions that can be documented and compared to the informed opinions of others are required. With sensible guidelines, informed opinion can be a reliable and valid way to document

Informed opinions must be based on direct experience with the child and his or her behavior across time, in various daily routines, and activities in home and community contexts.

the strengths and needs of young, vulnerable children whose capabilities are often concealed and thus not promoted.

In the following sections, we offer guidelines derived from practice-based evidence conducted in real-life settings (see Bagnato & Neisworth, 1990; Bagnato, Smith-Jones, Matesa, & McKeating-Esterle, 2006) to help structure or standardize procedures for using IO in a valid way to ensure the credibility of judgments and thereby promote its broader acceptance. These guidelines should meet most concerns regarding the use of IO to supplement or replace conventional testing.

What are Five Essential Features for Valid Use of Informed Opinions?

The TRACE Center for Excellence in Early Childhood Assessment (2002–2007), a research institute funded for five years by the Office of Special Education Programs (OSEP), was given the responsibility for researching the evidence base for early detection methods for early intervention eligibility. TRACE was funded by the federal government because OSEP determined that the national incidence of children with probable developmental delays was much higher than the number of children served in state early intervention programs. OSEP reached the conclusion that current conventional testing (i.e., use of tests and materials normed and standardized with and for children of typical development) for eligibility is ineffective and too costly; they called for

The research synthesis derived five practice features that were consistent across effective studies of clinical judgment to ensure reliability and validity of results.

research on the most promising practices to increase service eligibility and improve eligibility determination practices. Bagnato and colleagues at the Pennsylvania satellite for the TRACE Center published a research synthesis on clinical judgment, informed opinion, and determined that the method was a promising practice, which needed to be used and studied more often (Bagnato et al., 2006).

The definition which resulted from this research synthesis is that *clinical judgment* or *informed opinion* "refers to the knowledgeable perceptions of caregivers and professionals about the elusive and subtle capabilities of children in different settings that must be defined and quantified so that individuals or teams are able to reach accurate decisions about eligibility for early intervention" (Bagnato et al., 2006, p. 1). Most importantly, the research synthesis derived five practice features

Table 1
Five Essential Features of Informed Opinions and Associated Benefits

Feature	Benefit
Definitions for Judged Characteristics	Everyone understands what is being observed and judged.
Structured Opinions Using Uniform Tools	Everyone records opinions through ratings in the same way so they can be compared.
Information Across People, Places, and Time	A wide sample of the child's capabilities is observed across people to understand how the environment might influence behavior over time.
Consensus Process Among Parents and Professionals	A collective informed opinion across parents and professionals is reached through an egalitarian process
Training for all Raters or Judges	Everyone is trained to record their opinions in the same way to ensure rigor and consistency.

that were consistent across effective studies of clinical judgment to ensure reliability and validity of results. Table 1 shows these features and their benefits.

Guidepoints and Implications for Using Your Good Judgment

When conventional testing is not feasible or appropriate, informed opinion is an option in both federal and state Part C regulations for early intervention eligibility and has been proposed for expansion in the future IDEA re-authorization. The current IDEA legislation states use of informed clinical opinion is particularly warranted "when standardized instruments are unavailable, unreliable, or inappropriate for use in measuring developmental delay or evaluating a diagnosed condition such as autism spectrum disorder or pervasive developmental delay" (IDEA, 20 U.S.C. §303.300, 2004).

Recent proposed revisions to the implementing regulations §303.320(b)(2) would require that "the lead agency allow qualified personnel to use their informed clinical opinion to assess a child's present level of functioning in each of the developmental areas identified in the proposed §303.21(a)(1) and *to establish eligibility, even when other instruments fail to establish eligibility*" [emphasis added]. Moreover, the proposed revisions state that a child's medical and educational records can be reviewed to establish eligibility based on clinical judgment and informed clinical opinion regarding current functional capabilities without assessing either the child or family directly.

We suggest several guidelines for the appropriate and effective use of IO when making assessment decisions, including decisions related to eligibility. These guidelines and a rationale for their use are presented below.

1. **Specify the "credentials" of persons giving their informed opinions.** Not all opinions should be given the same weight; not all opinions might be convincing, accepted, or believable by decision-makers. What makes an opinion informed? Basically, there are two bases for being informed: (1) professional preparation and experience, and (2) familiarity with the child. Judgments about muscle tone, for example, are likely more credible when given by an experienced physical therapist rather than the opinion of the babysitter (although the babysitter's comments about other child aspects can be of significant value). Further, the opinion of someone who knows the child is desirable over the opinions of a stranger. The credibility of the opinion-giver, therefore, includes aspects such as professional preparation, direct experiences with various children, and extent of contact with and consistent knowledge of the child's behavior in everyday settings and routines.

2. **Identify the reasons for using IO.** All early intervention teams are required to give reasons why they are using selected procedures in assessment, intervention, and service delivery; the rationale for using informed opinion is no different. It is essential that both parents and professionals give their reasons why traditional and often mandated tests and testing procedures are considered inappropriate and not feasible (perhaps harmful) for a specific child. Observational descriptions of the child in daily routines and settings, and how and under what conditions they typically relate to their social and physical surroundings—their daily world—can be persuasive in showing that the use of tests requiring language, motor, and attention skills to complete decontextualized tasks "on demand" are inappropriate. Conventional testing can be detrimental in portraying the child's capabilities and thus, negatively influence developmental expectations of adults, which is another reason for using IO (Neisworth & Bagnato, 2004).

3. **Observe, sample, and record evidence about the child's capabilities across people, places, and times**. Ensure the collection of observations and opinions by using a multi-factor process: multiple methods (direct observation and caregiver reports), tools (checklists, rating scales), times (different days,

morning, afternoon), and situations (preschool, playground, supermarket, etc.). Children's functioning can vary considerably across time and circumstances. Proper sampling of behavior can yield important information about the child's competence in everyday situations.

4. **Pool and reconcile the diverse observations and opinions of parents and professionals on the team and reach consensus through respectful team processes**. It is important that the opinions of all team members (e.g., professionals, parents and family members, babysitters) about the child's competence are heard and respected rather than dismissed if they do not align with conventional wisdom or expectations. The team should be ready to consider "outliers" in the process and their reasons for disagreement. Often the outliers can provide compelling reasons for taking a second look at the child in a different way and for challenging conventional wisdom. For the most part, however, the team members can identify the most relevant or problematic child behaviors and functional capabilities and examine which aspects all agree on (as well as discrepancies). Through a respectful process, teams can resolve differences and reach consensus (i.e., agree on a point of view "they all can live with") about the child's eligibility for services or need for help.

5. **Use uniform tools and formats to structure and record opinions for comparisons**. We advocate for the use of available judgment-based tools and formats to ensure reliable, valid, and comparable informed opinions (see Table 2). The TRACE Center research synthesis identified and recommended (Bagnato et al, 2008) several appropriate and evidence-based clinical judgment instruments or formats for use by parents and professionals on early intervention teams. A team's use of the same tools for recording judgments can serve as the basis for confident decisions about child capabilities and needs for services or supports. The examples of judgment-based tools and formats in Table 2 are available to early intervention teams to structure informed opinions, have technical adequacy data available, and have been field-validated in early intervention for various assessment purposes (Bagnato et al., 2008).

For example, one uniform IO tool that has been field-validated and used by some state Part C programs to record informed opinions and to guide team-decision making is the SPECS (Bagnato & Neisworth, 1990; 2010). SPECS is a parent–professional, team decision-making system for

Figure 1
**Sample Developmental SPECS Judgment-Based Scales for
Receptive Language and Play**

RECEPTIVE LANGUAGE

**Understanding information as shown in various ways
such as following directions and identifying objects
and pictures.**

5 Typically understands information, especially speech
and gestures, as well as or better than most children
of the same age.

4 Usually understands most information expected of a
child about the same age.

3 Sometimes comprehends speech and gestures, but
shows observable problems in understanding.

2 Only occasionally understands; generally fails to
comprehend most speech and gestures.

1 Rarely shows any understanding of surrounding
events.

PLAY

**Exploration of the environment, appropriate use of
toys and objects, and cooperative interaction with
others just for the fun of it.**

5 Typically plays with toys and gets along with others as
well as or better than children of the same age.

4 Usually plays with toys and gets along with others in
an appropriate way, but is sometimes inappropriate.

3 Sometimes plays in an acceptable manner, but is often
immature, too repetitive, or destructive.

2 Only occasionally plays, or play is too repetitive,
immature, or destructive.

1 Hardly ever plays.

Figure 2
SPECS Individual Rater Profile for Team Decision-Making

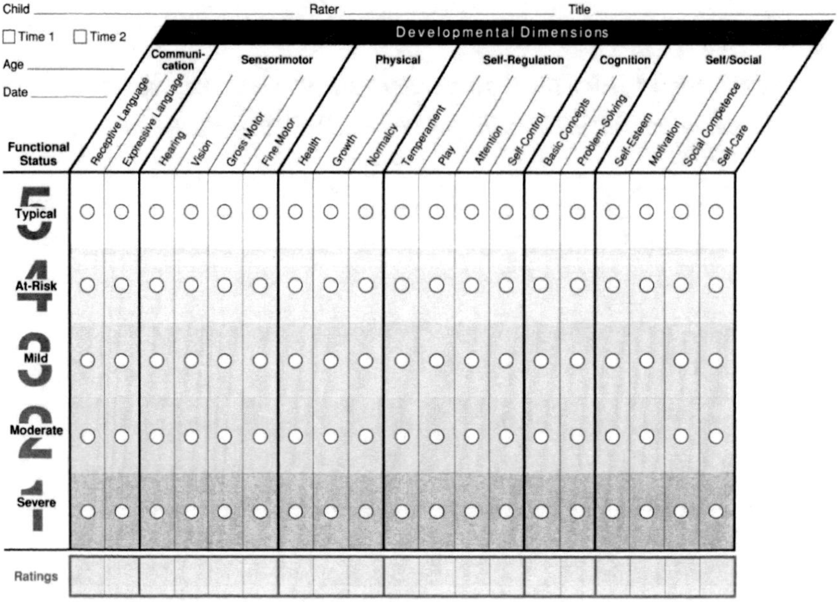

infants, toddlers, and preschool children from birth to 6 years of age which structures the use of informed opinions. SPECS was field-validated for use in early intervention with over 1,500 children, 800 parents, and 500 interdisciplinary professionals. Validity studies profiled results for young children with diverse delays and disabilities (Bagnato & Neisworth, 1990; 2010).

The SPECS materials are composed of judgment-based rating scales for parents and interdisciplinary professionals. The materials are written at a sixth grade reading level, using clear and simple descriptions of children's functional levels in areas such as communication, problem-solving, self-social, and sensorimotor (see Figure 1). Observers complete independent ratings of child capabilities based on their professional background and experience with the child. Independent ratings are subsequently used in a team decision-making process in which prominent differences in opinion are resolved and an aggregate consensus rating for 19 areas of functioning is generated and profiled as the "team's informed opinion" to justify service eligibility decisions (see Figure 2). In addition, the Program SPECS is a questionnaire in which a team of parents and professionals collaboratively answer 45 graduated questions about the intensity of services needed to promote the child's progress.

Table 2
Examples of Informed Opinion Instruments

Instrument	Author	Publisher	Age Range	Domains	Sample	Technical Adequacy Data Reported in Manual
ABAS (Adaptive Behavior Assessment System)	Harrison & Oakland (2004)	Western Psychological Services	0-89 years	Communication, Community use, School/home living, Functional pre-academics, Health & safety, Leisure, Self-care, Self-direction, Social, Motor	2100 children Validity studies included 126 children with at least 15 types of developmental disabilities	Internal consistency score reliability Inter-rater score reliability Construct validity of scores Convergent and discriminant score validity
ABILITIES Index[a]	Simeonsson & Bailey (1991)	University of North Carolina	Birth to 21 months	Audition, Behavior & Social Skills, Intellectual Function, Limbs, Intentional Communication, Tonicity, Integrity of Physical Health, Eyes, Structural Status	254 children, 213 parents, 133 teachers and 135 interdisciplinary professionals	Inter-rater score reliability Construct validity studies Internal consistency studies Classification accuracy studies
Ages & Stages Questionnaire (ASQ)	Bricker & Squires (1999)	Paul H. Brookes	4 months – 5 years	Communication, Gross motor, Fine motor, Problem solving, Personal-social	~1000 children	Test-retest score reliability Construct validity of scores Sensitivity and specificity

Table 2 (continued)

Instrument	Author	Publisher	Age Range	Domains	Sample	Technical Adequacy Data Reported in Manual
SPECS (System to Plan Early Childhood Services) • Infant • Developmental • Team • Program	Bagnato & Neisworth (1990; 2010)	Author Copyrights	Birth to 24 months 24 to 72 months	Communication, Sensorimotor, Physical, Self-regulation, Cognition, Self-social Developmental Support, Behavioral, Communication, Gross/fine Motor support, Vision, Hearing and Medical Support, Special, Transition Support and Teamwork	1300 children, 31% typical and 69% had developmental problems	Acceptable score reliability for all 19 dimensions Test-retest score reliability Content and construct score validity Classification accuracy
TABS (Temperament and Atypical Behavior Scale)	Bagnato, Neisworth, Salvia, & Hunt (1999)	Paul H. Brookes	11 to 71 months	Detached, Hyper-Sensitive/Active, Underreactive, Dysregulated	621 typical and 212 atypical developing children	Internal consistency score reliability for at-risk sample and for sample of children not at-risk Content and construct score validity

Note. Adapted from Valid Use of Clinical Judgment (Informed Opinion) for Early Intervention Eligibility by S. J. Bagnato, E. McKeating-Esterle, A. Fevola, P. Bortolamasi and J. T. Neisworth, 2008. Infants & Young Children, 21, 334-347. Copyright 2008 by Wolters Kluwer-Health/Lippincott Williams & Wilkins, and Research Foundations for Using Clinical Judgment for Early Intervention Eligibility by S. J. Bagnato, J. Smith-Jones, M. Matesa, E. Esterle, Cornerstones, 2(3), Copyright 2006 by TRACE Center, Orlena Hawks Puckett Institute. [a]Technical adequacy data for ABILITIES Index from published research reports.

Conclusion

Informed opinion (IO) is helpful and often necessary for informing decisions about a child's eligibility for early intervention services or supports. The use of IO is permitted under IDEA and the accompanying implementing early intervention regulations. The action guidelines outlined in this article will help to ensure the utility and credibility of IO as part of authentic assessment. Informed opinions, if properly structured through use of uniform processes and procedures, can be a reliable, valid, economical, and sensitive methodology for informed decision-making in assessment, particularly for early detection in early intervention and for more timely access to needed services and supports for young children.

Note
Direct queries to: Dr. Stephen J. Bagnato at Bagnatos@pitt.edu or Dr. John T. Neisworth at jtn1@psu.edu

References
Bagnato, S. J., McKeating-Esterle, E., Fevola, A. F., & Bartolomasi, A., Neisworth, J. T. (2008). Valid use of clinical judgment for early intervention eligibility. *Infants and Young Children, 20*, 334-347.

Bagnato, S. J., & Neisworth, J. T. (1990). *System to Plan Early Childhood Services (SPECS): Administration manual.* Circle Pines, MN: American Guidance Service.

Bagnato, S. J., & Neisworth, J. T. (2010). *SPECS for early intervention: A system for using informed opinions for valid team decision-making.* Pittsburgh, PA: Early Childhood Partnerships.

Bagnato, S. J., Neisworth, J. T., & McCloskey, G. (1994). *System to Plan Early Childhood Services (SPECS): Technical manual.* Circle Pines, MN: American Guidance Service.

Bagnato, S. J., Neisworth, J. T., & Pretti-Frontczak, K. (2010). *LINKing authentic assessment and early childhood intervention: Best measures for best practices.* Baltimore: Brookes.

Bagnato, S. J., Smith-Jones, J., Matesa, M. & McKeating-Esterle, E. (2006). Research foundations for using clinical judgment (informed opinion) for early intervention eligibility determination. *Cornerstones, 3*, 1-14.

Early Intervention Program for Infants and Toddlers with Disabilities (proposed rule). *Individuals with Disabilities Education Improvement Act* 34 CFR §303.320(b)(2). Retrieved September 12, 2011 from http://www.ed.gov/legislation/FedRegister/proprule/2007-2/050907a.html

Individuals with Disabilities Education Act (IDEA), 20 U.S.C. § 1432(5), 1435(a)(1), (1997).

Individuals with Disabilities Education Act (IDEA), 20, U.S.C. 303.300 (2004).

Neisworth, J.T., & Bagnato, S.J. (2004). The mismeasure of young children: the authentic assessment alternative. *Topics in Early Childhood Special Education, 17*, 198-212.

Using Digital Video to Enhance Authentic Assessment

Larry Edelman
University of Colorado School of Medicine

Carlos often finds it difficult to share materials and play with other children. When Joann, his preschool teacher, observes Carlos successfully sharing toys and playing cooperatively with a friend at school, she uses a camcorder to capture this interaction on video. Later, Joann reviews the clip, which helps her confidently rate an assessment item related to cooperative play with other children.

Megan, a physical therapist providing early intervention services, visits Dominic and his family at home. Dominic has very complex medical needs and family was spending a lot of time with medical professionals who were concentrating on his health issues. The family was focused on these issues and felt frustrated and anxious, wondering if he was making progress in other areas of his development. Using digital video, Megan was able to show the family videos she had taken over time of Dominic participating in typical family routines. These videos illustrated the skills he had been learning, which helped the family recognize his strengths and the progress that he had been making.

Kim, a preschool teacher, shows 3-year-old Amber videos of her participating in group reading time. As Kim listens to Amber discuss what she remembers and notices about the activity, she is able to document a number of Amber's communication and literacy skills that will help her complete an assessment tool.

After a rare southern California rainstorm, Michael, a preschool special educator, videos Oliver as he jumps in a puddle, counts forward and backward, and experiences the joys of playing in the rain. He uses this video footage to focus discussions with other team members about skills Oliver has mastered over the past several months.

He shares this and other clips of Oliver with the team members at the beginning of Oliver's next individualized education program (IEP) meeting. Watching Oliver's progress and discussing how the video images capture Oliver's strengths in the context of classroom activities and routines kicks off the meeting on a positive and celebratory note.

CeCe, a teacher in a child care program, observes Aurelius, who has autism spectrum disorder, reading a storybook out loud and comparing it with another book. CeCe, who has a digital video recorder nearby, records this activity and then edits the clip and posts it to Aurelius' online portfolio. CeCe uses the clip to help inform her ratings on an assessment tool. In addition, she shows the clip to Aurelius' mother, who is pleased to see visual evidence of his progress. His mother asks if she can have a copy of the video. CeCe is able to easily share the clip with Aurelius' mother who, in turn, forwards the clip to other family members.

These real-life stories illustrate the powerful ways that digital video is being used in early intervention, early childhood special education, and early care and education (these fields will collectively be referred to as *early childhood*). The purpose of this article is to describe how digital video is being used to enhance authentic assessment practices in early childhood. The article begins by defining *authentic assessment* and identifying its key features. Examples from two innovative projects that encourage and support early childhood providers to use digital video to enhance authentic assessment practices are provided. Next, considerations related to using digital video to enhance authentic assessment practices are identified and strategies for using video successfully are shared. Resources useful for using digital video to enhance authentic assessment practices in other contexts are shared.

Defining Authentic Assessment and Its Key Features

In order to understand how digital video can enhance authentic assessment practices, it is important to highlight the key features of authentic assessment. The Division for Early Childhood has identified 46 assessment standards (Sandall, Hemmeter, Smith, & McLean, 2005). Among these standards is authenticity, which includes gathering information to make informed decisions (i.e., conducting assessment) by observing children in natural and familiar situations (Neisworth & Bagnato, 2005). Neisworth and Bagnato (2004) have identified eight overarching standards that guide developmentally appropriate assessment. They define and describe the benefits of authentic assessment by noting that it

> ...*yields information about functional behavior in children's typical/natural settings, what they really know and do. The pitfalls of conventional testing, the unfamiliar adult, unrealistic test demands, and nonfunctional item content distilled through psychometric item selection are avoided. Information gathered in authentic settings, within the child's own developmental ecology, often provides us with a very different picture of strengths and needs. (p. 203)*

McAffee, Leong, and Bodrova (2004) have described authentic assessment as one type of performance assessment that uses tasks that are as close as possible to real-life situations. These authors acknowledge that assessment is a process of gathering information about children by using several different forms of evidence (including authentic assessment evidence) and then organizing and interpreting that information.

The Colorado Department of Education's Results Matter Program describes authentic assessment as a process for gathering "ongoing information about a child's progress to help parents and practitioners work together to support the child's learning and participation" (Results Matter, Colorado Department of Education, 2007) and identifies five primary features of authentic assessment: (1) it involves collecting information about a child on an *ongoing* basis, rather than being a one-time snapshot; (2) it looks at the *whole child*, instead of focusing on only one isolated skill or developmental area; (3) it is *naturalistic* and focuses on the child in the context of his or her participation in typical everyday routines, activities, and relationships, rather than in contrived situations; (4) it considers *multiple perspectives* from various people who are important in a child's life, not just one individual; and (5) it is *useful* in that information is collected, documented, and shared in ways that providers and families develop a more complete understanding of the child and can plan effective ways to support the child's learning and development (Results Matter, Colorado Department of Education, 2007).

These various definitions and descriptions are consistent in emphasizing that authentic assessment focuses on children's functional behaviors and skills within the context of their familiar and typical routines, activities, and relationships. Video captures both visual and auditory information and can facilitate the collection of information or evidence to document children's skills as well as the contexts in which they occur. Video is a very powerful strategy for authentic assessment documentation.

Use of Digital Video to Enhance Authentic Assessment Practices

Video is a compelling strategy for documenting young children's learning, development, and progress and enables us to capture the complex details of children's experiences, relationships, and skills. Once captured, the footage can be reviewed, shared, reflected on, and used to support key features of authentic assessment.

Due to recent innovations, practitioners and families have access to the use of digital video, which is more affordable, more accessible, and easier to shoot, edit, store, and share.

Video has been previously recommended for use in assessment, including in special education assessment (e.g., Greenwood & Rieth, 1994) and in early childhood assessment (e.g., Guidry, van den Pol, & Neilsen, 1996; Hong & Trepanier-Street, 2004). Forman (2010) has advocated for indexed video-clip databases of children's behavior as foundations for both documentation and accountability.

Despite these recommendations, video has not been universally adopted for use in early childhood assessment. Several reasons might be that, until recently, the use of video relied on equipment that was

relatively large and expensive and the footage was somewhat difficult to edit and share. These reasons are no longer significant barriers because video has evolved from analog (e.g., VHS tape) to digital. In addition, due to recent innovations, practitioners and families have access to the use of digital video, which is more affordable, more accessible, and easier to shoot, edit, store, and share. These innovations include the introduction of small, inexpensive, easy-to-use, low-cost digital camcorders that connect easily to computers; free (or low-cost) easy-to-use applications for editing and sharing video files; and small, inexpensive storage devices.

Digital video is accessible to almost everyone, opening up exciting new opportunities for its use in authentic assessment. Practitioners and families who have been using digital video find it to be transformative—it helps them better understand children's development and use of skills in context, and it enables them to work together more effectively to support and monitor their progress.

Two Initiatives Using Video to Enhance Authentic Assessment Practices

Two initiatives, one in Colorado and one in California, have been demonstrating ways that digital video can be used to enhance a variety of early childhood practices, particularly practices related to authentic assessment. Although both initiatives use digital video to support a wide range of early childhood practices (e.g., self-reflection, coaching, consultation, supervision, family support and education, individualized planning, professional development, video modeling), this article focuses primarily on exemplars related directly to authentic assessment.

Results Matter Digital Video Project. Results Matter is a program of the Colorado Department of Education that promotes the use of ongoing authentic assessment for more than 44,000 children served in a variety of Colorado's early childhood initiatives including preschool special education, Colorado Preschool Program, School Readiness Quality Improvement Program sites, family child care homes, child care centers, Early Head Start, Head Start, and charter school preschool programs.

Two initiatives, one in Colorado and one in California, have been demonstrating ways that digital video can be used to enhance a variety of early childhood practices, particularly practices related to authentic assessment.

According to the director of Results Matter,

> *The digital video project was a logical outgrowth given that Results Matter was built on the belief that ongoing observation and documentation are essential to accurate, valid, and useful assessment. Adding video documentation to notes, photos, and work samples results in assessment portfolios that have information to support "authentic" instructional planning and evaluation of progress. With advances in technology and increasing affordability, video documentation has become accessible to all early educators. As methods to edit and share video clips with ease progress, video documentation is expected to become the primary method for documentation in the Results Matter authentic assessment process. (N. Vendegna, personal communication, February 14, 2011)*

The Results Matter Digital Video Project started modestly in 2006, working with two preschool teachers and one early interventionist. Sixteen early childhood providers from eight different programs subsequently joined the project. Three additional programs and more than 30 participants were included in the project in 2010. To date, the project has included more than 100 participants from 16 programs. The work of the project is documented in the Results Matter Video Library, where video clips can be watched and downloaded for use in professional development activities (http://www.cde.state.co.us/resultsmatter/RMVideoSeries.htm).

Desired Results *access* Project Digital Video Initiative. The Desired Results system is the California Department of Education's accountability initiative to determine the effectiveness of its child development and early childhood special education programs. The Desired Results *access* Project (http://www.draccess.org) is funded by the Special Education Division of the California Department of Education to assist with the implementation of the Desired Results assessment system to measure the progress of California's preschool-age children with individualized education plans (IEPs). The Desired Results *access* Project has used video for quite some time to produce professional development and public awareness materials; the digital video initiative was designed to support practitioners' uses of digital video for authentic assessment and other practices.

The video initiative began by collaborating with administrators and teachers from the Los Angeles Unified School District. Based on their successes with using digital video to support authentic assessment and family support practices, the initiative expanded in 2011 by adding 18 practitioners from the Sacramento County Office of Education and the Santa Clara County Office of Education.

The director of training and product development for the Desired Results *access* project described how the digital video initiative is significant for the project.

> *Given that the Desired Results assessment system emphasizes authentic assessment practices, the use of digital video supports the administration and scoring of the Desired Results authentic assessment tools and facilitates a strengths-based approach to working as a team during the IEP process and collaborating with others to design and deliver instruction. Use of digital video provides opportunities for all individuals who should be informing an authentic assessment to contribute: parents, other caregivers, and service providers. By using video, we can observe and document what a child does within activities and across settings. The video initiative serves as a community of practice where providers can share their "lessons learned" and tips for successful practices—everyone benefits. (P. Salcedo, personal communication, February 12, 2011)*

Video documentation produced by this initiative can be viewed and downloaded for use in professional development activities on the Video

Initiative page of the Desired Results *access* Project Web site (http://www.draccess.org/videoinitiative/).

Practitioners' Reflections on Their Uses of Video to Enhance Authentic Assessment Practices

Based on observation, interviews with practitioners and families, and ongoing review of the video documentation, both the Colorado and California video projects have found that the use of digital video can enhance authentic assessment practices. The benefits of using digital video to enhance authentic assessment are reflected in the comments and feedback from practitioners who have participated in these initiatives. This section highlights reflections and the key lessons learned by these participants and illustrates a number of ways that digital video is being used to enhance authentic assessment. Although the practitioners set out to use video to enhance authentic assessment practices, they often described how a given video clip also helped enhance other practices, including planning, inclusion, collaboration, and family support and education.

A preschool special educator in the Los Angeles Unified School District, Michael Breaux, described his use of digital video for assessment as astonishing. In the video he stated,

First, the use of video recordings provided richer information than written observations, work samples, or photos of children meeting early learning standards. Second, children experienced sheer enjoyment and a sense of pride when watching themselves and their accomplishments. Third, as early childhood educators we can use the information to improve our teaching skills, make changes to the environment as needed and support children's learning. However, the most powerful outcome of using video recordings is the positive relationships we have been building with each child. The video recordings allowed me to see positive characteristics of children with more challenging behaviors and develop more positive relationships. (Edelman & Lopez-Breaux, 2010)

This teacher has suggested that every IEP meeting should start off with some kind of video clip showing the child being successful in the environment and further illustrates his use of video to support authentic assessment, team collaboration, family education, and individualized planning in *A Time for Oliver* (Edelman & Lopez-Breaux, 2010).

A teacher at Denver's Washington Park Early Learning Center, Christina DeVarona, described video as

a wonderful assessment tool, especially for assessing and documenting social interaction, language development, and problem-solving skills. Those to me are really challenging things to document by writing them down, or with just pictures. During the parent/teacher conferences I found it was a wonderful tool to be able to show the parents what their child was doing and be able to talk about it with them. When you are looking at a video you can pause it and talk about it and so I thought that was very helpful.

In *Sharing Video Documentation With Families* (Edelman, DeVarona, & Mogen, 2009), this teacher shows how revisiting a child's skills on video helped her achieve a more complete understanding of a child's learning style and share rich information at a parent-teacher conference.

Two coteachers in a Los Angeles Unified School District collaborative preschool classroom, Julia Chien and Marek Zielina, used digital video to create video portfolios for children. In *Using Video With the DRDP Assessments* (Edelman, Chien, & Zielina, 2009) one of these teachers described how video helps teachers revisit children's skills. She noted,

We've been able to make good use of video . . . now we can sometimes be able to go, "Oh, do you remember when Johnny was doing this? I think we videotaped that." And then we can pull out that video and we can actually see some evidence of that skill being exhibited, that "Oh, yes, Johnny did in fact do that" or "Oh, we thought he did it but he actually didn't do it."

A physical therapist and early member of the Results Matter video project in Colorado, Megan Klish Fibbe, described how she has used video as a strategy for authentic assessment in early intervention.

Video is a really nice complement to authentic assessment. It helps improve accuracy because it allows you to go back and check and see, "Did I see what I really thought I was seeing?" It also helps document progress over time so if you document the child in one particular skill you have the opportunity to document them later and really show the parents that amazing progress that the child might have made. When they're taking little baby steps toward that progress it is not as noticeable, but then when you can see over time it can be a really amazing thing. It also allows you to have a piece of information that you can share with another provider to get some additional feedback, or you can also share it with the family and get their input on the child's skills. Video also allows you to look at several different skill sets. I think that video helps you capture the richness and it's not something that you can take in all at one time, so then you can go through and take it apart and really absorb the richness of that routine. Sometimes families are more than happy to borrow a camera from me and use it for videotaping their child during routines that I can't be there for. There's no one else distracting from what's going on and you really get to see what happens when you're not there. (Edelman, Fibbe, & Eigsti, 2009)

Megan has described her work in a number of videos, including *Authentic Assessment in Early Intervention, Using Video to Share With Family Members*; *Using Video for REALLY Watching*; and *Using Video to Celebrate Progress* (Edelman, Fibbe, & Eigsti, 2009).

A preschool special educator in the Los Angeles Unified School District, Joann Hulkower, has focused her video efforts on authentic assessment and supporting inclusion and collaboration with families. She described how use of video has enhanced her authentic assessment practices.

I have gained an appreciation of the "whole" child that can be fostered better by viewing together a clip which "catches" the child's strengths. For example, I had one student whose parents' were overwhelmed when the psychologist gave an eligibility of autism. However, viewing the child demonstrating progress in class participation helped all IEP participants keep in mind the purpose of the meeting was to support the child's progress towards fulfilling her potential. When we use video clips as part of our authentic assessment tools, conducted in children's natural settings to make their ongoing progress visible to all participants in the learning endeavor, it facilitates our collaboration between all stakeholders to produce mutually desired results.

This practitioner's experiences are documented in several videos, including *A Proud Moment for Carlos; Using Video to Support Inclusion and Collaboration With Families;* and *The ABCs of Why We Use Video* (Edelman & Hulkower, 2010).

The director of the Emerald Preschool in Colorado's Boulder Valley School District, Kim Moroze, and her classroom team have been using video in a number of creative and effective ways. In *Documentation as a Habit* (Edelman & Moroze, 2010a), this director described the benefits of reviewing video. She noted, "I think that when we review the videos . . . we notice things that we wouldn't have noticed before. And then we can take additional notes on the video clips that we can't always get in that moment in time."

A classroom assistant in one of the Emerald preschool classrooms, Cyndy Reddy, described how video helps her remember what's happened:

you've got the pictures, you've got the sound, and it's a continuum so you don't have to write notes all the time—you can just reflect back as to what is going on and just continue with the lesson or the activity and the spontaneity of the kids as they are working together.

In *Watching Video Documentation With Children* (Edelman & Moroze, 2010b), the preschool director described how watching video documentation with children can be used as an assessment strategy:

We like using video and showing it to the children because their reaction is so amazing. It's a learning tool. They look at it again and they get re-engaged; the revisit of it is so valuable. To have them actually review a video, you can actually assess what they took away from that experience.

For me to assess what they got out of it the first time and to review it and see what they are getting out of it again, it's a whole other level that I haven't thought of previously, and I think it's amazing.

CeCe Sargent, a preschool teacher at Clayton Early Learning in Denver, CO, illustrated in *Aurelius Reading at Naptime* (Edelman & Sargent, 2010) how she used a digital camcorder to capture a unique illustration of a young boy's skills, compressed the clip using free software, posted the clip on an online portfolio, and then shared the clip with the child's mother in a way that she could easily share it with other family members. On the video, she described how digital video and related technology

enhances what's happening in the classroom. You live in the moment, and even if I'm telling the story to a parent, it isn't as rich as being able to show that clip. You just get to relive the experience and you get to actually see what exactly is happening rather than just talking about it.

Not all video is produced by dedicated digital camcorders. Teachers at SD27J preschool in Brighton, CO, have been using iPhones and iPod

Touch devices for recording video. In the video *Using the iPod Touch and iPhone to Record Video and Photographic Documentation* (Edelman & Ager, 2011) a preschool teacher, Bethany Ager, described how capturing video of children over time documents child progress to support accountability decisions.

> *It really shows how you're doing as a teacher and how the kids are learning . . . it's there for everybody to see. You can see the growth the children are making, especially if you are videotaping from the beginning of the year till the end of the year. You can see huge growth in them. And it's something that's irrefutable.*

Strategies for Ensuring Success When Using Digital Video to Enhance Authentic Assessment

Many valuable lessons have been learned from the Colorado and California digital video projects while supporting practitioners to use video to enhance authentic assessment practices. This section summarizes key lessons and strategies that have helped the projects and practitioners to succeed. These lessons learned and strategies might be useful for those interested in using digital video to enhance authentic assessment.

Administrative Support. Program administrators need to help practitioners find the time required to learn and practice the new skills associated with producing digital video and using video for authentic assessment. Each program should identify a resource specialist with experience, knowledge, and skill in producing and using digital video for assessment who can provide professional development and ongoing technical assistance.

Incremental Roll-out. It may be challenging to introduce the use of digital video program- or system-wide. Programs have found it helpful to initiate the use of video with a limited number of enthusiastic practitioners who share the evidence of their work and later on provide support to additional staff members.

Adequate Equipment. Practitioners need access to a digital video recorder and related supplies as well as an adequate computer with a number of applications installed. The equipment used by the Results Matter and the Desired Results *access* Project video initiatives has changed frequently as new video devices and computer applications

Table 1
Examples of Equipment for Use in Digital Video Initiatives

Type of Equipment	Purpose	Examples	Notes
Camcorder	Recording video and still pictures	Sanyo xacti VPC-CG20 Camcorder (also purchase accessories including a padded case, extra rechargeable battery, extra charger, and extra removable 4- or 8-GB SD cards)	The projects have used the Sanyo xacti line for several years, but frequently upgrade to newer models
Tripod	Stabilizing the camcorder	• Digipower TP-S010 Ultra Compact Mini Tripod • Joby Gorillapod Flexible Tripods (various models)	The Digipower can be purchased online for less than $3.00 and is often all that is required
External hard drive	For storing digital media	Samsung G2 Portable HX-MU050DC hard drive 500 GB/external	There are many good choices for external hard drives; this model has proven to work well on Macs and PCs
Media playing software	Playing video files	VLC Media Player (http://www.videolan.org/vlc/) QuickTime (http://www.apple.com)	These free media players work on both Macs and PCs and play a variety of media files
Media converter software	Basic editing functions including cut, copy, paste, trim, join, compress, and export to other file formats	MPEG Streamclip (http://www.squared5.com/) QuickTime Pro (http://www.apple.com)	MPEG Streamclip works well on both Macs and PCs. Must have QuickTime Player installed for this to work. A tutorial on its use can be found on the Results Matter Video Library
File-sharing software	Applications for sharing large video files	Dropbox.com Yousendit.com There are both free and fee-based versions of these applications.	Practitioners should consult their administrations before using any applications that transmit confidential data to ensure compliance with required regulations

become available. Both projects do their best to keep abreast of and test new products and applications in order to choose the equipment best suited for early childhood settings. The projects often select computer applications that are free or low-cost and that work on both PC and Apple platforms. Edelman (2011) periodically updates a document that describes the key features of low-cost digital video recorders that are useful for early childhood providers. Although the equipment used changes frequently, Table 1 shows examples of equipment and applications used at the time this article was written.

Initial Orientation. Practitioners new to digital video find it useful to attend a hands-on orientation workshop led by a resource specialist knowledgeable in using digital video for authentic assessment. To succeed, practitioners will eventually need to learn five sets of skills in order to use digital video effectively: (1) understanding the various ways that video might be used for authentic assessment; (2) shooting video; (3) transferring/naming/organizing video files and folders; (4) editing/compressing files; and (5) sharing files. These five sets of skills include too much new material to be digested in one orientation session. Therefore, the projects have found that the orientation session should be used to give the practitioners the video equipment and provide the first three skills in detail—just enough information to get them started in using video for authentic assessment. Learning the last two skill sets will occur over time. Before leaving the orientation, the practitioners can plan how they will continue learning on the job.

> *Many valuable lessons have been learned from the Colorado and California digital video projects while supporting practitioners to use video to enhance authentic assessment practices.*

Obtaining Consent. Practitioners obtain signed consent forms from families whose children participate in their programs. Such forms might be written to grant permission for the programs to use the video clips for a variety of purposes, including assessment, family education, supervision, coaching, consultation, professional development, and public awareness. The video projects have found it useful to include a cover letter to accompany the consent form that describes in lay language (as opposed to the more technical and legal language of the consent form) the intent of using video; to provide the cover letter and consent form in the primary languages spoken by families; and to explain to families the intended uses of video early on in the service-delivery process during face-to-face meetings such as parent-conferences and home visits. Consent forms and cover letters should be approved by a program's administrative or legal departments. No children or families should be video recorded unless they have signed consent forms.

Naming and Organizing Video Files. The video projects have found that it is very important for programs to identify consistent, if not uniform, conventions for titling video files and organizing files into folders before accumulating large number of files. Some useful tips include

- Create a system of folders for grouping files. Files might be organized into folders by children's names or identification numbers, assessment items, and so on.
- Be sure that each video file name ends with the correct suffix for the kind of file produced by your camcorder (e.g., .mp4)
- Use periods, dashes, or underscores to separate the sections of the file name. Do not use slashes (/).
- There are many ways that files might be named. Table 2 illustrates a sample file-naming convention that one program developed and found useful. One feature of this scheme is that it creates readable file names that line up nicely in folders for easy referencing.

Ongoing Learning Opportunities. Practitioners report that they master the use of the camcorders best by using video frequently and "learning by doing." As practitioners become comfortable with shooting, uploading, organizing, and using their video files for authentic assessment, they will want to learn the last two of the five skill sets: editing/compressing files and sharing files. Depending on the needs of practitioners, professional development in these skill sets might be provided in a variety of ways including face-to-face training sessions, Web conferences, and e-mail or telephone technical assistance. Many practitioners have found it useful to participate in a learning community that enables a group of practitioners to stay in touch through a password-protected platform established for providing technical assistance, problem solving, sharing information and files, and conducting online discussions. The platforms used to host these learning communities for the Colorado and

> Among the DEC recommended practices standards in assessment is authenticity, which includes gathering information to make informed decisions by observing children in natural and familiar situations.

Table 2

Example File-naming Convention

Date the Clip was Shot	Child's Name or Initials	Content	File-type Suffix
Month, day, and year, each in two digits, separated by periods, with no extra spaces, followed by a hyphen or underscore.	First name, followed by a period, then the capitalized first letter of the last name, followed by a hyphen or underscore.	Brief description of what is on the clip that makes it useful (e.g., behaviors, activity, assessment item, Individualized Family Service Plan (IFSP) or Individualized Education Plan (IEP) outcome, domain). Capitalize the first letter of each word with no spaces between words.	(e.g., .mp4, .mpeg4, .mov, .avi). The file format given in the identical way that the file was named when imported from the camcorder (e.g., .mp4). Be sure that the file format is always preceded by a period with no spaces afterward.
Example = 01.03.11- (January 3, 2011)	*Example* = John.S- (John Smith)	*Example* = UsingForkIndependently (ate lunch using a fork independently)	*Example* = .mp4

Example: An .mp4 video clip was taken on January 3, 2011, showing John Smith eating lunch and using a fork independently. The file was named 01.03.11-JohnS-UsingForkIndependently.mp4

California video projects have changed over time because both projects are continually searching for the best free platforms to host such learning communities. At the time when this article was authored, both projects were using Wiggio.com.

Modeling Authentic Assessment Practices. Both the California and Colorado video projects have produced brief videos for other practitioners that illustrate the various ways that digital video can be used in early childhood, particularly to enhance authentic assessment. These videos can be found on both the Colorado and California Web sites (http://www.cde.state.co.us/resultsmatter/RMVideoSeries.htm; http://www.draccess.org/videoinitiative/).

Summary

Participants in two projects have demonstrated creative and effective ways that digital video can be used to enhance authentic assessment practices. The strategies that were shared in this article for using digital video to enhance authentic assessment practices were gathered from the literature, from the experiences of practitioners who participated in the digital video projects, and from the expertise and experiences of the author. Digital video is a powerful tool that has the potential to help improve authentic assessment practices by capturing information about children's functional behavior in everyday settings. In the past, the relatively high cost and difficulty in using video made it somewhat challenging to adopt. Now that it is affordable and relatively easy to use, the use of digital video to enhance authentic assessment practices is accessible to many more early childhood practitioners and programs.

Note

I wish to acknowledge Nan Vendegna, Anne Kuschner, and Patty Salcedo for their clear vision and ongoing support of the video projects and to thank Nan and Patty for their review and suggestions of early drafts of this article.

Correspondence about this article should be addressed to Larry Edelman, Department of Pediatrics, University of Colorado School of Medicine, Aurora, CO, 80045. E-mail: larry.edelman@ucdenver.edu

References

Edelman, L. (2011). *Comparison and recommendations for low-cost digital video recorders in early intervention and early care and development.* Denver, CO: Author. Retrieved 09/30/11 from http://exploringtech.wordpress.com/lo-cost-digital-camcorders-for-ei-and-ece/

Edelman, L. & Ager, B. (2011). *Using the iPod Touch and iPhone to record video and photographic documentation* [Video file]. Retrieved 09/30/11 from http://www.cde.state.co.us/resultsmatter/RMVideoSeries.htm

Edelman, L., Chien, J., & Zielina, M. (2010). *Using video with the DRDP assessments* [Video file]. Retrieved 09/30/11 from http://www.draccess.org/videoinitiative/

Edelman, L., DeVarona, C., & Mogen, S. (2009). *Sharing video documentation with families* [Video file]. Retrieved 09/30/11 from http://www.cde.state.co.us/resultsmatter/RMVideoSeries.htm

Edelman, L., Fibbe, M. K., & Eigsti, H. J. (2009). *Authentic assessment in early intervention* [Video file]. Retrieved 09/30/11 from http://www.cde.state.co.us/resultsmatter/RMVideoSeries.htm

Edelman, L. & Hulkower, J. (2010). *Using video to support inclusion and collaboration with families* [Video file]. Retrieved 09/30/11 from http://www.draccess.org/videoinitiative/

Edelman, L. & Lopez-Breaux, M. (2010). *A time for Oliver* [Video file]. Retrieved 09/30/11 from http://www.draccess.org/videoinitiative/

Edelman, L. & Moroze, K. (2010a). *Documentation as a habit.* [Video file]. Retrieved 09/30/11 from http://www.cde.state.co.us/resultsmatter/RMVideoSeries.htm

Edelman, L. & Moroze, K. (2010b). *Watching video documentation with children* [Video file]. Retrieved 09/30/11 from http://www.cde.state.co.us/resultsmatter/RMVideoSeries.htm

Edelman, L. & Sargent, C. (2011). *Aurelius reading at naptime* [Video file]. Retrieved 09/30/11 from http://www.cde.state.co.us/resultsmatter/RMVideoSeries.htm

Forman, G. (2010). Documentation and accountability: The shift from numbers to indexed narratives. *Theory Into Practice, 49*(1), 29-35.

Greenwood, C. R. & Rieth, H. J. (1994). Current dimensions of technology-based assessment in special education. *Exceptional Children, 61*, 105-113.

Guidry, J., van den Pol, R., Keeley, E., & Neilsen, S. (1996). Augmenting traditional assessment and information: The Videoshare model. *Topics in Early Childhood Special Education, 16*, 51-65.

Hong, S. B. & Trepanier-Street, M. (2004). Technology: A tool for knowledge construction in a Reggio Emilia inspired teacher education program. *Early Childhood Education Journal, 32*, 87-94.

McAfee, O., Leong, D. J., & Bodrova, E. (2004). *Primer on early childhood assessment: What every teacher should know.* Washington, DC: National Association for the Education of Young Children.

Neisworth, J. T. & Bagnato, S. J. (2004). The mismeasure of young children: The authentic assessment alternative. *Infants & Young Children, 17*, 198-212.

Neisworth, J. T. & Bagnato, S. J. (2005). Recommended practices in assessment. In S. Sandall, M. L. Hemmeter, B. J. Smith, & M. McLean (Eds.), *DEC recommended practices: A comprehensive guide for practical application in early intervention/early childhood special education.* Longmont, CO: Sopris.

Results Matter, Colorado Department of Education. (2007). *What is authentic assessment?* [Video file]. Retrieved 09/30/11 from http:// www.cde.state.co.us/resultsmatter/RMVideoSeries.htm

Additional Resources

The videos included as part of the initiatives described in this article can be viewed and downloaded online at no cost for use in educational and professional development activities from the following sites.

Results Matter Video Library
http://www.cde.state.co.us/resultsmatter/RMVideoSeries.htm

Recommended Videos Related to the use of Video in Authentic Assessment:
- *What Is Authentic Assessment?*
- *Sharing Video Documentation With Families*
- *Authentic Assessment in Early Intervention*
- *Using Video to Share With Family Members.*
- *Using Video for REALLY Watching*
- *Using Video to Celebrate Progress*
- *Documentation as a Habit*
- *Watching Video Documentation With Children*
- *Using the iPod Touch and iPhone to Record Video and Photographic Documentation*
- *Aurelius Reading at Naptime*

Desired Results *access* Project Digital-video Initiative http://www.cde.state.co.us/resultsmatter/RMVideoSeries.htm

- *Recommended Videos Related to the Use of Video in Authentic Assessment:*
- *A Time for Oliver*
- *Using Video with the DRDP Assessments*
- *A Proud Moment for Carlos*
- *Using Video to Support Inclusion and Collaboration With Families*
- *The ABCs of Why We Use Video*

Bringing Pieces Together: Assessment of Young Children's Social-Emotional Competence

Rosa Milagros Santos,

Michaelene M. Ostrosky,

Tweety Yates,
University of Illinois at Urbana-Champaign

Angel Fettig,
University of North Carolina-Chapel Hill

Gregory Cheatham,
University of Kansas

LaShorage Shaffer,
University of Michigan-Dearborn

The development of social-emotional competence during the early childhood years is an important foundation for later success. Researchers have noted that the emphasis on cognitive and academic preparedness often overshadows any importance placed on children's social-emotional development in the early years (Raver, 2002). "Young children's emotional adjustment matters. Children who are emotionally well-adjusted have a significantly greater chance of early school success while children who experience serious emotional difficulty face grave risks of early school difficulty" (Raver, p. 3).

Supporting social-emotional skills can help children feel more confident and competent in developing relationships, building friendships, resolving conflicts, persisting when faced with challenges, coping with anger and frustrations, and managing emotions (Parlakian, 2003; Shonkoff & Phillips, 2000). A young child who relates positively to others, is motivated to learn, and can calm him- or herself or be calmed by others will be ready to learn and experience success in school and in life. However, not all children readily acquire the skills to engage in positive social

A young child who relates positively to others, is motivated to learn, and can calm him- or herself or be calmed by others will be ready to learn and experience success in school and in life.

interactions, and some children may even engage in challenging behaviors that can further prevent them from forming positive relationships with their peers and caregivers. It is important to note, however, that not all children with language and/or social-emotional delays will engage in challenging behaviors. Nor do all children who engage in challenging behaviors have social or language delays. What is unfortunate is that many children who do exhibit challenging behaviors often do not receive the supports needed to help them develop the social-emotional skills necessary to succeed in school, at home, and in the community (Kazdin & Kendall, 1998).

There is evidence that the trajectory of a child's social-emotional development can be changed (Powell, Dunlap, & Fox, 2006; Shonkoff & Phillips, 2000). Howes (2000) found that the quality of the preschool climate (i.e., teacher-child relationships) and the environment (i.e., access to highly engaging materials) were highly predictive of children's social-emotional competence during the second grade. She noted that children's social-emotional competence with their peers in the later years were related positively to the quality of the children's relationship with their preschool teachers, the opportunities for engagement with peers during preschool, and the perceptions preschool teachers have about children's behaviors, including challenging behaviors. The Howes study highlights how the tone set by early care and education professionals within their programs can have a lasting influence on children's social-emotional competence.

Assessing infants, toddlers, and young children not only helps identify their social-emotional needs, but also helps early care and education professionals better understand and support each child in their care. The assessment of young children gives early care and education professionals insights into children's behaviors, helps professionals understand how children react to their environment, and is useful in monitoring children's progress. Knowledge generated from assessing every child can lead to more responsive interactions and stronger relationships with all children.

There is evidence that the trajectory of a child's social-emotional development can be changed.

Therefore, it is important for early childhood professionals to critically examine their assessment practices, particularly in the area of social-emotional development. Early identification of children with social-emotional needs ensures that supports can be put in place for children who may need them to succeed not only while in an early childhood program but in the future as well.

In this article, we discuss evidence-based practices in assessing the social-emotional competence of young children. Throughout, we use the term *assessment* in its broadest form to include screening, diagnosing, evaluating for eligibility purposes and curricular needs, and monitoring progress. See Table 1 for definitions of key assessment terms and links to social-emotional competence. It is beyond the scope of this article to discuss in more detail general information related to assessment. However, we recommend McLean, Wolery, and Bailey (2004), Ostrosky and Horn (2002), and Sandall, Hemmeter, Smith, and McLean (2005) as starting points for basic information on assessment processes and practices in early childhood.

Table 1
Definition of Key Terms

Term	Definition	Link to Social-Emotional Competence
Assessment	A dynamic process of systematically gathering information from multiple sources and settings, over numerous points in time, and reflecting a wide range of child experiences.	The functional assessment process provides detailed information on the purpose of a child's challenging behavior and includes a set of observations and questions that enable professionals and family members to critically evaluate the meaning of the child's challenging behavior.

Table 1 (*continued*)

Term	Definition	Link to Social-Emotional Competence
Curriculum-based assessment	A process for assessing a child's abilities on a pre-determined sequence of objectives; used to link assessment, intervention, and evaluation.	A curriculum-based assessment might provide ideas for linking what and how to teach a child critical peer relationship skills, such as sharing and turn taking.
Evaluation	Procedures used to determine initial and continuing eligibility for early intervention/early childhood special education services.	An evaluation tool might lead to the initial diagnosis of autism, noting difficulties in social interaction.
Norm-referenced assessment	Compares a child's performance with that of similar children who have taken the same test.	A norm-referenced tool can help professionals and family members notice when a social-emotional behavior falls outside the boundaries of "typical development" for a child of a similar age (i.e., it is not unusual for an 18-month-old to bite occasionally, yet it is unusual for a 4-year old to resolve peer conflicts by biting).
Screening	A process of identifying children who may need a more comprehensive evaluation.	A parent might bring her child to a screening because she is worried about the frequency and intensity of her young daughter's temper tantrums at bedtime.
Ongoing monitoring	Used to track critical skills that you want to measure.	An early care and education professional might track a child's engagement during circle time, following changes in the classroom environment such as the placement of the child and the addition of visual supports.

Also, throughout this article we use the term *early care and education professionals* to refer to a variety of personnel who are affiliated with early care settings including teachers, child care workers, mental health consultants, psychologists, student service coordinators, allied medical providers, special education consultants, and developmental therapists. Using a question-and-answer format, we (a) provide a brief overview of

social-emotional competence in young children, (b) discuss considerations when selecting social-emotional assessment tools, (c) describe the roles and responsibilities of families and early care and education professionals in the assessment process, and (d) discuss ways to use the information gathered through the assessment process.

Overview of Social-Emotional Competence in Young Children

The accurate assessment of young children's skills is an important component of high-quality early childhood programs, and information obtained from assessments should be used to understand and support children's development, to determine curricula and individual learning objectives, and to evaluate program effectiveness. Thus, it is important that early care and education professionals have the necessary skills to understand their roles in assessing young children (e.g., evaluation team member, referral agent, assessor). Furthermore, in order to effectively assess social-emotional skills, early care and education professionals should have a clear understanding of what social-emotional competence means for young children.

What Is Social-Emotional Competence?

Social-emotional competence is the "developing capacity of the child from birth through five years of age to form close and secure adult and peer relationships; to experience, regulate, and express emotions in socially and culturally appropriate ways; and to explore the environment and learn in the contexts of family, community, and culture" (Zero to Three, 2001, as cited in Center on the Social Emotional Foundations for Early Learning, 2008, p. 14). In the first 5 years of life, children experience rapid growth across all areas of development, including the social-emotional domain. Key to children's ability to gain skills across developmental domains is the quality of relationships they form with responsive adult caregivers. Through their caregivers, children learn about themselves and how to interact with others and their environment.

Key to children's ability to gain skills across developmental domains is the quality of relationships they form with responsive adult caregivers.

How Does Social-Emotional Competence Support Children's Overall Development? Beginning at birth, developmental domains are intertwined (Dodge, Rudick, & Berke, 2006; Fogel, 2009; Squires & Bricker, 2007). For infants, social interactions with significant adults support not only their ability to communicate (e.g., babbling and cooing) but also motivate them to explore their environment (e.g., turning of the head, reaching for a toy, crawling toward the caregiver).

Early experiences influence how young children begin to understand, control, and master their world and how they form perceptions of self (Fogel, 2009). Infants initially express their wants and needs by crying, smiling, and turning toward or away from what they like or dislike. When these needs are met consistently, children are more easily comforted, pay increased attention to what is going on around them, are more open

to exploring their environments, and are better able to calm themselves and regulate their emotions. Young children learn that they can affect others through their actions and begin to develop secure attachments with their caregivers and peers.

How Does Culture Influence Children's Social-Emotional Development? Culture plays a large role in determining the acceptability of specific social-emotional behaviors. Recognizing how culture is intertwined with social-emotional skills can help professionals better understand children's behaviors (Cheatham & Santos, 2005). With the changing demographics, early care and education professionals need to develop a foundational understanding of how culture and language interact with social-emotional competence. This knowledge is critical in order to accurately identify delays or disabilities as

> *Recognizing how culture is intertwined with social-emotional skills can help professionals better understand children's behaviors.*

well as understand nuanced behaviors that are reflective of children's social competence within their home and the larger community.

In fact, emphasis should be placed on viewing children's home behaviors (including language) as adaptive to the environments in which they live (e.g., a child engages in minimal eye contact with adults as a sign of respect). Professionals should recognize that some children might need to develop new social-emotional skills to successfully navigate their day across different settings (Cheatham & Santos, 2005).

How Does a Child's English-Language Ability Impact the Assessment Process? Children's linguistic abilities can impact the outcome of any assessment, including one that focuses on social-emotional skills. For instance, children who attend programs in which their home language is not used and who do not yet have high levels of English proficiency may show delays in social-emotional development (Chang et al., 2007; Tabors, 2008). They may

also engage in behaviors that appear atypical to professionals (i.e., not giving eye contact to an adult when responding to a question, rarely interacting with peers). In fact, children's social-emotional competence is often linked to language ability (Shonkoff & Phillips, 2000), and therefore, assessing social-emotional competence without considering communication abilities may result in inaccurate findings. Assessment procedures for children who are linguistically diverse must by necessity be different from typical assessment procedures (Espinosa, 2005; Lund & Duchan, 1993; Mattes & Omark, 1991; Overton, Fielding, & Simonsson, 2004; Roseberry-McKibbin, 1994). Recommendations for assessing children from linguistically diverse backgrounds are provided in Box 1.

Box 1.
Recommendations for Assessing Linguistically Diverse Children

McLean (2005, p. 28-29) recommends the following strategies when assessing linguistically diverse children:

1. Complete an assessment of language proficiency and dominance before planning further assessment. Language proficiency refers to the child's fluency and competence in using a particular language; language dominance refers to the language that the child prefers to speak.
2. Conduct formal testing with the assistance of an interpreter or translator and a cultural guide who works in conjunction with the assessment team in administering and interpreting screenings and assessments.
3. Examine assessment tools for cultural and linguistic bias. Modifications can be made so that items are culturally and linguistically appropriate; however, this may invalidate the scoring. In this case, the test can be used as a descriptive measure rather than for reporting scores.
4. Use informal methods such as observations, interviews of family members and caregivers, and play-based assessments conducted in comfortable, familiar settings, in addition to formal methods of assessment.

Selecting Social-Emotional Assessment Tools

The effective assessment of children's social-emotional competence requires not only an understanding of the characteristics of social-emotional development but also the careful selection of assessment tools. Different assessment tools are used for different purposes, and care must be taken to carefully and critically select assessment tools that match the intended purpose. For example, a screening tool such as the Ages and *Stages Questionnaire–Social Emotional* (ASQ-SE; Squires, Bricker, & Twombly, 2002) may be used to determine whether a child may be in need of further evaluation. Likewise, the *Autism Diagnostic Observation Schedule* (ADOS; Lord, Rutter, DiLavore, & Risi, 2002) may be used to form a clinical diagnosis and determine eligibility for services, and a functional assessment interview form (Center on the Social Emotional Foundations for Early Learning, 2010) may be used to pinpoint a child's needs and lead to designing an appropriate intervention. Obtaining assessment information from a variety of sources, across a variety of settings, and using a variety of methods is recommended practice and increases the accuracy of the assessment results (Sandall, Hemmeter, Smith, & McLean, 2005). Early care and education professionals should remember that due to differences across settings and sources, each piece of information gathered, whether it be for screening, diagnosing, or monitoring, may present a slightly different picture of the child and should be interpreted with caution (Merrell, 2001). It is the whole picture of the child, the joining of all the pieces of information that gives early care and education professionals the most accurate picture of a young child's strengths and needs.

What Are Some Social-Emotional Assessment Tools to Use With Young Children?

There are many commercially available social-emotional assessment tools. Some tools are specific to social-emotional development (e.g., ASQ-SE; Squires, Bricker, & Twombly, 2004), whereas others include a social-emotional component (e.g., *Assessment, Evaluation, and Programming System for Infants and Children*, 2nd edition; Bricker & Pretti-Frontczak, 2002).

Although states and programs may have specific requirements for assessing infants, toddlers, and young children, standardized or norm-referenced assessments are generally used for screening, diagnosing, and evaluating for eligibility purposes. Alternative forms of assessments such as curriculum-based and observational data gathering are used for program planning and monitoring progress. Examples of some of the available norm-referenced tools for assessing social-emotional competence are included in Table 2. Additional tools can be found in Ringwalt (2008; http://www.nectac.org/~pdfs/pubs/screening.pdf). Space limitations prevent us from providing an exhaustive list of tools in this article. Additional information on selecting tools to screen social emotional competencies can be found in Henderson and Strain (2009). Finally, our table is intended simply as an information source and not a critical analysis or endorsement of any specific tool.

Table 2
Sample Norm-Referenced Assessment Tools

Instrument, Author, and Publisher (publication date)	Ages	Purpose
Ages & Stages Questionnaire: Social Emotional (ASQ-SE) by Squires, Bricker, & Twombly Brookes (2002)	6–60 months	Screens and monitors for social-emotional behaviors: parents complete ratings.
Behavior Assessment System for Children (BASC-II) by Reynolds & Kamphaus American Guidance (1992)	2–5 years	Assesses behavior functioning and identification of behavior problems (aggression, hyperactivity, conduct problems) of children 2–21 years.
Devereux Early Childhood Assessment Program (DECA) by LeBuffe & Naglieri Kaplan Press (1999)	2–5 years	Assesses positive and problem behaviors. Infant & Toddler version also available.
School Social Behavior Scales, 2nd Edition, by Merrell Assessment-Intervention Resources (2002)	5–18 years	Identifies social competence and antisocial behavior problems of children and youth for intervention planning.
Social Skills Improvement System (SSiS) by Gresham & Elliott Pearson Assessments (2008)	3–18 years	Measures social skills and problem behaviors of children and adolescents via teacher, parent, and student reports. Provides support for the development of appropriate interventions.
Temperament & Atypical Behavioral Scale (TABS) by Bagnato, Neisworth, Salvia, & Hunt Brookes (1999)	11–71 months	Identifies critical temperament and self-regulation problems to determine services for special education eligibility, planning of education and treatment programs, monitoring child progress and program effectiveness.

Administration	Language	Information on the Cultural and Linguistic Backgrounds of the Norming Population
15–20 minutes May be administered by parents or caregivers and scored by professionals	English, Spanish	59% = White; 9% = Black; 9% = Hispanic; 6% = Asian/ Pacific Islander; 2% = Native American; 16% = Mixed
10–20 minutes	English, Spanish	"Sample closely matched the 2001 Current Population Survey with respect to sex, socioeconomic status (as indicated by mother's education level), race/ ethnicity, geographic region, and special education classification" (Tan, 2007, p. 122)
15–20 minutes May be administered by parents or caregivers and scored by professionals	English, Spanish	25% = Low-income families; 69% = White, 17% = Black; 4% = Asian/Pacific Islander; 1% = Native American; 9% = Other
5–10 minutes Completed by teachers and other school personnel	English	"SSBS-2 norm sample corresponded more closely to the U.S. population . . . [however] several groups were either oversampled (e.g., Whites, special education status, the West region) or undersampled (e.g., Hispanics, kindergartners)" (Alfonso, Rentz, Orlovsky & Ramos, 2007, pp. 84-85)
10–25 minutes for each questionnaire	English, Spanish	"The U.S. Census Bureau's *Current Population Survey* (2006) was used as a matching source for the U.S. population (in regard to geographic region, race/ethnicity, and socioeconomic status) for each of the norming groups" (Crosby, 2011, p. 293)
5–30 minutes Administered by parents/ caregivers	English	"Sample not nationally representative, limited demographic information available about sample" (Henderson & Strain, 2009, p. 13)

What Do Early Care and Education Professionals Need to Consider When Selecting a Norm-Referenced Social-Emotional Assessment Tool?

Early care and education professionals need to thoughtfully examine assessment tools in order to choose ones that are most appropriate for the purpose for which they are being used, as well as for the individual needs of the children and families served by the program. Many norm-referenced assessment tools have not included children who are culturally and linguistically diverse in their norming population. In addition, some assessment tools were not normed on a population of children but instead have relied on developmental milestones taken from other assessment tools or research involving primarily children from Euro-American middle-class backgrounds (Bailey, 2004). Even assessment tools that have been normed on children from diverse populations may not be appropriate for a particular child. Therefore, early care and education professionals should make sure that the assessment process fits the child as opposed to making the child fit into their assessment process. A related article featured in this monograph by Duran, Cheatham, and Santos (2011) provides

information on assessment considerations for children from culturally and linguistically diverse backgrounds.

Finally, early care and education professionals need to know that there are a limited number of norm-referenced tools and items for social-emotional assessment within existing tools. Due to the complexity of young children's social-emotional skill development, looking at a score gleaned from a limited number of items gives us just one piece of the puzzle. As mentioned earlier, it is essential to use a variety of sources to get an accurate picture of a child's social-emotional competence. For example, repeated observations during naturally occurring interactions might not only reinforce assessment scores/ results, but also allow for more accurate interpretation and understanding of the individual child in his or her natural environments. Repeated observations can reveal the uniqueness of a child's temperament and how the child regulates emotions, as

Repeated observations can reveal the uniqueness of a child's temperament and how the child regulates emotions, as well as how he or she communicates and expresses emotions.

well as how he or she communicates and expresses emotions. This gives valuable information that might be overlooked when using traditional assessment tools that might rely heavily on information gathered from a single point in time.

The Role of Families in the Assessment Process

The assessment of children's social-emotional skills should be a shared experience between early care and education professionals and families. This is especially important because social-emotional skills develop within the context of a child's family, community, and cultural expectations (Parlakian, 2003). Family members tend to regularly interact with their young children and, therefore, see their children's abilities in a range of contexts. As a result of this insider's perspective, families are key members of the evaluation team and can assist the team in understanding their child's social-emotional development.

What Do Families Contribute to the Assessment Process?

Utilizing families' knowledge as a source of information about their children's social-emotional skills is valuable to the assessment process. Family members usually know their young child better than other members of the assessment team and often have unique knowledge not available to other team members. Including family members' knowledge of their child can enhance the reliability and validity of the assessment process (Squires, 1996).

Furthermore, parents can be accurate assessors of their young children's development, including language, communication, and social-emotional competence (Bricker & Squires, 1989; Diamond & Squires, 1993; Henderson & Meisels, 1994; Sachse & Suchodoletz, 2008). Family

members might participate in an assessment by eliciting particular behaviors from their child, or they might gather information about their child's behavior at home or confirm that a particular assessment was representative of their child's social-emotional competence. Banks, Santos, and Roof (2003) describe specific strategies that can assist early care and education professionals gather information from families in ways that are respectful and sensitive to their cultural, linguistic, and personal beliefs and practices.

What Can Families Gain From Being a Part of the Assessment Process?

Involving families as members of the assessment team acknowledges the value of their perspective and the important information they have to share. Also, encouraging families to be active members on assessment teams can help them learn about their children's social-emotional strengths and needs. When families take an active role in the assessment process, it increases their knowledge and understanding of their children's social-emotional competence, allowing them to better support their children's growth and development. Because families play a major role in fostering children's social-emotional competence, this is critical. Additionally, keeping families informed of important developmental milestones is likely to increase their engagement in their children's educational program (Turnbull, Turnbull, Erwin, Soodak, & Shogren, 2011).

How Does Family Involvement in the Assessment Process Benefit Children?

The presence and participation of family members in the assessment process can help children establish trust and rapport with members of the assessment team. Young children's feelings of safety and security are key to accurately assessing their social-emotional competence; therefore, having caregivers or familiar adults who support feelings of comfort present can enhance assessment outcomes.

The Role of Early Care and Education Professionals in the Assessment Process

The role of early care and education professionals in the assessment process is multifaceted. They may administer tests to children; gather information using observations, artifacts (e.g., portfolios, work samples), and interviews; implement interventions based on the assessment results; and conduct ongoing monitoring of children's behaviors and reactions to interventions. Unlike other assessment team members (e.g., psychologists, social workers), early care and education professionals may have direct contact and access to children and families on a regular basis. As such, they can serve as a natural bridge between the children and their families and the other members of the assessment team.

What Can Early Care and Education Professionals Do to Support Family Involvement in the Assessment Process?

Communication between families and other members of the assessment team is key to ensuring a successful assessment process. Researchers suggest that early care and education professionals explain each part of the assessment process to family members in oral and/or written formats and in the family's language (Grisham-Brown, Hemmeter, & Pretti-Frontczak, 2005; Ostrosky, Lee, & McMahon, 2008; Turnbull et al., 2011). It also is important that all members of the assessment team, including family members, have a shared understanding about social-emotional competence and the importance of assessing these skills.

Early care and education professionals play a critical role in encouraging family involvement in the assessment process. Early care and education professionals also need to build on the strengths that families bring to the assessment process. Flexibility is important so families feel comfortable with the amount and type of participation they would like to engage in during the assessment process. Early care and education professionals need to take into account individual family's preferences and styles when providing family members with options for involvement at each stage of the assessment process. For example, in some cultures parents may not typically engage in "playful" interactions with children. Thus, asking a mother to sit on the floor and sing or do a finger play with her child may feel awkward and unnatural, especially when unfamiliar adults are observing the interaction. Likewise, family members might consider educators the experts on children's development and may feel uncomfortable offering their opinions about their children's strengths and areas of need.

Family members might participate in an assessment by eliciting particular behaviors from their child, or they might gather information about their child's behavior at home or confirm that a particular assessment was representative of their child's social-emotional competence.

Finally, early care and education professionals can set the tone among members of the assessment team. A respectful tone can be accomplished by encouraging nonjudgmental attitudes, acknowledging differing points of view, and valuing and validating the different backgrounds and beliefs that each member of the team brings to the table.

What Is the Best Way for Early Care and Education Professionals to Share Assessment Results With Families?

The assessment team should strive to present assessment results to families in family-friendly formats. Whether information is shared during or soon after an assessment, it is important that it is presented in a way that is useful and meaningful to families, in a manner that promotes feelings of competence and confidence. Additionally, assessment information should be shared in an objective and nonjudgmental manner.

It is also important that team members share assessment results using language that does not appear to blame anyone. Often, discussions around a child's social-emotional skills, especially challenging behavior, result in adults blaming one another (i.e., professionals blaming parents and vice versa). It is critical that assessment teams work together and build supportive, trusting relationships in order to provide the best services for children and their families.

Finally, it is critical that early care and education professionals reconnect with families after family members have had an opportunity to review and digest the assessment results. Early care and education professionals need to be sensitive to the fact that the assessment process can be a very stressful and emotional time for families. Family members need to know that they can ask questions and share any concerns they have about their child or the assessment process. It is important for families to have a safe environment where they feel that their input and questions are valued. Follow-up conversations can provide such a context. A summary of strategies and recommendations for working with families during the assessment process can be found in Table 3.

Whether information is shared during or soon after an assessment, it is important that it is presented in a way that is useful and meaningful to families, in a manner that promotes feelings of competence and confidence.

Table 3
Summary of Recommendations for Working With Families During the Assessment Process

Theme	Recommendations
Encouraging families' meaningful participation in the assessment process	• Take into account individual family preferences and styles when providing family members with options for how they would like to be involved at each stage of the assessment process.
	• Encourage family members' participation in assessments by asking them to (a) elicit particular behaviors from their child, (b) collect information about their child's behavior at home, or (c) confirm that a particular assessment was representative of their child's social-emotional competence.
	• Include family members' knowledge of their child to enhance the reliability and validity of the assessment process.
	• Encourage the presence and participation of family members to support children's feelings of comfort.

Table 3 (*continued*)

Theme	Recommendations
Supporting families' roles in the assessment team	• Encourage families to be active members of the assessment team, in roles they feel comfortable assuming.
	• Be sensitive to the fact that the assessment process can be a very stressful and emotional time for families.
	• Utilize families' knowledge as a source of information about their children's social-emotional skills.
	• Build on the strengths that families bring to the assessment process.
	• Set a respectful tone among members of the assessment team by (a) encouraging nonjudgmental attitudes, (b) acknowledging different points of view, and (c) valuing and validating the different backgrounds and beliefs.
	• Work together and build supportive, trusting relationships in order to provide the best services for children and their families
Sharing information with families before, during, and beyond assessment	• Keep families well-informed to increase their engagement in their children's educational program.
	• Ensure a shared understanding with families about social-emotional competence and the importance of assessing these skills.
	• Explain each part of the assessment process to family members in oral and/or written formats and in the family's language
	• Share assessment information in an objective and nonjudgmental manner.
	• Present assessment results to families in family-friendly formats—useful and meaningful to families and in a manner that promotes feelings of competence and confidence.
	• Let family members know that they can ask questions and share any concerns they have about their child or the assessment process.
	• Reconnect after family members have had an opportunity to review and digest the assessment results.

Using Social-Emotional Assessment Information

Meaningful assessment information should inform what early care and education professionals do on a day-to-day basis with young children

(Bricker, Davis, & Squires, 2004; McConnell, 2000). How information is used should be based on the purpose of the assessment process (e.g., screening, diagnosis, ongoing monitoring). Some of the primary reasons for the initial and ongoing assessment of young children's social-emotional competence are to use the information gathered to guide curricula and planning decisions, to develop goals and individualized plans for

children, and to determine program effectiveness. Based on a review of assessment information, goals for strengthening a child's social-emotional competence are selected, and learning opportunities are embedded into daily interactions and routines using carefully chosen materials and activities (Dichtelmiller & Ensler, 2004; Pretti-Frontczak & Bricker, 2004). Without linking assessment information, intentional teaching, and the evaluation of instructional programming, early care and education professionals cannot adequately support children's social-emotional competence.

Summary

Given the importance of early identification and intervention in changing the trajectory of children's social-emotional development (Shonkoff & Phillips, 2000), the need to critically examine assessment practices around social-emotional competence cannot be taken lightly. Why we assess, how we assess, where we assess, the tools we select, and how this information is used are important variables to consider so that the assessment process leads to positive social-emotional outcomes as well as academic benefits for all infants, toddlers, and young children (Hyson, 2004).

When discussing future directions for promoting social-emotional competence, Siperstein and Favazza (2008) refer to an idea initially offered by Frances Horowitz in the late 1980s (Horowitz, 1989, 2000): creating programs that place children "at promise" instead of "at risk." We might look at the concept of "at promise" to help us not only identify children with social-emotional needs, but also to assist us as we learn more about each child's strengths (characteristics and early experiences), which in turn should guide our day-to-day practices in promoting social-emotional competence and preventing later social-emotional challenges.

Notes

This article was adapted from the "Research Synthesis on Screening and Assessing Social-Emotional Competence" by Yates, Ostrosky, Cheatham, Fettig, Shaffer, and Santos (2008) and published by the Center on the Social and Emotional Foundations for Early Learning, http://vanderbilt.edu/csefel

Development of this article was supported by the Center on the Social and Emotional Foundations for Early Learning (Administration for Children and Families, U.S. Department of Health and Human Services, Cooperative Agreement #90YD0215/01).

References

Alfonso, V. C., Rentz, E., Orlovsky, K., & Ramos, R. (2007) Test review: School Social Behavior Scales, second edition. *Journal of Psychoeducational Assessment, 25,* 82-100.

Bagnato, S. J., Neisworth, J. T., Salvia, J., & Hunt, F. (1999). *Temperament and Atypical Behavior Scale (TABS): TABS Screener.* Baltimore: Brookes.

Bailey, D. B. (2004). Tests and test development. In M. McLean, M. Wolery, & D. B. Bailey (Eds.), *Assessing infants and preschoolers with special needs* (3rd ed., pp. 22-44). Upper Saddle River, NJ: Pearson Education.

Banks, R., Santos, R. M., & Roof, V. (2003). Discovering family concerns, priorities, and resources: Sensitive family information gathering. *Young Exceptional Children, 6*(2), 11-19.

Bricker, D., Davis, M. S., & Squires, J. (2004). Mental health screening in young children. *Infants and Young Children, 17*(2), 129-144.

Bricker, D. & Pretti-Frontczak, K. (2002). *Assessment, evaluation, and programming system for infants and children (AEPS)* (2nd ed.). Baltimore: Brookes.

Bricker, D. & Squires, J. (1989). The effectiveness of parental screening of at-risk infants: The Infant Monitoring Questionnaires. *Topics in Early Childhood Special Education, 9,* 67-85.

Center on the Social Emotional Foundations for Early Learning (2008). Handout 1.2 definition of social emotional development. *CSEFEL Infant-Toddler Module 1.* Retrieved September 6, 2008, from http://www.vanderbilt.edu/csefel/in ftodd/mod1/1.2.pdf

Center on the Social Emotional Foundations for Early Learning (2010). Handout 3a.6 Functional Assessment Interview Form–Young Child. *CSEFEL Preschool Module 3a.* Retrieved July 19, 2011, from http://csefel.vanderbilt.edu/modules/module3a/ handout6.pdf

Chang, F., Crawford, G., Early, D., Bryant, D., Howes, D., & Burchinal, M., et al. (2007). Spanish-speaking children's social and language development in prekindergarten classrooms. *Early Education and Development, 18,* 243-269.

Cheatham, G. A. & Santos, R. M. (2005). A-B-Cs of bridging home and school expectations for children and families of diverse backgrounds. *Young Exceptional Children, 8,* 3-11.

Crosby, J. W. (2011). Test review: F. M. Gresham & S. N. Elliott Social Skills Improvement System Rating Scales. Minneapolis, MN: NCS Pearson, 2008. *Journal of Psychoeducational Assessment, 29,* 292–296.

Diamond, K. & Squires, J. (1993). The role of parental report in the screening and assessment of young children. *Journal of Early Intervention, 17*(2), 107-115.

Dichtelmiller, M. L. & Ensler, L. (2004). New insights in infant/toddler assessment: Experiences from the field. *Young Children,* 59, 30-33.

Dodge, D. T., Rudick, S., & Berke, K.(2006). *The Creative Curriculum for Infants, Toddlers, and Twos* (2nd ed.). Washington, DC: Teaching Strategies.

Espinosa, L. M., (2005). Curriculum and assessment considerations for young children from culturally, linguistically, and economically diverse backgrounds. *Psychology in the Schools, 42,* 837-853.

Fogel, A. (2009). *Infancy: Infant, family, and society* (5th ed.). Cornwall-on-Hudson, NY: Sloan Publishing.

Gresham, F. M. & Elliott, S. N. (2008). *Social Skills Improvement System (SSiS).* Minneapolis, MN: NCS Pearson.

Grisham-Brown, J., Hemmeter, M. L., & Pretti-Frontczak, K. (2005). *Blended practices for teaching young children in inclusive settings.* Baltimore: Brookes.

Henderson, L. & Meisels, S. (1994). Parental involvement in the developmental screening of their young child: A multiple source perspective. *Journal of Early Intervention, 18*(2), 141-154.

Henderson, J. & Strain, P. S. (2009). *Screening for delays and problem behavior (Roadmap to Effective Intervention Practices).* Tampa: University of South Florida, Technical Assistance Center on Social Emotional Intervention for Young Children.

Horowitz, F. D. (1989). *The concept of risk: A re-evaluation.* Invited address at the Biennial Meeting of the Society for Research in Child Development, Kansas City, MO.

Horowitz, F. D. (2000). Child development and the PITS: Simple questions, complex answers, and developmental theory. *Child Development, 71,* 1-10.

Howes, C. (2000). Social-emotional classroom climate in child care, child-teacher relationships and children's second grade peer relations. *Social Development, 9*(2), 191–204.

Hyson, M. (2004). *The emotional development of young children.* New York: Teachers College Press.

Kazdin, A. E. & Kendall, P. C. (1998). Current progress and future plans for developing treatments: Comments and perspectives. *Journal of Clinical Child Psychology, 27,* 217–226.

LeBuffe, P. A. & Naglieri, J. A. (1999). *DECA: Devereux Early Childhood Assessment.* Lewisville, NC: Kaplan Press.

Lord, C., Rutter, M., DiLavore, P. C., & Risi, S. (2002). *Autism diagnostic observation schedule.* Los Angeles: Western Psychological Services.

Lund, N. & Duchan, J. (1993). *Assessing children's language in naturalistic contexts.* Englewood Cliffs, NJ: Prentice Hall.

Mattes, L. & Omark, D. (1991). *Speech language assessment for the bilingual handicapped.* Oceanside, CA: Academic Communications Associates.

McConnell, S. R. (2000). Assessment in early intervention and early childhood special education: Building on the past to project into our future. *Topics in Early Childhood Special Education, 19,* 43-48.

McLean, M. (2005). Conducting child assessments. In S. A. Fowler, R. M. Santos, & R. M. Corso (Eds.), *Appropriate screening, assessment, and family information gathering* (pp. 23- 35). Longmont, CO: Sopris West.

McLean, M., Wolery, M., & Bailey, D. B. (2004). *Assessing infants and preschoolers with special needs* (3rd ed.). Upper Saddle River, NJ: Pearson Education.

Merrell, K. W. (2001). Assessment of children's social skills: Recent developments, best practices, and new directions. *Exceptionality, 9*(1-2), 3-18.

Merrell, K. W. (2002). *School social behavior scales,* (2nd ed.). Assessment-Intervention Resources. Baltimore: Brookes.

Ostrosky, M. & Horn, E. (Eds., 2002). *Young exceptional children monograph series no. 4: Assessment: Gathering meaningful information.* Missoula, MT: Division for Early Childhood of the Council for Exceptional Children (DEC).

Ostrosky, M. M., Lee, S. Y., & Ehmen McMahon, D. (2008). Infant and toddler portfolios as an assessment tool: Considerations when getting started. In C. A. Peterson, L. Fox, & P. M. Blasco (Eds.), *Young exceptional children monograph series on early intervention for infants and toddlers and their families: Practices and outcomes* (pp. 33-46). Missoula, MT: DEC.

Overton, T., Fielding, C., & Simonsson, M. (2004). Decision making in determining eligibility of culturally and linguistically diverse learners: Reasons given by assessment personnel. *Journal of Learning Disabilities, 37*(4), 319-330.

Parlakian, R. (2003). *Before the ABCs: Promoting school readiness in infants and toddlers.* Washington, DC: Zero to Three.

Powell, D., Dunlap, G., & Fox, L. (2006). Prevention and intervention for the challenging behaviors of toddlers and preschoolers. *Infants and Young Children, 19*(1), 25-35.

Pretti-Frontczak, K. & Bricker, D. (2004). *An activity-based approach to early intervention.* Baltimore: Brookes.

Raver, C. (2002). Emotions matter: Making the case for the role of young children's emotional development for early school readiness. *Social Policy Report of the Society for Research in Child Development, 16*(3), 1-20.

Reynolds, C. R. & Kamphaus, R. W. (1992). *Behavior assessment system for children.* Circle Pines, MN: American Guidance Service.

Ringwalt, S. (2008). *Developmental screening and assessment instruments with an emphasis on social and emotional development for young children ages birth through five.* Chapel Hill: The University of North Carolina, FPG Child Development Institute, National Early Childhood Technical Assistance Center.

Roseberry-McKibbin, C. (1994). Assessment and intervention for children with limited English proficiency and language disorders. *American Journal of Speech-Language Pathology, 3,* 77-88.

Sachse, S. & Suchodoletz, W. V. (2008). Early identification of language delay by direct language assessment or parent report? *Journal of Developmental & Behavioral Pediatrics, 29*(1), 34-41.

Sandall, S., Hemmeter, M. L., Smith, B. J., & McLean, M. E. (2005). *DEC recommended practices: A comprehensive guide.* Longmont, CO: Sopris West.

Shonkoff, J. P. & Phillips, D. A. (2000). *From neurons to neighborhoods: The science of early childhood development.* Washington, DC: National Academy Press.

Siperstein, G. N. & Favazza, P.C. (2008). Placing young children "at promise": Future directions for promoting social competence. In W. H. Brown, S. L. Odom, & S. R. McConnell (Eds.), *Social Competence of Young Children: Risk, Disability, and Intervention* (pp. 321-332). Baltimore: Brookes.

Squires, J. (1996). Parent completed developmental interviews: A low cost strategy for child-find and screening. *Infants and Young Children, 9*(1), 16-28.

Squires, J. & Bricker, D. (2007). *An activity-based approach to developing young children's social emotional competence*. Baltimore: Brookes.

Squires, J., Bricker, D., & Twombly, L. (2004). *The Ages & Stages Questionnaires: Social Emotional (ASQ-SE). A parent-completed, child-monitoring system for social-emotional behaviors*. Baltimore: Brookes.

Tabors, P. O. (2008). *One child, two languages: A guide for preschool educators of children learning English as a second language* (2nd ed.) Baltimore: Brookes.

Tan, C. S. (2007). Test review: Reynolds, C. R., & Kamphaus, R. W. (2004). Behavior assessment system for children (2nd ed.). Circle Pines, MN: American Guidance Service *Assessment for Effective Intervention, 32*, 121-124.

Turnbull, A., Turnbull, R., Erwin, E. J., Soodak, L. C. & Shogren, K. A. (2011). *Families, professionals, and exceptionality: Positive outcomes through partnership and trust*. Upper Saddle, NJ: Pearson Education.

Evaluating Young Children Who Are Dual Language Learners: Gathering and Interpreting Multiple Sources of Data to Make Informed Decisions

Lillian K. Durán, Ph.D.,
Utah State University

Gregory A. Cheatham, Ph.D.,
University of Kansas

Rosa Milagros Santos, Ph.D.,
University of Illinois at Urbana-Champaign

The growing number of children and families served in early childhood programs who speak languages other than English has raised many questions in the field of Early Intervention and Early Childhood Special Education (EI/ECSE) about appropriate and relevant assessment practices with children who are dual language learners (DLLs; See Box 1 for current demographic information). Many special educators struggle to accurately distinguish developmental delays from cultural and linguistic differences (Klingner & Harry, 2006). Over the years, several resources have become available that outline appropriate special education evaluation procedures for culturally and linguistically diverse (CLD) populations (e.g., Cartledge, Gardner, & Ford, 2009; de Valenzuela & Baca, 2004; Figueroa, 2002; Rhodes, Ochoa, & Ortiz, 2005; Paradis, Genesee, & Crago, 2010; García & Dray, 2007; Guiberson, 2009; Hart, 2009). However, many of these resources focus on school-age populations and, although many broad themes and recommendations apply across age groups, there are considerations unique to early childhood practice (Espinosa, 2005).

In this article, we will describe evidence-based practices for the appropriate and effective evaluation of children who are DLLs. Our aim is to provide EI/ECSE providers with guidance as they conduct evaluations.

Box 1
Current Demographic Information on Dual Language Learners

- Close to 20% of all Americans speak a language other than English, a significant increase since 1980.

- Next to English, Spanish is the most common language spoken in the U.S. today (U.S. Census Bureau, 2010).

- Young DLLs (0–5 years old) are one of the fastest growing segments of the U.S. population (U.S. Census Bureau, 2010).

- Approximately, 20% of children six years and under live in homes in which one parent is foreign born. The majority of these children live in a home where English is spoken fluently. However, a significant number (26%) live in households where no one over 13 years old speaks English fluently (Hernandez, Denton, & Macartney, 2008).

- The US Department of Education Office of Special Education Programs (OSEP) currently does not collect data specifically on the number of immigrant families served.

- With the reauthorization of IDEA in 2004, states are now mandated to begin collecting data on the number of DLLs (OSEP uses the term Limited English Proficient) served in Part B programs, ages 3–21.

- According to OSEP 490, 949 DLLs are served under all Part B programs, but data specifically for 3–5 year-olds are not available (Data Accountability Center, 2008).

Box 2
Juana, Gloria, and Raul

Ms. Brunner, the ECSE teacher receives a referral on a bilingual Spanish-speaking 4-year-old girl named Juana who has been in an English-only Head Start classroom for 6 months; this has been her first exposure to preschool. Her family moved to the U.S. from Mexico two years ago, and she has two older siblings attending school. Her sister, Josefa, is in the 2nd grade, and her brother Angel is in the 3rd grade. Her mother, Gloria, and father, Raul, only speak Spanish, but her siblings are introducing more English into the home. Head Start administered the Developmental Indicators for the Assessment of Learning–3 (DIAL–3; Mardell & Goldenberg, 1998) in Spanish for screening and Juana scored in the "refer" range. Gloria has concerns regarding Juana's development, including that she does not seem to use as much language in Spanish as her other children did at the same age. As well, Gloria worries that she can no longer understand what Juana is saying to her because since she began attending Head Start she is often choosing to use English at home. Her Head Start teacher has also expressed concerns about her ability to follow directions and learn new concepts.

Note: This case study was developed by the first author and represents a composite of many actual referrals.

Throughout the article, we will refer to a problem-solving process via a case study that we describe in Box 2. We will follow Juana and her family through the evaluation process to illustrate eight recommended practices we generated from the literature and that follow the recommended practices outlined in the DEC Position Paper, *Responsiveness to ALL Children, Families, and Professionals: Integrating Cultural and Linguistic Diversity into Policy and Practice* (Division for Early Childhood, 2010). To ensure that children who are DLLs are assessed effectively and properly identified, EI/ECSE providers need to understand the process of acquiring a new or second language, how languages develop for children growing up in bilingual or multilingual homes, the influence of culture on development, how to work effectively with interpreters, and how to collaborate with

Ideally, an interdisciplinary evaluation planning team should include the family, the EI/ECSE provider or teacher, a Speech and Language Pathologist, an English Language Learning (ELL) specialist, and a cultural liaison and/or interpreter.

and gather information from a broad range of families in a culturally responsive manner. To develop a deep understanding of these issues, early childhood providers need considerable content knowledge and the acquisition of specific skills that may not have been addressed during preservice preparation. The following recommendations will provide information related to each of these content areas, but for a more thorough understanding, readers are encouraged to seek additional information from the references provided in Box 3.

Recommendations When Evaluating Young Children Who Are Dual Language Learners

Recommendation 1:
Form an Interdisciplinary Evaluation Planning Team

Ideally, an interdisciplinary evaluation planning team should include the family, the EI/ECSE provider or teacher, a speech and language pathologist, an English Language Learning (ELL) specialist, and a cultural liaison and/or interpreter. Teams may also include occupational and/or physical therapists, and school psychologists as necessary. When assessing children who are DLLs, it is important to collaborate with ELL specialists in school districts, although this has not been common practice in ECSE

Box 3
Resources on Dual Language Learners

The following references will provide more information to help you effectively evaluate and serve children who are DLLs:

Barrera, I. & Kramer, L. (2009). *Using skilled dialogue to transform challenging interactions: Honoring identity, voice, & connection*. Baltimore: Brookes.

Castro, D., Ayankoya, B., & Kasprzak, C. (2011). *The New Voices~Nuevas Voces: Guide to cultural and linguistic diversity in Early Childhood*. Baltimore: Brookes.

Howes, C., Downer, J. T., & Pianta, R. C. (2011). *Dual language learners in the early childhood classroom*. Baltimore: Brookes.

Kohnert, K. (2008). *Language disorders in bilingual children and adults*. San Diego: Plural.

Lynch, E. W. & Hanson, M. J. (2011). *Developing cross-cultural competence: A guide for working with children and their families* (4th ed.). Baltimore: Brookes.

Minnesota Department of Education. (2011). *Talk with me manual: A resource guide for speech-language pathologists and educators working with linguistically diverse young children and their families*. Retrieved August 23, 2011, from http://education.state.mn.us/mdeprod/groups/EarlyLearning/documents/Manual/020994.pdf

Paradis, J., Genesee, F., & Crago, M. B. (2010). *Dual language development and disorders: A handbook on bilingualism and second language learning*. Baltimore: Brookes.

Tabors, P. O. (2008). *One child, two languages: A guide for preschool educators of children learning English as a second language* (2nd ed.). Baltimore: Brookes.

(Guiberson, 2009). These professionals have knowledge about assessing language proficiency and testing adaptations that can be made for children with limited English proficiency. Another team member that has not been common is a "cultural liaison." Some states, such as Minnesota, have created a funding source for cultural liaisons who can serve as a bridge between EI/ECSE personnel and the family. These liaisons can help the team understand the family's culture and the adaptations to the evaluation process that may be necessary to facilitate active family engagement and to gather accurate data regarding the child's development. A definition of and example roles for a cultural liaison are provided below:

"Cultural liaison" means a person who is of the same racial, cultural socioeconomic, or linguistic background as the *child*, and who:

• Provides information to the IEP team about the child's race, cultural, socioeconomic, and linguistic background;

- Assists the IEP team in understanding how racial, cultural, socio-economic, and linguistic factors impact educational progress; and
- Facilitates the parents' understanding and involvement in the special education process.

Cultural liaisons are recommended when teams are concerned that cultural or linguistic issues are affecting the overall special education process (Minnesota Department of Education, 2003, p. 37).

Recommendation 2:
Ensure Active and Meaningful Family Participation

A family-centered approach to service delivery is emphasized in Public Law 108-446, the most recent reauthorization of the Individuals with Disabilities Education Act (IDEA, 2004). It is mandated that parents are informed at every step of the special education process and that they are provided the opportunity to be active members of their child's special education team. The Division for Early Childhood of the Council for Exceptional Children also emphasizes that families are mandatory partners during the evaluation process (Neisworth & Bagnato, 2005).

Meaningful participation of families in the assessment process and determination of eligibility for special education services is vital in identifying and understanding children's strengths and areas of need.

Unfortunately, researchers have suggested that professionals often have difficulty communicating and collaborating with families who speak languages other than English and whose cultural backgrounds are differ-

Box 4
Questions to Ask Prior to an Evaluation

The evaluation planning team should answer the following questions prior to initiating the evaluation:

1. How can the team promote active family engagement and culturally responsive information gathering?
2. Where and how will observations in the child's natural settings be conducted?
3. How will the team determine the child's language proficiency in the child's home language(s) and English?
4. How will the team locate an interpreter and/or a cultural liaison? What training or guidance will be provided to the interpreter or cultural liaison prior to the evaluation?
5. How will the team decide what assessments to use and what language or languages to assess in? What other data will be gathered?

ent from their own (Harry, 2008; Klingner & Harry, 2006; Salas, 2004). Differences in language and culture present a challenge for building relationships between EI/ECSE providers and families, and researchers have identified several culture- and language-related factors that impact relationships between them (Barrera & Kramer, 2009; Cheatham & Santos, 2009; Kalyanpur & Harry, 1999; Chen, McLean, Corso, & Bruns, 2005; Lynch & Hanson, 2011). For example, Barrera and Kramer (2009) noted that negotiating issues of power and differences in values assigned to behaviors and child rearing practices play a critical role in developing successful relationships between EI/ECSE providers and families from diverse cultural and linguistic backgrounds. Special care and attention is required during collaborative evaluations to ensure that parents are not simply "recipients of professionals' decisions" (Turnbull, Turnbull, Erwin, Soodak, & Shogren, 2010, p. 99). For parents who speak languages other than English, language interpreters and cultural liaisons provide critical links within the evaluation team. Language interpreters should be qualified to interpret special education procedural information and technical terms to facilitate meaningful parent participation and informed consent. Meaningful participation of families in the assessment process and determination of eligibility for special education services is vital to the identification and understanding of children's strengths and areas of need. Often, families hold crucial information that allows for an accurate diagnosis and assessment of their children's skills. As such, members of the evaluation team must recognize and consider factors that facilitate and hinder the development of positive relationships with families. The assessment process provides multiple opportunities for members of the evaluation team and families to begin to build rapport and further develop a positive relationship.

One way to build relationships with families is to use an interview format to gather necessary information. The use of interview techniques has been well documented as an effective strategy in gathering information from families in research and practice (Banks, Santos, & Roof, 2003; Lynch & Hanson, 2011). Open-ended and informal interviews provide families with the flexibility about when and how much information to share about themselves and their children at any given time (Banks et al., 2003). When implemented effectively, informal, open-ended interviews also allow EI/ECSE providers to build rapport that is necessary to allow them to access additional information about the children and families at a later time (Cartledge et al., 2009; Dunst, Trivette, & Deal, 1995). Interviews can be used to learn from families about their life experiences, expectations of their children, preferences (e.g., language), and their goals and hopes for their children's future.

Finally, gathering information about language use patterns in the home is critical to determine whether the child is a simultaneous bilingual (i.e., learning two languages at the same time) or sequential bilingual (i.e., primarily speaking one home language and is being or will be introduced to English through home visits or preschool) (Paradis et al., 2010). This information will help the evaluation team better understand the child's language proficiency based on the relative amount of input and interaction that the child has had in each language. Appendix A is a sample family language background questionnaire that providers can use to gather language information through an interview format. Another home language and literacy interview form is available at no cost online at http://www.cpsd.us/BELA/belamaterials.htm.

Ms. Brunner schedules her initial home visit with Gloria and Raul in the evening because Raul works long hours, mostly in the daytime. She adjusts her schedule to meet when both parents can be available. She makes sure that she has also scheduled an interpreter and plans to meet her 30 minutes before the home visit to review the purpose of the visit and special education due process and evaluation procedures so that the interpreter is prepared and understands her role at the meeting. Ms. Brunner's goal is to initiate a positive working relationship with Gloria and Raul, as well as to gather information about their family background and their perspectives regarding Juana's development.

To accomplish this goal, she comes prepared with open-ended questions such as:

"Tell me some of Juana's favorite activities at home."

"Do you have any concerns about how well she is learning or talking?"

"What would help me to know Juana and your family better?" and

"What are your hopes for Juana?"

During the home visit, Gloria and Raul both share information about Juana and their family. They traveled from Michoacán, Mexico to this area two years ago to live with Raul's sister. It has been difficult for Raul to find work, but he recently found a job in a meat packing plant. The hours are long, but he is happy to be supporting his family. Gloria stays home to care for their three children.

As they begin to talk about Juana they share that she likes to play outside with her siblings and she especially likes to play chasing games. They report that she struggles to communicate with her family in Spanish, she is difficult to understand, and she does not seem to talk like their other children did at her age. They want her teachers to know that she is an energetic and happy child who is eager to please. They do report, however that she sometimes gets frustrated when she is trying to explain or ask for something and no one can understand her. They also explain that although Juana understands mostly Spanish they have noticed that since she has been attending Head Start, she is coming home and using more English with her siblings and is even trying to communicate with them in English.

Ms. Brunner also comes prepared with a list of some things the Head Start teacher has included in the referral. She shares with them Juana's favorite activities (e.g., music and book reading), how she's learning the routines, and friendships she has developed since she started in the program. For Gloria and Raul, it is really important for them to know how well Juana is adjusting to the program.

Ms. Brunner realizes that she may not get most of the information she needs on her first visit so her goal is to learn a few things at a time and most importantly gain the family's trust. She makes sure, however, that she has thoroughly explained the special education evaluation process through the interpreter and she has all appropriate initial paperwork signed. She also interviews Gloria and Raul to complete the home language background questionnaire (found in Appendix A) at this meeting. Before she leaves, she also schedules her next visit at a time that is convenient for the family and when Juana will be home so that she can observe her in her home environment.

Recommendation 3:
Observe the Child's Language Use in Natural Environments

Informal and systematic observation is important in the evaluation of children who are DLLs (Cartledge et al., 2009; National Association for the Education of Young Children [NAEYC], 2005). For most children, observations of children's language use and behavior should be completed in both the home and in their early care and education environment (e.g., preschool) to more fully understand their linguistic competencies in one or both of their languages. EI/ECSE professionals can informally observe and document ways in which the child uses language, linguistic input, and the kinds of linguistic expectations within their natural environment(s).

Informal and systematic observation is important in the evaluation of children who are DLLs.

Furthermore, EI/ECSE providers can observe and document children's use and understanding of home language and English syntax (i.e., grammar), phonology (i.e., speech sounds), semantics (i.e., words, their meanings, and their relationships), and pragmatics (i.e., appropriate language in use), in addition to nonverbal communication (Crais & Roberts, 2004). For instance, when a child is playing with a sibling, notes can be taken on vocabulary and associated sounds used, sentence length and grammar, and the child's ability to understand unstated meanings (e.g., the child responds to the brief request, "Red one" by handing the sibling a red block saying, "Here it is").

In addition to informal observations, systematic observation tools (e.g., rating scales, criterion-referenced assessments) can be employed to ensure a complete understanding of children's language competencies (NAEYC, 2005). Some examples might include the Assessment, Evaluation, and Programming System (AEPS; Bricker et al., 2002) or the Hawaii Early Learning Profile (HELP; Teaford, Wheat, & Baker, 2010).

During observations, special attention should be paid to children's code switching (i.e., mixing two or more languages within and/or across sentences), as well as to that of the others in home and school environments. Importantly, code switching typically does not indicate a lack of competence in one language. Instead, code switching is a sign of high language proficiency in both languages and should be viewed as a means by which children are resourcefully and skillfully communicating their exact meanings with others who speak both of their languages (Paradis et al., 2010). As a rule-governed system, code switching demands appropriate choices of words, phrases, and discourse as a reflection of socio-cultural factors, such as relationships, affiliation, and comfort with another speaker (Myers-Scotton, 2006). Given the importance of code switching and other culture-based communication behaviors to a comprehensive understanding of bilingual children's communication abilities, individuals who speak in both of the child's languages should be asked to conduct or participate in and interpret observations to determine if code switching follows family and/or community code-switching language norms, in addition to helping to determine the child's functioning in the areas of language mentioned above.

Ms. Brunner also prepares herself to conduct an observation of Juana in her home environment. She schedules an interpreter and meets with her again prior to the home visit to share the questions that will be asked during the meeting, as well as the information she may need to provide when Ms. Brunner is conducting the observation, such as helping to accurately record Juana's utterances in Spanish.

After the home language observation, Ms. Brunner also schedules a time to conduct an observation in Juana's Head Start classroom and to interview her teacher. She observes Juana during naturally occurring routines and documents her utterances in English and Spanish (schedule an interpreter if necessary or, if available, bilingual Head Start staff might also assist). She also carefully observes her engagement in activities and her interactions with both peers and the teacher. She takes time to interview the Head Start teacher about Juana's progress in the program and asks her to compare Juana's development to other Spanish-speaking children she has taught in her classroom.

Recommendation 4:
Determine Child's Language Proficiency in Home Language(s) and English

Language proficiency testing has not traditionally been part of the special education evaluation process; however, the Individuals with Disabilities Education Improvement Act (2004) and earlier versions of the law require that assessments "Are provided and administered in the child's native language or other mode of communication and in the form most likely to yield accurate information on what the child knows and can do academically, developmentally, and functionally, unless it is clearly not fea-

sible to so provide or administer" (IDEA, 2004). Language proficiency is not easily determined and requires attention to measurement. Once a home language questionnaire is completed, testing the child's language proficiency is the important next step to ensure accuracy. When testing for language proficiency, it is critical that all languages the child speaks are assessed separately and, if possible, by different assessors. It must be noted that many children who are DLLs are sensitive to which language to speak with different communicative partners and in different contexts. This ability is called "interlocutor sensitivity" (Pettito et al., 2001).

To obtain the most accurate measure of a child's language ability in each of his/her language(s), the evaluation team needs to conduct proficiency testing in one language and then provide the same opportunity in the other language(s). Language proficiency testing is not conducted to determine eligibility for special education. It is conducted to determine which language or languages to target for assessment, and how much and what kind of assessment to conduct in each language. Young children who are DLLs vary widely in their proficiency in each language (Kohnert, Bates, & Hernandez, 1999; Kohnert & Bates, 2002). Some are simultaneous bilinguals and may have relatively balanced proficiency in both of their languages. Others may be sequential bilinguals and have much more proficiency in their home language with only emerg-

To obtain the most accurate measure of a child's language ability in each of his/her language(s), the evaluation team needs to conduct proficiency testing in one language and then provide the same opportunity in the other language(s).

ing skills in English (Paradis et al., 2010). For the simultaneous bilingual, full assessment in each language is considered the best approach to determine the child's functioning and to measure overall linguistic abilities. For the sequential bilingual who has little proficiency in English, emphasis on measurement in the home language will be critical in determining language or developmental delays because the child's English ability may be insufficient to distinguish delay from stages of second language acquisition. Overall, more research needs to be conducted to provide more solid recommendations on determining language proficiency in young children who are DLLs, but currently in the field, the recommended approach is to use multiple data sources and clinical judgment. Data sources include home language background information from the child's family; language samples and observation in natural settings; parent, care provider, and teacher reports; and language proficiency testing when possible.

The following are some measures that are available to measure language proficiency in children who are DLLs. Each measure presented has strengths and weaknesses and the choice of instruments needs to match the child's developmental level. Additionally, while there are standardized measures for Spanish and English, norm-referenced measures for other languages are not available. For example, the Pre-IDEA Proficiency Test (Pre-IPT; Ballard, Tighe, & Dalton, 1991) and the Pre-Language Assessment Scale (Pre-LAS; Duncan & De Avila, 2000) are designed for Spanish-speaking children ages 3–5 who are typically developing. A child with a significant cognitive or language delay may not be able to complete many of the items and a basal may not be achieved. However, the Pre-IPT (Ballard et al., 1991) or Pre-LAS (Duncan & De Avila, 2000) might be a good measure for a child who is near kindergarten age with a mild to moderate speech and language impairment or motor delay. The Bilingual Early Language Assessment (BELA; Tabors & Heise-Baigorria, 2004) might be a better choice for a younger child or one with more significant delays. It is also designed for children ages 3–5, but many of the test items are simple pointing or naming tasks. It is available at no cost online (http://www.cpsd.us/BELA/index.htm), but there is no published normative data for the assessment and practitioners must use clinical decision-making to infer relative language proficiency between the child's languages. It is currently available in Arabic, Bangla, Chinese, Haitian Creole, Portuguese, and Spanish. Hmong, Oromo, Russian, and Somali versions are available online at no cost through the Minnesota Department of Education (http://education.state.mn.us/MDE/Learning_Support/Early_Learning_Services/Early_Childhood_Programs/Help_Me_Grow_Prog_Serv/Administration/index.html). The authors of the instrument also encourage practitioners to have the test translated into other languages, and new translations can be posted on their website. Overall, it is important for the assessor to spend time getting to know these instruments to decide which might work best within their specific community and for each referred child's developmental abilities.

If no standardized measures exist in the child's home language, then EI/ECSE providers may need to administer a standardized test that was developed in English through the use of an interpreter.

For children under age 3, the best approach to determining language proficiency is through gathering and analyzing language samples and parent reports. A good tool for gathering information about receptive and expressive vocabulary for a child age 8–37 months is the MacArthur-

Bates Communication Development Inventories, 2nd Edition (Fenson et al., 2007). There is also a published Spanish version, the MacArthur-Bates Inventarios del Desarollo de Habilidades Comunicativas (Jackson-Maldonado et al., 2003). Additionally, the MacArthur-Bates Communication Development Inventories are available online in 47 different languages (http://www.sci.sdsu/cdi/adaptations_ol.htm).

Juana was administered the BELA (Tabors & Heise-Baigorria, 2004) in English and Spanish, and the team found that although she has some limited expressive and receptive language abilities in English (e.g., words related to pre-academic content such as color names, numbers, and shapes), her overall receptive and expressive language in Spanish was still significantly higher. The parents also reported significantly more Spanish use in the home than English during the home language interview. Therefore, Spanish was determined to be her dominant language with emerging skills in English.

Recommendation 5:
Create a Culturally and Linguistically Responsive Evaluation Plan

After information about the child's language proficiency and home language environment is gathered, the evaluation team can make an informed decision about which language(s) to use for testing. If no standardized measures exist in the child's home language, then EI/ECSE providers may need to administer a standardized test that was developed in English through the use of an interpreter. We highlight below three complications to translating English measures that MUST be considered:

1. The standard scores will NOT be valid. If an English language assessment is translated into another language and administered through the use of an interpreter, the norms and standard scores will not apply to the child being assessed. These assessments were not normed through the use of an interpreter and bilingual children were not included in the sample.

2. There will be cultural and linguistic bias in the assessment. Items on the test may not be familiar to children from different cultural backgrounds such as common foods, household items, or animals. Additionally, language items may not be "functionally equivalent" because developmental trajectories in languages differ. In some languages children may learn more verbs before nouns, or certain grammatical structures may be more common and develop more

quickly (Paradis et al., 2010; Peña, Bedore, & Rappazzo, 2003; Peña & Kester, 2004). Simply translating a test from one language to another does not account for these technical and complex differences between languages and cultures (see Peña, 2007 for a full discussion of these issues).

3. If the person interpreting the assessment into another language is not trained in early childhood assessment, the interpretation of the items and how the child's responses are reported may be inaccurate. Therefore, there is considerably more potential for error and sources of confound in the results obtained through this method.

Given the limited number of technically adequate assessments available in languages other than English, many EI/ECSE practitioners find themselves in the position of administering assessments designed for monolingual English speakers through the use of an interpreter. (For a listing of assessments and screening instruments available in languages other than English, see The Midwest Equity Assistance Center of Kansas State University's Web site, http://www.meac.org/documents/Publications/Assessment_instrument.pdf.) In this case, the EI/ECSE provider will need to use caution in interpreting the results. The child's performance on the items administered can be described, but multiple data sources (e.g., parent and teacher report, observations in natural settings, language samples, and criterion-referenced assessments) are also necessary to determine eligibility for special education services. Additionally, practitioners may use techniques such as dynamic assessment or testing to the limits to gather more information about a child's learning potential and range of abilities without being confined to standardized test administration (For a full description of these approaches see de Valenzuela & Baca, 2004 and Gutiérrez-Clellan & Peña, 2001).

Because Juana is dominant in Spanish, the team agreed that the majority of her testing should be conducted in Spanish with supplemental data gathering in English to further document her emerging skills. Thus, Juana's assessment battery includes: (1) Preschool Language Scale–4, Spanish (PLS–4; Zimmerman, Steiner, & Pond, 2002); (2) Learning Accomplishment Profile–Diagnostic, 3rd Edition, Spanish (LAP–D; Hardin, Peisner-Feinberg, Weeks, 2005); (3) language samples recorded in Juana's Head Start classroom as well as teacher reports about her English language usage gathered over time (such as a running record for one week of all of the English utterances that the Head Start teacher can record and examples of the types of requests Juana can respond to in English); (4) completion of an AEPS to investigate Juana's skills in English and the developmental skills she demonstrates in the classroom; and (5) language samples collected in her home with the assistance of an interpreter through observation of a family routine, such as mealtime or at play with siblings.

Recommendation 6:
Conduct Testing with Bilingual EI/ECSE Professionals or a Trained Interpreter

To effectively administer tests in the child's dominant language, it is important that the evaluation team includes a staff member who is proficient in the child's dominant language. An interpreter may be used if bilingual staff is not available. Today, interpreters may be found in the community (e.g., via immigrant centers), local colleges or universities, churches, and businesses. Utilizing nonprofessional interpreters and translators poses a different set of challenges that the evaluation team must address before moving forward with the assessment.

It is important that the interpreter has been given ample training and time to review the tests before being expected to administer them. Specific training in expectations during the administration of the assessment is often needed to ensure that an accurate measure of children's skills and knowledge is obtained (e.g., the level of prompting that is acceptable during the test, what skills are being measured so that he/she will report more accurately how the child responded, and appropriate types of communication with the family about the assessment). See Ohtake, Santos, and Fowler (2000) and Cheatham (2011) for other helpful strategies when working with interpreters or translators.

To effectively administer tests in the child's dominant language, it is important that the evaluation team includes a staff member who is proficient in the child's dominant language.

The team has identified Mrs. Vargas, a paraprofessional in the kindergarten program next door to Head Start to assist with administering the PLS–4 (Zimmerman et al., 2002) and the LAP–D (Hardin et al., 2005). Mrs. Vargas is fluent in both English and Spanish and has worked in the schools for over five years. While she has some experience administering curriculum based assessments to the kindergarteners, Mrs. Vargas is unfamiliar with the PLS–4 and LAP–D. Thus, Mr. Kraft, the speech language pathologist, and Ms. Brunner meet with Mrs. Vargas to teach her to administer the test. While Mrs. Vargas practices administering the test with Ms. Brunner, Mr.

Kraft coaches and provides her with feedback throughout the prac-tice session. For her time learning to administer the tests and the time she spent with Juana during the actual testing, Mrs. Vargas was provided a previously agreed upon hourly compensation. Ms. Brunner is present during the assessment, but because she does not speak Spanish she allows Mrs. Vargas to administer the items under her supervision. Ms. Brunner realizes that to obtain the most accurate results it is best to use one target language during the test-ing session rather than switching back and forth between English and Spanish.

Recommendation 7:
Analyze and Compare Data Collected Across Each of Child's Languages and from Multiple Sources

Data collected from multiple sources should be used to create a develop-mental and linguistic "profile" for the child (Oller, Pearson, & Cobo-Lewis, 2007). It is necessary for the team to have a measure of the relative amount of input and interaction the child receives in each language, the child's actual language proficiency in English and home language(s), standardized test results if appropriate, observa-tions in natural settings, reports from parents and other care providers if appropriate (e.g., Head Start teacher, child care provider, etc.), and possibly a criterion-based measure. Multiple sources of data provide the team with the opportunity to corroborate results and note patterns that may have emerged across the different contexts and assessments.

Multiple sources of data provide the team with the opportunity to corroborate results and note patterns that may have emerged across the different contexts and assessments.

If a child has developmental delays, one would expect similar scores or reports from multiple data sources. Currently, interpreting and analyz-ing bilingual data and assessment results is not an exact science. Most of the assessment tools available on the market were primarily normed on monolingual children and will need to be interpreted with caution (Peña & Kester, 2004). Children who are DLLs are known to generally score lower when each of their languages is compared to monolingual norms. Thus, the evaluation team needs to analyze results from assessments that have been administered in both (or all) of the child's languages and inves-tigate the skills that are distributed across all languages, such as size of vocabulary using conceptual scoring (see Bedore, Peña, García, & Cortez,

2005 for a full description) and sophistication of the child's syntax in each language. Of course, the child's proficiency in each language will also be dependent on the amount of input they have had in each (Paradis, et al. 2010; Oller et al., 2007).

The following statement was generated by the evaluation team to discuss Juana's need for special education services under developmental delay criteria. "The standards and procedures (standardized, norm-referenced scores) used with the majority of children were not used with Juana, as these English instruments are not normed on bilingual children who speak languages other than English. Although Juana is demonstrating emerging skills in English, her dominant language was determined to be Spanish as measured by the Bilingual Early Language Assessment and therefore norm-referenced scores on English measures are not considered valid. Standardized instruments were administered in Spanish to document Juana's expressive and receptive language, cognitive, gross and fine motor, social/emotional, and self-help development. Overall, the objective data used to conclude that Juana has a developmental delay and is in need of specialized instruction include: parent and Head Start teacher reports, standardized testing in Spanish, Head Start and ECSE teacher reports on the AEPS, and observations and language samples collected in her home and Head Start setting. Juana was found to have delays as measured by the PLS–4 and the LAP–D in Spanish; her scores fell below -1.5 standard deviations in expressive and receptive language on both measures and in cognition on the LAP-D. The other data collected support these results. She therefore qualifies for Special Education services under the criteria for developmental delay.

Recommendation 8:
Discuss with Families the Importance of Home Language Development

Families may approach their children's home language acquisition and retention in various ways. Studies illustrate that many parents place high value on the home language as a link to family, culture, and community (Garcia, Mendez-Perez, & Ortiz, 2000; Perez, 2000). However, other parents may emphasize the acquisition of English because they believe it ensures their children's academic and subsequent occupational success in their new country. The latter families may be making the "English-only" choice based on inaccurate messages they have received from the media or others in the community that the acquisition of English must be at the expense of maintaining their child's home language.

This warrants research-based discussions with families and providing
families with information regarding
the importance of home language
maintenance. EI/ECSE professionals
can help families understand that
bilingualism is beneficial and that
home language development can
actually support children's acquisition of English language and literacy
(August & Shanahan, 2006; Cheatham,
Santos, & Ro, 2007; Rolstad, Mahoney,
& Glass, 2005; Slavin & Cheung, 2005). From this perspective, parents can
understand that adding another language (i.e., English) does not have
to result in subtracting their home language. Indeed, children with and
without disabilities can become bilingual without cost to either of their
languages when provided with appropriate support (Barnett, Yarosz,
Thomas, Jung, & Blanco, 2007; Durán, Roseth, & Hoffman, 2010; Feltmate
& Kay-Raining Bird, 2008; Kohnert, Yim, Nett, Kan, & Durán, 2005;
Thordardottir, Ellis-Weismer, & Smith, 1997).

> EI/ECSE professionals can help
> families understand that bilin-
> gualism is beneficial and that
> home language development
> can actually support children's
> acquisition of English language
> and literacy.

Similarly, EI/ECSE professionals can help families understand implications of home language loss for children and families, a common experience when children come from homes in which English is not spoken
(Anderson, 2004; Tabors, 2008; Tse, 2001). As the child gradually loses
ability in the home language, disconnects can occur with those family
members who do not speak English or have limited proficiency in English.
Moreover, parents may be limited in their ability to take the role of primary socializer due to their minimal communication and shared culture
with their child (Wong-Fillmore, 2000). Ultimately, of course, EI/ECSE
professionals must listen to and respect the family's priorities and goals
regarding their child's language use.

*Juana has qualified for Special Education services under the criteria
for developmental delay and over the school year, as Ms. Brunner
continues to meet with Gloria and Raul both in school and at home,
she reminds them about how important it is for them to continue
to use Spanish with Juana at home. Every week, Juana selects a
Spanish-language book to bring home that she and her family can
read together. Through the classroom monthly newsletter (that is
translated into Spanish), she shares with Gloria, Raul, and the other
families in the program the importance of native language development and suggests some simple strategies for supporting their chil-*

dren's language development that they can easily implement at home and in the community (See Appendix B). Ms. Brunner also schedules bimonthly home visits and brings an interpreter who models activities in Spanish that the family can engage in with Juana to promote her native language development.

Conclusion

The appropriate and unbiased evaluation of young children who are DLLs takes time and careful consideration. EI/ECSE providers need to be aware of the complexity involved in determining children's language proficiency and how this proficiency will in turn influence their results on standardized instruments. We need to take the guesswork out of this process and incorporate targeted measurement practices to ensure our evaluation findings are accurate. The child's family is also integral to the evaluation, and new strategies must be learned to gather information from all of the families we serve. Practitioners may need more training on culturally responsive practices that foster collaborative relationships with families. EI/ECSE providers also need access to more information on dual language development so that they can better understand differences associated with bilingual development. In addition to mastering new content, EI/ECSE providers will need to be flexible and receptive to changes in practice.

More time and energy may need to be initially invested as new procedures are implemented when evaluating young children who are DLLs. However, the trade-off will hopefully be that the special education team will gather more accurate and unbiased information about the children and their families to responsibly answer the question, "Does this child have a developmental delay or are concerns related to linguistic and/or cultural differences?" Ultimately, there is no substitute for gathering high quality and accurate data to inform any decision regarding a child's need for special education services.

References

Anderson, R. T. (2004). First language loss in Spanish-speaking children: Patterns of loss and implications for clinical practice. In B. A. Goldstein (Ed.), *Bilingual language development and disorders in Spanish-English speakers* (pp. 187-212). Baltimore: Brookes.

August, D., & Shanahan, T. (Eds.) (2006). Developing literacy in second language learners: Report of the national literacy panel on language-minority children and youth. Mahwah, NJ: Lawrence Erlbaum.

Ballard, W. S., Tighe, P. L., & Dalton, E. F. (1991). *IDEA language proficiency test*. Brea, CA: Ballard & Tighe.

Banks, R., Santos, R. M., & Roof, V. (2003). Discovering family concerns, priorities and resources: Sensitive family information gathering. *Young Exceptional Children, 6*(2), 11-19.

Barnett, W. S., Yarosz, D. J., Thomas, J., Jung, K., & Blanco, D. (2007). Two-way and monolingual English immersion in preschool education: An experimental comparison. *Early Childhood Research Quarterly, 22*, 277-293.

Barrera, I., & Kramer, L. (2009). *Using skilled dialogue to transform challenging interactions: Honoring identity, voice, and connection*. Baltimore: Brookes.

Bedore, L. M., Peña, E. D., García, M., & Cortez, C. (2005). Conceptual versus monolingual scoring: When does it make a difference? *Language, Speech, and Hearing Services in the Schools, 36*, 188-200.

Bricker, D., Capt, B., Pretti-Frontczak, K., Johnson, J., Slentz, K., Straka, E., et al. (2002). *Volume 2: AEPS® Test for Birth to Three Years and Three to Six Years*. Baltimore, MD: Brookes.

Cartledge, G., Gardner, R., & Ford, D. Y. (2009). *Diverse learners with exceptionalities: Culturally responsive teaching in the inclusive classroom*. Upper Saddle River, NJ: Pearson.

Castro, D., Ayankoya, B., & Kasprzak, C. (2011). *The New Voices~Nuevas Voces: Guide to cultural and linguistic diversity in Early Childhood*. Baltimore: Brookes.

Cheatham, G. A. (2011). Language interpretation, parent participation and young children with disabilities. *Topics in Early Childhood Special Education, 31*, 78-88.

Cheatham, G. A., & Santos, R. M. (2009). "Why won't they just cooperate?" Understanding how cultural values impact how we team with families. In C. Peterson, L. Fox, & A. Santos (Eds.), *Young Exceptional Children Monograph Series 11*, Quality Inclusive Services in a Diverse Society (pp. 107-121). Missoula, MT: Council for Exceptional Children Division for Early Childhood.

Cheatham, G. A., Santos, R. M., & Ro, Y. E. (2007). Home language acquisition and retention for young children with special needs. *Young Exceptional Children, 11*, 27-39.

Chen, D., McLean, M., Corso, R. M., & Bruns, D. (2005). Working together in early intervention: Cultural considerations in helping relationships and service utilization. In R. M. Corso, S. A. Fowler, & R. M. Santos (Eds.), *CLAS Collection 2: Building healthy relationships with families* (pp. 39-58). Longmont, CO: Sopris West.

Crais, E. R., & Roberts, J. E. (2004). Assessing communication skills. In M. Mclean, M. Wolery, & D. B. Bailey (Eds.), *Assessing infants and preschoolers with special needs* (pp. 345-411). Upper Saddle River, NJ: Pearson.

Data Accountability Center. *Individuals with Disabilities Education Act Data: Part B Data and Notes*. (2008). Retrieved from https://www.ideadata.org/PartBData.asp

de Valenzuela, J. S., & Baca, L. (2004). Procedures and techniques for assessing the bilingual exceptional child. In L. Baca & H. Cervantes (Eds.), *The bilingual special education interface* (pp. 184-201). Upper Saddle River, NJ: Pearson.

Division for Early Childhood. (2010). *DEC Position Paper: Responsiveness to all children, families, and professionals: Integrating cultural and linguistic diversity into policy and practice*. Missoula, MT: Author.

Duncan, S. E., & De Avila, E. A. (2000). *PreLAS 2000*. Monterey, CA: CTB/McGraw-Hill.

Dunst, C. J., Trivette, C. M., & Deal, A. G. (1995). *Enabling and empowering families: Principles and guidelines for practice.* Cambridge, MA: Brookline Books.

Durán, L. K., Roseth, C., & Hoffman, P. (2010). An experimental study comparing English-only and transitional bilingual education on Spanish-speaking preschoolers' early literacy development. *Early Childhood Research Quarterly, 25,* 207-217.

Espinosa, L. (2005). Curriculum and assessment considerations for young children from culturally, linguistically, and economically diverse backgrounds. *Psychology in the Schools, 42,* 837-853.

Feltmate, K., & Kay-Raining Bird, E. (2008). Language learning in four bilingual children with Down syndrome: A detailed analysis of vocabulary and morphosyntax. *Canadian Journal of Speech-Language Pathology and Audiology, 32,* 6-20.

Fenson, L., Marchman, V. A., Thal, D. J., Dale, P. S., Reznick, J. S., & Bates, E. (2007). MacArthur-Bates, Communicative Development Inventories (2nd Ed.). Baltimore, MD: Brookes.

Figueroa, R. A. (2002). Toward a new model of assessment. In A. J. Artiles & A. A. Ortiz (Eds.), *English language learners with special education needs: Identification, assessment, and instruction* (pp. 51-64). McHenry, IL: Center for Applied Linguistics and Delta Systems.

García, S. B., & Dray, B. J. (2007). Bilingualism and special education. In F. E. Obiakor (Ed.), *Multicultural special education* (pp. 18-33). Upper Saddle River, NJ: Pearson.

García, S. B., Mendez-Perez, A. M., & Ortiz, A. A. (2000). Mexican American mothers' beliefs about disabilities: Implications for early childhood intervention. *Remedial and Special Education, 21,* 90-100.

Guiberson, M. (2009). Hispanic representation in special education: Patterns and implications. *Preventing School Failure, 53*(3), 167-176.

Gutiérrez-Clellen, V., & Peña, E. (2001). Dynamic assessment of diverse children: A tutorial. *Language Speech and Hearing Services in Schools, 32,* 212-224.

Hardin, B., Peisner–Feinberg, E. S., & Weeks, S. W. (2005). *Learning Accomplishment Profile-Diagnostic* (3rd ed). Lewiston, NC: Kaplan Early Learning Company.

Harry, B. (2008). Collaboration with culturally and linguistically diverse families: Ideal versus reality. *Exceptional Children, 74,* 372-388.

Hart, J. E. (2009). Strategies for culturally and linguistically diverse students with special needs. *Preventing School Failure, 53,* 197-206.

Hernandez, D., Denton, N., & Macartney, S. (2008). *Children in Immigrant Families—The U.S. and 50 States: National Origins, Language, and Early Education.* Retrieved from http://www.fcdus.org/resources/resources_show.htm?doc_id=479561

Howes, C., Downer, J. T., & Pianta, R. C. (2011). *Dual language learners in the early childhood classroom.* Baltimore: Brookes.

Individuals with Disabilities Education Act (IDEA), 20 U.S.C. § 1400 (2004).

Jackson-Maldonado, D., Thal, D. J., Fenson, L., Marchman, V. A., Newton, T., & Conboy, B. (2003). *MacArthur inventarios del desarrollo de habilidades comunicativas.* Baltimore, MD: Brookes.

Kalyanpur, M., & Harry, B. (1999). *Culture in special education.* Baltimore, MD: Brookes.

Klingner, J. K., & Harry, B. (2006). The special education referral and decision-making process for English language learners: Child study team meetings and placement conferences. *Teachers College Record, 108,* 2247-2281.

Kohnert, K. (2008). *Language disorders in bilingual children and adults.* San Diego: Plural.

Kohnert, K., & Bates, E. (2002). Balancing bilinguals II: Lexical comprehension and cognitive processing in children learning Spanish and English. *Journal of Speech, Language, and Hearing Research, 45,* 347-359.

Kohnert, K., Bates, E., & Hernandez, A. (1999). Balancing bilinguals: Lexical-semantic production and cognitive processing in children learning Spanish and English. *Journal of Speech, Language, and Hearing Research, 42,* 1400-1413.

Kohnert, K., Yim, D., Nett, K., Kan, P. F., & Durán, L. (2005). Intervention with linguistically diverse preschool children: A focus on developing home language(s). *Language, Speech and Hearing Services in the Schools, 36*(3), 251-263.

Lynch, E. W., & Hanson, M. J. (Eds.) (2011). *Developing cross-cultural competence: A guide for working with children and their families* (4th ed.). Baltimore: Brookes.

Mardell, C., & Goldenberg, D. S. (1998) *Developmental Indicators for the Assessment of Learning–3.* Birmingham, AL: Psychcorp.

Minnesota Department of Education. (2003). *ELL Companion to Reducing Bias in Special Education Evaluation.* Retrieved August 23, 2011, from http://education.state.mn.us/mdeprod/groups/SpecialEd/documents/Manual/003103.pdf

Minnesota Department of Education. (2011). *Talk with me manual: A resource guide for speech-language pathologists and educators working with linguistically diverse young children and their families.* Retrieved August 23, 2011, from http://education.state.mn.us/mdeprod/groups/EarlyLearning/documents/Manual/020994.pdf

Myers-Scotton, C. (2006). How codeswitching as an available option empowers bilinguals. In M. Putz, J. A. Fishman & J. Neffvan Aertselaer (Eds.), *Along the routes to power: Explorations of empowerment through language* (pp. 73-84). Berlin, Germany: Mouton de Gruyter.

National Association for the Education of Young Children (NAEYC). (2005). *Screening and assessment of young English-language learners: Supplement to the NAEYC and NAECS/SDE joint position statement on early childhood curriculum, assessment, and program evaluation.* National Association for the Education of Young Children. Retrieved August 23, 2011, from http://www.naeyc.org/files/naeyc/file/positions/ELL_Supplement_Shorter_Version.pdf

Neisworth, J. T., & Bagnato, S. J. (2005). Assessment. In S. Sandall, M. L. Hemmeter, B. J. Smith, & M. McLean (Eds.), *DEC recommended practices: A comprehensive guide for practical application* (pp. 45-69). Longmont, CO: Sopris West.

Ohtake, Y., Santos, R. M., & Fowler, S. A. (2000). It's a three-way conversation: Families, service providers, and interpreters working together. *Young Exceptional Children, 4*(1), 12-18.

Oller, D. K., Pearson, B. Z., & Cobo-Lewis, A. (2007). Profile effects in early bilingual language and literacy. *Applied Psycholinguistics, 28,* 191-230.

Paradis, J., Genesee, F., & Crago, M. B. (2010). *Dual language development and disorders: A handbook on bilingualism and second language learning.* Baltimore, MD: Brookes.

Peña, E. D. (2007). Lost in translation: Methodological considerations in cross-cultural research. *Child Development, 78*(4), 1255-1264.

Peña, E., Bedore, L. M., & Rappazzo, C. (2003) Comparison of Spanish, English, and bilingual children's performance across semantic tasks. *Language, Speech, and Hearing Services in Schools, 34,* 5-16.

Peña, E., & Kester, E. S. (2004). Semantic development in Spanish-English bilinguals: Theory, assessment, and intervention. In B. A. Goldstein (Ed.), *Bilingual language development and disorders in Spanish-English speakers* (pp. 187-212). Baltimore: Brookes.

Perez, A. M. (2000). Mexican American mothers' perceptions and beliefs about language acquisition in infants and toddlers with disabilities. *Bilingual Research Journal, 24,* 225-242.

Pettito, L. A., Katerelos, M., Levy, B. G., Guana, K., Tétreault, K., & Ferraro, V. (2001). Bilingual signed and spoken language acquisition from birth: Implications for the mechanisms underlying early bilingual acquisition. *Journal of Child Language, 28,* 453-496.

Rhodes, R. L., Ochoa, S. H., & Ortiz, S. O. (2005). *Assessing culturally and linguistically diverse students: A practical guide.* New York, NY: Guilford.

Rolstad, K., Mahoney, K., & Glass, G. (2005). The big picture: A meta-analysis of program effectiveness research on English language learners. *Educational Policy, 19,* 572-594.

Salas, L. (2004). Individualized education plan (IEP) meetings and Mexican-American parents: Let's talk about it. *Journal of Latinos in Education, 3,* 181-192.

Slavin, R. E., & Cheung, A. (2005). A synthesis of research on language of reading instruction for English language learners. *Review of Educational Research, 75,* 247-284.

Tabors, P. O. (2008). *One child, two languages: A guide for preschool educators of children learning English as a second language,* (2nd ed.). Baltimore: Brookes.

Tabors. P. O., & Heise-Baigorria, C. (2004). *Bilingual Early Language Assessment.* Retrieved August 23, 2011, from www.cpsd.us/BELA/

Teaford, P., Wheat, J., & Baker, T. (2010) *HELP 3–6 Assessment Manual (2nd Ed.).* Palo Alto, CA: Vort Corporation.

Thordardottir, E., Ellis-Weismer, S., & Smith, M. (1997). Vocabulary learning in bilingual and monolingual clinical intervention. *Child Language Teaching and Therapy, 13,* 215-227.

Tse, L. (2001). *"Why don't they learn English?" Separating fact from fallacy in the U.S. language debate.* New York: Teachers College.

Turnbull, A., Turnbull, R., Erwin, E. J., Soodak, L. C., & Shogren, K. A. (2010). *Families, professionals and exceptionality: Positive outcomes through partnership and trust.* Boston, MA: Pearson.

U.S. Census Bureau. (2010). *Language use in the United States: 2007.* Retrieved from http://www.census.gov/population/www/socdemo/language/ACS-12.pdf U.S.

Wong-Fillmore, L. (2000). Loss of family languages: Should educators be concerned? *Theory into Practice, 39,* 203-210.

Zimmerman, I. L., Steiner, V., & Pond, R. E. (2002) *Preschool Language Scale–4.* Birmingham, AL: Psych Corp.

Appendix A
Questionnaire for the Family Home Language and Education

Date____/____/____

Child's Name_____ Child's Date of Birth___/___/___ Child's age:_____

Name of the person completing this form:_____ Relationship to the child:_____

1. (a) At what age did your child begin to attend any early childhood program? _____
    (b) In what type of educational programs has you child participated? (for example preschool, childcare, Head Start) Were they bilingual programs or English-only settings?
    _____

2. (a) Does your child speak _____? YES   NO
   (b) If so, at what age did your child begin to speak _____? _____
   (c) Does he/she speak _____ often? YES   NO
   (d) With whom does your child speak _____? _____

3. (a) Does your child speak English? YES   NO
   (b) If so, at what age did your child begin to speak English? _____
   (c) Does he/she speak English often? YES   NO
   (d) With whom does your child speak English? _____

4. (a) In what language(s) do you speak at home?_____
   (b) Please list the people that live in your home, and the languages that each person speaks. (For example: grandmother-Spanish, older brother-English and Spanish, etc.)

5. Does your child have any medical problems that you know of? YES   NO

6. In comparison with other children of the same age, do you feel that your child has any problems in speaking?   YES   NO

7. Do you have any concerns regarding your child's development, behavior, language or learning level? YES   NO

How many years of schooling has the child's mother completed? _____
In what country?_____

How many years of schooling has the child's father completed? _____
In what country?_____

Appendix B

Sources for Materials to Provide to Families to Support Home Language Development

Hennepin County Library
www.hclib.org/BirthTo6/EarlyLit.cfm
• Family resources for early literacy in multiple languages

¡Colorín Colorado!
www.colorincolorado.org
• A bilingual site for families and educators of dual language learners

Teaching for Change
http://www.teachingforchange.org/node/144
• *How to Maintain Your Home Language* handout in English and Spanish

Washington Learning Systems
http://www.walearning.com/resources/
• Handouts in English and Spanish as well as other languages on learning activities in natural environments

Sources for General Information in Languages other than English Related to Special Education

March of Dimes
http://www.nacersano.org/
• Companion website all in Spanish about health during pregnancy, prematurity, birth defects, and some other pregnancy and newborn information

Zero to Three
http://www.zerotothree.org/site/PageServer?pagename=ter_par_parenthandouts
• Parent handouts on child development available in Spanish

PACER Center
http://www.pacer.org/translations/index.asp
• Translated materials about Special Education and school into Hmong, Somali, and Spanish

Minnesota Department of Education
http://education.state.mn.us/MDE/Accountability_Programs/Compliance_and_Assistance/Recommended_Due_Process_Forms/index.html
• Due Process forms in ten different languages
http://education.state.mn.us/MDE/Learning_Support/Special_Education/Evaluation_Program_Planning_Supports/Cultural_Linguistic_Diversity/index.html
• English-Somali and English-Hmong Special Education Glossary
• Guidelines on alternative procedures for conducting an evaluation in Spanish and with an interpreter
http://www.parentsknow.state.mn.us/parentsknow/index.html
• Information on many different disabilities and child development in Spanish, Hmong, and Somali

Using Goal Attainment Scaling to Monitor the Developmental Progress of Young Children with Disabilities

Laurie A. Dinnebeil,

Margie Spino,

William F. McInerney,
University of Toledo

Sheila is just beginning her second year as a full-time itinerant early childhood special education (IECSE) teacher. She travels to children's homes or schools and partners with parents and teachers on ways to address the goals and objectives of young children with special needs. During her first year as an itinerant teacher, she struggled with all the progress monitoring forms, checklists, charts, and communication logs she used for the children on her caseload. She wants a better method to monitor each child's progress and to summarize progress in a way that can be easily communicated to other team members. She also wants to find a way to better support the parents and early childhood teachers with whom she partners.

Monitoring children's progress towards meeting their individualized family service plan (IFSP) or individualized education plan (IEP) goals or outcomes is critical for making sound decisions about the use of intervention strategies. The Division of Early Childhood of the Council for Exceptional Children (DEC, 2007) has emphasized the need for "feedback spirals" to inform and guide practices that support the development of young children with disabilities (p. 7). To make informed team-based decisions, there must be effective ways for team members to communicate about children's developmental or pre-academic progress. Family members, educators, and therapists must be able to share assessment information about children's progress in a way that promotes shared accountability and understanding. In addition, given the movement towards consultative or triadic service delivery models in early childhood education, it is important to monitor adults' use of child-focused intervention strategies, and to communicate that information in an efficient and effective manner (Buysse & Wesley, 2005; Dinnebeil & McInerney, 2011). The purpose of this paper is to describe how early childhood teams can use Goal Attainment Scaling (GAS: Kiresuk, Smith, & Cardillo, 1994) to manage and provide information about a child's progress towards meeting intended goals, objectives, or outcomes. Examples of how to plan for and use this progress monitoring approach also are provided.

Monitoring children's progress towards meeting their individualized family service plan (IFSP) or individualized education plan (IEP) goals or outcomes is critical for making sound decisions about the use of intervention strategies.

What is Goal Attainment Scaling (GAS)?

GAS (Kiresuk et al., 1994) is an effective strategy to rate children's progress towards meeting IFSP/IEP goals or objectives. GAS differs from a traditional rating scale in that, as part of a six-step process (Roach & Elliott, 2005), team members *jointly* develop a scoring rubric using detailed or operational definitions of specific behaviors that must occur in order for the team to determine that progress is occurring. They use the scoring rubric as a way to monitor children's progress and then share that information with each other in order to evaluate the success of the child-focused intervention strategies they use to support the child's learning or developmental progress. The GAS rating scale enables team members to communicate effectively and efficiently about children's progress.

GAS involves the use of numerical ratings, along with the scoring rubric that describes specific dimensions of a key behavior or skill to track an individual's progress towards meeting a goal, objective, or outcome.

GAS involves the use of numerical ratings, along with the scoring rubric that describes specific dimensions of a key behavior or skill to track an individual's progress towards meeting a goal, objective, or outcome. Itinerant

Figure 1
Blank GAS Worksheet

Goal Attainment Scale Worksheet

Student Name: **Date:**

Parent(s):   **Teacher:**

Consultant: **Site:**

Target Behavior:

Goal Attainment Scale	Indicators
+2	
+1	
0	
−1	
−2	

Graph of Progress:

GAS Ratings										
+2										
+1										
0										
−1										
−2										
Day	1	2	3	4	5	6	7	8	9	10
Date	M	T	W	R	F	M	T	W	R	F

Comments:

Adapted from Roach, A.T. & Elliott, S.N. (2005). Goal attainment scaling: An effective and efficient approach to monitoring student progress. Teaching Exceptional Children, 37, 8–17.

professionals and other members of the IFSP/IEP team (e.g., parents, general ECE teachers) jointly develop the scoring rubric; consequently they use a common system for monitoring behavior. Developing the scoring rubric can support a child or family because it facilitates team members' work toward defining and scaling common goals, objectives, or outcomes.

The GAS scoring rubric begins with "0" as a scale anchor and consists of both negative and positive ratings (i.e., –2, –1, 0, +1, +2). If desired, the scoring rubric can be made even more specific by using fractional ratings (e.g., +1, +1.5, +2). Assigning numerical values to qualitative features of a behavior provides a common metric for team members to use when making informed decisions about progress. A blank GAS worksheet is shown in Figure 1. Detailed steps for completing the worksheet, as well as examples of each step involved in GAS, are described in subsequent sections.

Support for the Use of GAS

The earliest discussions of GAS (Kiresuk et al., 1994) occurred in the mental health community when the process was viewed as a more personalized tool to gauge patient response to treatment (Holroyd & Goldenberg, 1978; Kiresuk & Sherman, 1968). GAS was also described in the early childhood special education literature where it was proposed as a viable planning and evaluation tool that could be used to document the outcomes of early intervention services for infants and families (Simeonsson, Bailey, Huntington, & Brandon, 1991; Simeonsson, Huntington, & Short, 1982). Of particular interest to the field were the concrete and pragmatic features of the GAS, and the potential correspondence of GAS with traditional evaluation information.

Bailey and colleagues (1986) described the practical features of GAS (Kiresuk et al., 1994). GAS promised to serve as the focal point of a pragmatic planning process. This process would include developing early intervention service goals that were specific to a family or child, implementing these services and, finally, evaluating the effectiveness of these services via the use of discrete rating rubrics. GAS was embraced as an example of the application of the "goodness-of-fit" concept to individualization of goals. Bailey and colleagues noted that GAS was a simple and logical way to describe young children's progress towards meeting goals or objectives. The effects of intervention efforts would be "scaled" or evaluated based on incremental improvement in child and family function that could be attributed to specific interventions.

GAS has also been described and reviewed in the special education literature. Carr (1979) described GAS as an important component of a process that included developing a set of goals with members of the planning team, assigning weights or priorities to these goals, creating outcomes that could be linked to each goal, rating or scoring the relative success or failure in meeting these outcomes, and determining a summary "score" across all goals. Roach and Elliott (2005) suggested GAS could become an efficient and effective scaling method to monitor student progress. Gliner, Ross, and Spencer (1999) cited the use of GAS as an option in assessing student success in transitioning from school to work environments.

The GAS model also has been applied in other disciplines. Palisano, Haley, and Brown (1992) and Palisano (1993) described GAS as an individualized, criterion-referenced measure of change that could address important features of child development for the physical therapist. GAS offered opportunities to detect minor changes in the motor skills of infants. GAS offered a rational model for analysis of idiosyncratic motor skill development in some children, including children with the most severe disabilities (Jones et al., 2006). This unique feature of GAS provided an advantage in measurement of subtle motor development, compared with less sensitive norm-referenced scales that focused on more global indicators. The use of GAS as an adjunct tool in evaluation of occupational therapy gains (Mailloux et al., 2007), and in the evaluation of the effectiveness of speech pathology services were also proposed (Schlosser, 2004). GAS also has been demonstrated to be useful within a behavioral consultation approach (Sladeczek, Elliott, Kratochwill, Robertson-Mjaanes, & Stoiber, 2001), as well as a team-based intervention program (Oren & Ogletree, 2000). Roach and Elliott (2005) described the utility of GAS in documenting change in educational and social behaviors.

Applying Goal Attainment Scaling in the Context of Progress Monitoring

We believe that GAS merits consideration by IFSP or IEP teams because it offers an option to describe and document changes in a child's performance that is jointly defined by all members of a team. DEC (2007) has emphasized the importance of individualizing assessment efforts and notes that effective assessment efforts "contribute to intervention outcomes" (p. 11) and reflect an individualized problem-solving approach to gathering and using information about children's progress in order to make curricular and intervention decisions. GAS enables users to individualize assessment progress monitoring efforts by focusing on key dimensions or indicators of a behavior or skill. The dimensions that are scaled can be qualitative or quantitative

> *We believe that GAS consideration by IFSP or IEP teams because it offers an option to describe and document changes in a child's performance that is jointly defined by all members of a team.*

in nature, making GAS a useful tool across a variety of developmental domains or classes of behavior.

The foundation of GAS lies in the team's joint decision to identify goals, objectives, or outcomes and determine their operational definitions. For example, as detailed below, an IEP team consisting of the itinerant ECSE teacher, the ECE partner teacher, the child's parent, and school psychologist might identify the independent use of verbal requests for objects or activities as a priority outcome for a preschooler soon to be entering kindergarten. Not only would the team identify that particular outcome, they would also jointly determine "what it looks like" and "what it doesn't look like," so that everyone on the team shares the same perspective. This discussion is critical to the success of GAS (and, for that matter, any team-based intervention strategy) because different team members might have different perspectives about what it means to independently request an object or an activity.

Six steps involved in GAS identified by Roach and Elliott (2005) are (1) identify concerns, (2) analyze concerns, (3) plan instruction or intervention, (4) construct the goal attainment scale, (5) implement instruction or intervention, and (6) evaluate the success of the instruction or intervention.

Roach and Elliott (2005) outlined six steps involved in GAS that mirror practices that the fields of early intervention and early childhood special education consider to be recommended practices (Sandall, Hemmeter, Smith, & McLean, 2005). Specifically, readers will note the consistency between the steps outlined below and the recommended practices for interdisciplinary teaming and early childhood assessment. The six steps outlined by Roach and Elliott are:

1. **Identify concerns.** The first step in GAS is to identify specific dimensions of the child's progress that are of concern to the IEP or IFSP team. This involves discussing the child's strengths, needs, and present levels of performance specific to a particular goal, objective, or outcome. The team uses data collected from a variety of sources (e.g., observations, standardized assessments, permanent products) to identify issues or concerns.

To illustrate each step in the GAS process (Roach & Elliott, 2005), we return to the story of Sheila, the itinerant ECSE teacher. We meet Delisa, an ECE partner teacher and Jorge, one of the preschoolers who Sheila serves. Jorge is 5 years old and will be entering kinder-garten next year. Jorge's team consists of his parents, Sheila, Delisa, Tom (Jorge's speech/language pathologist), and Sylvia, the school psychologist employed by the school district. Jorge's team has deter-mined that it's important for him to learn how to request objects or activities verbally instead of grabbing them from others. They realize that in order to be successful in kindergarten, Jorge not only needs to be able to request items and activities, he also needs to do it indepen-dently, without any prompting or other forms of adult support.

Delisa tells Sheila that Jorge enjoys eating crackers, playing with puzzles and cars, and any art activity. Delisa has noticed, though, that Jorge will either just grab an item from another person or stand and cry when he is unable to get what he wants. During the past week, Sheila observed Jorge in the classroom and noted that Jorge did not make a request independently, but he did make a request if an adult told him to do it. Jorge's parents also told the team that Jorge did not ask for snacks, drinks, or preferred toys at home.

2. **Analyze concerns.** Based on the results of Step 1, members of the team jointly identify a target behavior that is operationally defined so that team members agree on salient dimensions of the behavior. In addition to identifying key dimensions of the target behavior, the team also jointly identifies the desired outcome of intervention in operational terms. In doing so, team members would identify spe-cific circumstances or conditions under which salient dimensions of the behavior are likely to occur.

In our example, the team spends some time discussing exactly what they mean by "independently request something." They agree that the request must be verbal and can be made to other children or to any adult. Jorge should say something like, "More crackers" or "Car please." They also concur that the request must precede any negative behavior. For example, if Jorge cries, Delisa asks what's wrong, and then he requests more crackers, this would not be rated as an inde-pendent request because Delisa's question would be considered a prompt. They also identify certain times during the day that requests would be more likely—snack time, art, and free play.

3. **Plan instruction or intervention.** Once the team reaches con-sensus about a target behavior and the desired outcome of inter-vention, members of the team discuss and plan how they will

intervene or provide systematic instruction to support the child's progress. While we recognize the emphasis that the field has placed on using embedded learning opportunities as a recommended practice for child-focused intervention strategies (Wolery, 2005), we also acknowledge that instruction or intervention can reflect a variety of approaches or other models (e.g., direct instruction as described by Cole, Dale, Mills, & Jenkins, 1993). It is important to remember that intervention should take place across different environments (e.g., home or school) and, as such, the team must identify intervention strategies that can be embedded in different routines or activities.

The team plans how they will support Jorge in making requests. They decide to use incidental teaching strategies during snack, art, and free play, providing at least three opportunities each day. For example, at snack time Delisa would only give Jorge two crackers (the strategy of giving a little bit) to set the occasion for him to request more crackers. During art, each child might be given only one decoration (e.g., sticker, feather, button) so each child would need to request items from the other children in order to complete their picture. They hope that these learning opportunities will provide the motivation Jorge needs to independently ask for objects or activities.

4. **Construct the Goal Attainment Scale.** The fourth step in the process involves developing the specific GAS. Team members work together to develop the scale. They first operationally define what they believe would be indicators of the Best Possible Outcome, the Worst Possible Outcome, and No Change. These detailed descriptions are anchored to numerical ratings as follows: +2 for Best Possible Outcome, −2 for Worst Possible Outcome, and 0 for No Change. In addition to these anchors, team members also develop scoring rubrics for the ratings of +.5, +1, +1.5 and −.5, −1, and −1.5.

In developing the scale anchor indicators, Roach and Elliott (2005) recommended considering the desired outcome of the behavior. For example, do the desired results include having a child engage in the behavior more frequently? Less frequently? With diminishing levels of support? For a longer or shorter period of time? With more accuracy? Answering these questions will help the team determine the Best Possible Outcome and the steps along the way to achieving that outcome.

In our example of making requests, the team asks Sheila and Delisa to work together to develop the scale. Delisa suggests that she would

Figure 2
GAS Worksheet for Jorge

Goal Attainment Scale Worksheet

Student Name: Jorge   **Date:** September 12

Parent(s): Mitch & Luisa   **Teacher:** Delisa

Consultant: Sheila   **Site:** Central School

Target Behavior: Jorge will independently make requests of other adults and children without any prompting.

Goal Attainment Scale	Indicators
+2	Jorge makes more than 3 independent requests.
+1	Jorge makes 1-3 independent requests.
0	Jorge makes no independent requests but does make more than 3 requests after receiving a prompt.
−1	Jorge makes 1-3 requests after receiving a prompt.
−2	Jorge makes no requests even with prompting.

Graph of Progress:

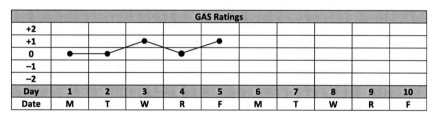

GAS Ratings										
+2										
+1										
0										
−1										
−2										
Day	1	2	3	4	5	6	7	8	9	10
Date	M	T	W	R	F	M	T	W	R	F

Comments:

Adapted from Roach, A.T. & Elliott, S.N. (2005). Goal attainment scaling: An effective and efficient approach to monitoring

student progress. *Teaching Exceptional Children, 37,* 8–17.

like to see Jorge make more requests, and Sheila agrees, so they create the scale anchor indicators based on frequency. Given the data indicated that Jorge never independently made requests but did so after adult prompting, they used this as the indicator for the 0 or No Change rating. They considered the best possible outcome would be if Jorge made more than three independent requests each day. This would mean he not only made a request during each planned oppor-

tunity but that he also made an additional request. This best possible outcome indicator would be matched to the numerical rating of +2. Next, they consider what would be the worst possible outcome. Delisa immediately replies that the worst outcome would be if Jorge makes no requests, even after being prompted. So this outcome is assigned a numerical rating of −2. After more discussion, they match indicators to the ratings of +1 and −1. Figure 2 shows the completed worksheet.

5. **Implement instruction or intervention.** Once team members have developed the GAS, they implement the instruction or intervention planned in Step 3 and use the scale to monitor the child's progress. As stated above, using GAS helps team members to track progress easily. Individuals responsible for implementing the intervention rate the child's progress on a systematic basis and use the numerical ratings to communicate efficiently with other team members.

In our example, Sheila and Delisa created at least three opportunities each day for Jorge to make requests. After each opportunity, Delisa noted whether he made the request independently or required prompting. At the end of the day, she assigned a numerical rating. She used the section at the bottom of the GAS Worksheet to record his progress. By the third day, Jorge was independently making 3 requests, so Delisa put a dot in the +1 box for Day 3. When Sheila arrived the next week, she reviewed the GAS Worksheet while Delisa was working with the children. Sheila was quickly and easily able to see exactly how Jorge was doing by looking at the numerical ratings that Delisa had recorded at the bottom of the worksheet.

6. **Evaluate the success of the instruction or intervention.** The final step is using the data collected through GAS to inform progress-monitoring decisions and to evaluate the degree to which the intervention is supporting attainment of specified goals, objectives, or outcomes. At this step, it can be helpful to graph the data in order to obtain a clearer picture of trends or patterns. If team members are implementing the intervention in multiple settings, comparing GAS data across settings can help them determine if there are effects specific to the setting that influence attainment of goals, objectives, or outcomes. As with any evaluation, using GAS data will help the team decide whether to continue, revise, or discontinue the intervention.

Delisa and Sheila share the data with the rest of the team. They examine the numerical ratings at the bottom of the worksheet. Sheila connects the dots to help them see Jorge's progress. They can clearly see that Jorge has begun to make more requests. Days 1, 2, and 4 were at 0, while Days 3 and 5 were at +1. Sheila notes that they're off to a good start. Delisa agrees and says that Jorge is responding well to the intentional learning opportunities. He did not exhibit any frustration or distress when his access was limited or he was only given a little bit. They decide to continue with the intervention. During the second week, Delisa will ask her classroom assistant to help her observe during other times of the day to see if Jorge is making more requests.

Benefits and Limitations of GAS

As with any progress monitoring strategy, GAS has benefits and limitations (Kiresuk et al., 1994). Roach and Elliott (2005) have identified a number of these upon which we will elaborate.

Benefits. Perhaps the greatest benefit of GAS is the degree to which it promotes communication and collaboration across team members. Because members of the team jointly construct the scale, they are more likely to reach consensus on important features and operational descriptions of a particular behavior. This discussion can facilitate a shared understanding crucial to achieving a high level of congruence across team members (Dinnebeil & Rule, 1994). Family participation and involvement in assessment and intervention processes is strongly recommended by the field (Bagnato & Neisworth, 2005; DEC, 2007), and required under federal legislation. The GAS process promotes family participation and involvement because all team members jointly develop the GAS rating rubric, thereby agreeing on important outcomes as well as intermediary measures of progress.

In addition to promoting communication and shared expectations for desired outcomes, GAS is easy to use once the team members construct the scale. Because it requires minimal time to record a rating, GAS can be a tool that parents or teachers can use to measure developmental or learning progress. It also provides information that is easy to share with others, enabling team members to quickly and efficiently "check in" with each other regarding children's progress. The data GAS generates is easy to understand and can be especially helpful when displayed in a graph.

GAS is an individualized, criterion-based approach to assessment. As such, it can be tailored to address salient features of a behavior and record not only the mastery of a certain skill, but degrees of progress towards mastering a skill or behavior. Because GAS is developed by team members, users can be assured that is appropriate for a particular child, behavior, or situation.

Limitations. As with most progress monitoring methods, GAS (Kiresuk et al., 1994) also has limitations. Perhaps the greatest limitation is its inherently subjective nature and the degree to which observer bias might influence user's ratings. This is an issue for many types of rating scales and checklists that rely on others' interpretations of a child's behavior (*see* Neisworth & Bagnato, this issue). Team members can minimize the effects of bias by creating scoring rubrics that contain objective and specific behavioral descriptions that all users understand, endorse, and value. In addition, GAS is not a standardized or norm-referenced method of assessment that allows users to compare one child's performance relative to another child's performance. GAS is a form of criterion-referenced assessment that can be valuable for making progress monitoring decisions and evaluating the effectiveness of a specific intervention strategy (DEC, 2007). Finally, while it is relatively easy and efficient to use the scoring rubric to document and communicate progress, because it is individualized, it takes time to construct the scale. The development of a range of rubrics, however, might result in certain efficiencies from extensive use of similar developmental rubrics across children, when appropriate.

Another Example of the Use of GAS to Monitor Children's Progress

Heather and Stevie

Heather is a 5-year-old girl who has Down syndrome. She attends an all-day, inclusive preschool. Stevie, the classroom teacher, has been meeting with Sheila (the IECSE) since the beginning of the school year to support Heather's progress towards meeting her IEP goals. The two have decided to use GAS to monitor Heather's progress in counting objects.

Step 1: Identify Concerns. Stevie tells Sheila that she's a bit frustrated because she's been working one-on-one with Heather but has not been successful in getting Heather to count objects. While Heather enjoys playing and socializing with the other students and adults in the classroom, she is less interested with one-on-one instruction or "seat" work. Stevie is also concerned because Heather's behavior and performance seem to decline when she is not successful. Stevie reviews previous records and relates that when asked, Heather correctly counts one and two objects 100% of the time, counts three objects correctly about 70% of the time, and four objects correctly less than 50% of the time. At the last parent conference, Heather's mother related that she could never get Heather to count anything at home.

Step 2: Analyze concerns. Based on the information shared, Sheila and Stevie decide that Heather's target behavior will be to count four objects accurately and independently. When Stevie asks "how many," Heather is to point to each item and say the number name (e.g., "one, two, three, four"). They also discuss when it would be best to provide the instruction during the school day and decide to embed the counting in different routines and activities. For example, during art, Stevie could ask Heather to count four stickers and then ask Heather to give one sticker to four other children. Stevie says that she could easily find five opportunities, each day, to embed counting.

Step 3: Plan instruction or intervention. Because Heather does better when she can be successful, Sheila and Stevie discuss using an error-less learning strategy where prompts are faded during instruction while reinforcement also is provided (Wolery, Ault, & Doyle, 1992). They agree on using the constant time delay strategy (Walker, 2008). Because this strategy greatly reduces the child's errors, they'll focus on the levels of support Heather requires to be successful rather than percent of correct responses when they develop the scale.

Step 4: Construct the Goal Attainment Scale. Next, they work on developing the scale for the GAS worksheet. Sheila asks Stevie what she would consider to be the Best Possible Outcome, and both agree that it would be Heather independently providing the correct number of objects all of the time. They assign this statement a numerical rating of +2. Sheila and Stevie decide that the Worst Possible Outcome would be if Heather required full support to count the objects and assign this a rating of –2. For the No Change statement rated 0, they use the baseline data Stevie provided. They spend some time discussing the level of support required for the +1 and –1 rated statements. As they reach consensus on the content of each section of the rating form, Stevie records the results on the GAS worksheet.

Step 5: Implement instruction or intervention. Sheila and Stevie review the classroom schedule and identify five times each day during which counting could be embedded. Throughout the next 2 weeks, Delia uses the constant time delay strategy to support Heather's counting during embedded activities. At the end of each day, Stevie rates Heather's progress and records this on the worksheet.

Figure 3
GAS Worksheet for Heather

Goal Attainment Scale Worksheet

Student Name: Heather   **Date:** February 10

Parent(s): Ami & Gao   **Teacher:** Delisa

Consultant: Sheila   **Site:** Central School

Target Behavior: When asked, Heather will accurately and independently count 4 objects.

Goal Attainment Scale	Indicators
+2	Heather independently provides the correct number of objects every time (5 out five times).
+1	Heather independently provides the correct number of objects most of the time and requires a verbal prompt the remaining times.
0	Heather requires a verbal prompt most of the time to provide the correct number of objects and independently provides the correct number the remaining times.
−1	Heather requires a verbal prompt every time to provide the correct number of objects (5 out of 5 times).
−2	Heather requires hand-over-hand assistance and verbal modeling some of the time to provide the correct number of objects.

Graph of Progress:

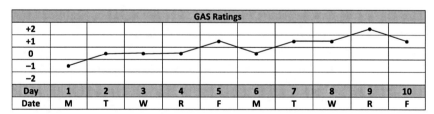

GAS Ratings										
+2										
+1										
0										
−1										
−2										
Day	1	2	3	4	5	6	7	8	9	10
Date	M	T	W	R	F	M	T	W	R	F

Comments:

Adapted from Roach, A.T. & Elliott, S.N. (2005). Goal attainment scaling: An effective and efficient approach to monitoring

student progress. *Teaching Exceptional Children, 37,* 8–17.

Step 6*: Evaluate the success of the instruction or intervention. When Sheila visits after the first week, she and Stevie discuss the effectiveness of the intervention for Heather by reviewing the data on her worksheet. Both agree that the intervention appears to be working, and they will continue collecting data for another week without any changes. Stevie smiles as she comments that not only was it quick* *and easy to record the ratings, but that it also shortened the time they needed to meet to discuss Heather's progress. When Sheila returns after the second week, they both remark on the steadily upward progress indicated on the graphs (Figure 3). Stevie notes that not only is Heather more independent in counting four objects, but she appears more engaged with the counting activities. Stevie also tells Sheila that she has shared the GAS graph of progress with Heather's parents, and they are interested in learning the constant time delay strategy so that they can support counting opportunities at home.*

Conclusion

GAS (Kiresuk et al., 1994) addresses the "value-added" aspects of reflection; analysis of key elements of a goal, objective, or outcome in relation to a task; and consensus building among members of the child support team. The value of this aspect of GAS cannot be underestimated. If, for example, members of a team can agree on observable indicators of child progress, then all members of the team can endorse a strategy to support the child in attaining this skill or demonstrating this behavior. The implications for adults charged with implementation of intentional instruction strategies are equally apparent as an outcome of using GAS to plan and monitor. The team has determined which observable behaviors are consistent with appropriate instruction. GAS provides the template for periodic review of progress as the result of consistent use of a specific intervention strategy.

The primary purpose of GAS (Kiresuk et al., 1994) is not to create a series of isolated snapshots of progress in developing a particular set of skills. The intent of GAS is to provide an opportunity to "check" on the progress of the child and, more importantly, to use this information to inform the teaching and learning process. GAS is a useful tool in informal and individualized assessment of child progress. GAS continues to hold promise as a valuable option in assessing the development of young children with special needs and in gauging the effectiveness of engagement of those adults prominent in their lives.

Note

E-mail address for corresponding author: laurie.dinnebeil@utoledo.edu. You may also reach Dr. Dinnebeil at 2801 West Bancroft St, MS 954, Toledo, OH 43606.

References

Bagnato, S. J. & Neisworth, J. (2005). Recommended practices in early intervention/early childhood special education assessment. In S. Sandall, M. L. Hemmeter, B. J. Smith, & M. E. McLean (Eds.), *DEC recommended practices in early intervention/early childhood special education* (pp. 17-28). Longmont, CO: Sopris.

Bailey, D. B, Simeonsson, R. J., Winton, P. J., Huntington, G. S., Comfort, M., Isbell, P., et al. (1986). Family-focused intervention: A functional model for planning, implementing, and evaluating individualized family services in early intervention. *Journal of Early Intervention, 10,* 156-171.

Buysse, V. & Wesley, P. A. (2005). *Consultation in early childhood settings.* Baltimore: Brookes.

Carr, R. A. (1979). Goal attainment scaling as a useful tool for evaluating progress in special education. *Exceptional Children, 46,* 88-95.

Cole, K. N, Dale, P. S., Mills, P. E, & Jenkins, J. R. (1993). Interaction between early intervention curricula and student characteristics. *Exceptional Children, 60,* 17-28.

Dinnebeil, L. A. & McInerney, W. F. (2011). *Guide to itinerant early childhood special education services.* Baltimore: Brookes.

Dinnebeil, L. A. & Rule, S. (1994). Congruence between parents' and professionals' judgments about the development of young children with disabilities: A review of the literature. *Topics in Early Childhood Special Education, 14,* 1-25.

Division for Early Childhood (DEC). (2007). *Promoting positive outcomes for children with disabilities: Recommendations for curriculum, assessment, and program evaluation.* Missoula, MT: Author.

Gliner, J. A., Ross, T., & Spencer, K. C. (1999). The use of goal attainment scaling to evaluate student involvement in transition. *Journal for Vocational Special Needs Education, 21,* 27-33.

Holroyd, J. & Goldenberg, I. (1978). The use of goal attainment scaling to evaluate a ward treatment program for disturbed children. *Journal of Clinical Psychology, 34,* 732-739.

Jones, M. C., Walley, R. M., Leech, A., Paterson, M., Common, S., & Metcalf, C. (2006). Using goal attainment scaling to evaluate a needs-led exercise programme for people with severe and profound intellectual disabilities. *Journal of Intellectual Disabilities, 10,* 317-335.

Kiresuk, T. J. & Sherman, R. E. (1968). Goal attainment scaling: A general method for evaluating comprehensive community mental health programs. *Community Mental Health Journal, 4,* 443-453.

Kiresuk, T. J., Smith, A., & Cardillo, J. E. (Eds.). (1994). *Goal attainment scaling: Applications, theory and measurement.* Hillsdale, NJ: Erlbaum.

Mailloux, Z., May-Benson, T. A., Summers, C. A., Miller, L. J., Brett-Green, B., Burke, J. P., et al. (2007). Goal attainment scaling as a measure of meaningful outcomes for children with sensory integration disorders. *American Journal of Occupational Therapy, 61,* 254-259

Oren, T. & Ogletree, B. T. (2000). Program evaluation in classrooms for students with autism: Student outcomes and program processes. *Focus on Autism and Other Developmental Disabilities, 15,* 170-175.

Palisano, R. J., Haley, S. M., & Brown, D. A. (1992). Goal attainment scaling as a measure of change in infants with motor delays. *Physical Therapy, 72,* 432-437.

Palisano, R. J. (1993). Validity of goal attainment scaling in infants with motor delays. *Physical Therapy, 73,* 651-685.

Roach, A. T. & Elliott, S. N. (2005). Goal attainment scaling: An efficient and effective approach to monitoring student progress. *Teaching Exceptional Children, 37*(4), 8-17.

Sandall, S., Hemmeter, M. L., Smith, B. J., & McLean, M. (Eds.). (2005). *DEC recommended practices: A comprehensive guide for practical application in early intervention/early childhood special education.* Missoula, MT: Division for Early Childhood.

Schlosser, R. W. (2004). Goal attainment scaling as a clinical measurement technique in communication disorders: A critical review. *Journal of Communication Disorders, 37,* 217-239.

Simeonsson, R. J., Bailey, D. B., Huntington, G. S., & Brandon, L. (1991). Scaling and attainment of goals in family-focused early intervention. *Community Mental Health Journal, 27,* 77-83.

Simeonsson, R. J., Huntington, G. S., & Short, R. J. (1982). Individual differences and goals: An approach to the evaluation of child progress. *Topics in Early Childhood Special Education, 1,* 71-80.

Sladeczek, I. E., Elliott, S. N., Kratochwill, T. R., Robertson-Mjaanes, S., & Stoiber, K. (2001). Application of goal attainment scaling to a conjoint behavioral consultation case. *Journal of Educational and Psychological Consultation, 12,* 45-58.

Walker, G. (2008). Constant and progressive time delay procedures for teaching children with autism: A literature review. *Journal of Autism and Developmental Disorders, 38,* 261-275.

Wolery, M. (2005). DEC Recommended practices: Child-focused practices. In S. Sandall, M. L. Hemmeter, B. J. Smith, & M. E. McLean (Eds.), *DEC recommended practices: A comprehensive guide for practical application* (pp. 71-106). Longmont, CO: Sopris.

Wolery, M., Ault, M. A., & Doyle, P. M. (1992). *Teaching students with moderate to severe disabilities: Use of response prompting strategies.* New York: Longman.

Building Good Assessment into Accountability Systems for Early Childhood Programs

Kathleen Hebbeler,

Lauren Barton,

Cornelia Taylor,

Donna Spiker,
SRI International

Andrea teaches 4-year-olds in one of her school district's state-funded prekindergarten classes. Of the 20 children she teaches, five have individualized education programs (IEPs). Over the past several years, she has attended several workshops on the state's new observation-based online assessment system and has also received assistance and feedback from the district's early childhood coordinator. She is becoming increasingly more proficient at observing, scoring, and documenting children's performance on the assessment. For the five children with IEPs in her classroom, Andrea and other team members will meet to summarize how these children are functioning in three outcome areas relative to same-age peers using multiple sources of information, including the online assessment data. They will apply specific criteria to decide jointly on a summary rating that reflects the child's functioning across settings in each outcome area. Andrea has also received training and additional follow-up supervision about this summary rating process.

The information that Andrea provides to the district will serve multiple purposes. The process of gathering information through the online assessment helps Andrea learn more about each child she teaches and helps her plan how to best support each child's development. In addition, the district early childhood coordinator examines the assessment scores from all of the prekindergarten classes to identify strengths and potential areas for improvement across the classes to plan for professional development. The state is using the data to compare the performance of children in full-day and half-day programs, and to report to the legislature on the extent of progress children make in the state pre-K program. The data have proven to be especially valuable in recent years when state budget discussions have focused on the need for funding cuts. The rating data on Andrea's children with IEPs are combined with data for other preschoolers with IEPs in her district to produce an overall picture on how much progress children make while receiving special education. The state combines the data across all districts to produce the same information at the state level. The state identifies targets and compares its performance to its targets and also compares district performance to the state target. The goal of the comparisons is to identify districts that might need additional support to better meet the needs of young children with disabilities.

One basic principle of good early childhood assessment is that scores from an assessment tool should have established technical adequacy for the intended use (Division for Early Childhood, 2007; National Association Early Childhood Specialists in State Departments of Education & National Association for the Education of Young Children, 2003; Shepard, Kagan, & Wurtz, 1998). Applying this principle to the design of accountability systems for early childhood programs presents an interesting dilemma because nearly all currently available assessment tools for collecting information about young children were not designed to provide information for making inferences in accountability systems. Nevertheless, all states and territories have had to address this dilemma as they developed accountability systems for a federal requirement to provide data on outcomes for children receiving early intervention (EI) or early childhood special education (ECSE) services.

The Government Performance and Results Act (Government Performance and Results Act of 1993, Pub. L. No 103-62, §20, 107 Stat. 285) requires the U.S. Department of Education to report on the outcomes achieved through all federal programs, including the early childhood programs funded under the Individuals with Disabilities Education Act (IDEA). In these times of tight budgets, data on outcomes are essential for all federal programs to justify continued funding. Since 2007, the U.S. Department of Education has required that all states report data on children's progress in EI and ECSE for three outcomes: having positive social relationships; acquiring and using knowledge and skills; and using appropriate behaviors to meet their needs (see Hebbeler & Barton, 2007, for more information on the federal reporting requirement).

The federal reporting requirement resulted in EI and ECSE leading the way in building statewide accountability systems. Other segments of the early care and education system also are facing these issues because accountability questions about how well programs are serving young children are being asked of all early childhood programs (Harbin, Rous, & McLean, 2005). A national coalition advocating for improved data recently released 10 essential elements that characterize a good early childhood state data system. One of the elements is information on how children are developing (Early Childhood Data Collaborative, 2010). Building measurement systems to gather this information means that program leaders will be making decisions about how information about children's development and learning will be used and which assessment tool(s) will be used to collect it.

Collecting data to inform accountability decisions provides an opportunity for early childhood programs, such as EI and ECSE, Early Head Start, Head Start, state prekindergarten, and family support programs, to demonstrate that they are effective and that the investment supporting the program is money well spent.

We begin this paper with a brief overview of key issues in accountability in early childhood, especially as these relate to EI and ECSE. Next we detail the considerations for designing assessments systems that are critical for accountability purposes. This is followed by a brief review of the principles of good assessment and a discussion of options and challenges for using early childhood assessment instruments in accountability systems. We close with recommendations for the next generation of assessment tools. Much of the content of the paper applies to all early childhood programs, but we use examples from EI and ECSE because these two programs have more advanced measurement systems for child outcomes than many other early childhood programs.

Accountability and Early Childhood Programs

Accountability involves documenting results or outcomes from a program or activity to inform decision making by public or private program designers, funders, and other stakeholders (Stecher et al., 2010). Collecting data to inform accountability decisions provides an opportunity for early childhood programs, such as EI and ECSE, Early Head Start, Head Start, state prekindergarten, and family support programs, to demonstrate that they

Figure 1
Example of How Data are Aggregated for Different Levels of Accountability Decision Making and Reporting.

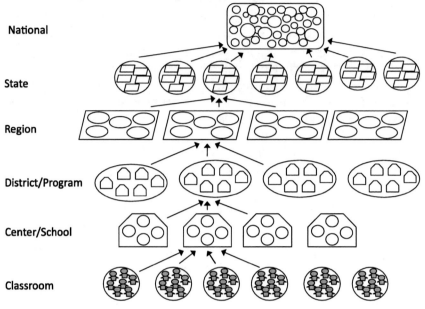

National

State

Region

District/Program

Center/School

Classroom

are effective and that the investment supporting the program is money well spent. The National Research Council (2008) identified assessment for accountability as one of the four purposes of assessment in early childhood. Historically, few early childhood programs have regularly reported the child outcomes achieved by their programs (Meisels, 2007; Schultz & Kagan, 2007).

Under the system established by No Child Left Behind, accountability in the K–12 system came to be prominently associated with sanctions for poor performance (Mintrop & Sunderman, 2009). Sanctions, however, are only one of several policy options that can follow from information on program performance. Actions also might include continuing or increasing funding to support programs shown to be achieving intended objectives. When results are mixed, actions might include targeting technical assistance, professional development, or studying and refining the program models or practices being implemented. For programs that consistently do not produce results, removal or reduction of funding might be justified. However, sanctions should never be decided solely on assessment results; rather, multiple forms of data, including data about program quality, should be reviewed and used to inform decision making (National Research Council, 2008; Schultz & Kagan, 2007).

Recognition of the need for accountability is widespread given investments being made in early childhood programs, but there is less agreement about the level at which information should be produced and the level at which programs[1] should be held accountable. Accountability can exist at many levels from the classroom or local program level all the way up to the federal level. As illustrated in Figure 1, classrooms are nested within schools or centers, schools are nested within districts, which might be nested in regional administrative units, which are nested in states. The name and number of levels between child and state varies across states and between EI and ECSE, but the concept of units nested within units within a state holds across all states for both EI and ECSE.

Assessment information about children who received services can be combined, or aggregated, and used for decision making at any of these levels. Consensus exists that accountability for outcomes at the national and state level is necessary. A task force on early childhood accountability was divided, however, on using child assessment data for accountability at the local level because of the possibility of misuse and negative consequences (Schultz & Kagan, 2007). Concerns identified by members of the task force included the limitations of available assessment tools, the difficulty of implementing large scale assessment efforts including issues of consistent administration and cost, and the possibility of negative consequences for the child, such as narrowing of the curriculum and teaching to the test.

Other members of the task force believed that child assessment data can be helpful to the state in understanding and improving the performance of local programs, and thus, could have a positive influence on local program performance. Supporters of the use of child assessment for accountability acknowledge the challenges and potential for misuse, but believe these issues can be addressed with proper safeguards. They also maintain that instructional practices could benefit from a state-initiated child assessment effort by increasing awareness of children who are not progressing at the expected rate (National Research Council, 2008; Schultz & Kagan, 2007). Clearly, users of child assessment data need to be vigilant to ensure that these data are collected and used appropriately to support informed decision making related to improving program performance. The U.S. Department of Education requires that state EI and ECSE publicly report aggregated data on child outcomes at the state and at the program (EI) or local education agency level (ECSE), and the Department

---

[1] As is the custom in early childhood, the word "program" is used in this paper to refer to programs at many different levels. For example, ECSE is a program within IDEA, the state administers the state's program, a county might operate a program for infants, toddlers and their families, and a school district might have a program for children with hearing impairments. Accountability information can be examined at any of these program levels. Throughout the paper, we have tried to make clear from the context which level of program is being discussed.

expects that the data will be used to examine program performance at both state and local levels.

Special Considerations for Gathering Assessment Data for Use in Informing Accountability Decisions

Gathering assessment data for use in accountability differs from other kinds of assessment in several ways. These include: a focus on aggregated data as opposed to the traditional focus on information about an individual child; the need for alignment between the content of the assessment and program objectives; and identification of criteria against which to evaluate program performance. These differences constitute additional considerations for assessment selection that must be considered by those developing accountability systems.

First, in assessment for accountability, the focus is on the outcomes for a group, likely a very large group, of children rather than for an individual child (see Figure 1 for possible groupings). When administering screening or diagnostic assessments, results typically are used to make decisions at an individual child level, such as whether or not a child needs additional assessment or meets established criteria for a delay. Assessments designed to inform decisions about planning instruction or intervention are used to address the unique needs of a child, small groups of children in a classroom, or all children in a classroom. In accountability systems, assessment data are combined across many children so that the performance of a group of children yields aggregated summary information about program performance at a particular level (e.g., classroom, school, region, etc.), and are used to inform decisions at that level of interest. How "program level" is defined varies depending on the focus of the decision. For a school district making decisions about ECSE meeting program objectives, the program level would include all children in the district. For a state making decisions about program effectiveness, the program level would include all children in the state participating in the program. Because both EI and ECSE programs are supported with federal IDEA funding, these data also are being collected and reported at the federal program level. Across these various levels, a key point is that the basis for decision making is aggregated, not individual, data.

A second consideration in using assessment information to make accountability decisions is the need to ensure that what is being assessed aligns with the intended objectives of the program, and those objectives must be clearly stated. For example, measuring children's gains in literacy would be inappropriate for reporting on a program focused on developing children's social skills. If the objective of the program is vaguely defined, such as "to promote children's development and learning," then it would be difficult to identify and reach consensus on what to measure to inform decision making about whether the program is meeting its objectives. Although this consideration seems obvious, the limited number of assessment instruments available to gather reliable and valid data useful for informing accountability decisions means that measures used for accountability can be those whose content is not well aligned with what the program is trying to do. In 2003, for example, Head Start instituted a National Reporting System (NRS) to provide child outcome data. The NRS was criticized for several reasons, including failing to identify clearly the intended purpose of the data collection. A second criticism was that only early literacy and math skills were assessed, which was insufficient for a program also intended to address other facets of child well-being such as social-emotional skills, nutrition, and health (Meisels & Atkins-Burnett, 2004; Zigler & Styfco, 2004).

A third consideration related to use of assessment instruments in an early childhood accountability system is the comparison of program level data to an external criterion to determine if programs are meeting their objectives (National Research Council, 2008). Identifying the appropriate program level criteria is challenging in early childhood because it requires categorizing performance of children in the program relative to a standard. The early childhood field does not have a history of comparing children's performance to a standard. This is quite controversial due, in part, to the fact that early development is quite variable and characterized by change (Meisels, 2007). A challenge in designing early childhood accountability systems is identifying both a reasonable child level standard and a reasonable criterion at the program level.

One possible criterion might be the percentage of children who have achieved the state's early learning guidelines (ELG). ELGs are statements of what children are expected to know and be able to do (also referred to as early learning standards, foundations, benchmarks, and other terms in different states). Nearly all states have developed ELGs for both infants and toddlers and for preschoolers (Scott-Little, Kagan, Stebbins Frelow, & Reid, 2009; The National Child Care Information and Technical Assistance Center, n.d.). Unfortunately, many ELGs are too general with regard to content and age-related expectations to function as a standard at the child level, and few, if any, assessment instruments have been developed to align directly with or measure a state's ELGs. Similarly, Head Start recently released a new child outcomes framework consisting of 11 domains, but, like many ELGs, it does not provide information as to expected performance for children of different ages (U.S. Department of Health and Human Serivces, 2010).

Table 1

Federal Reporting Categories for Child Outcomes Data for Early Intervention and Early Childhood Special Education Programs under the Individuals with Disabilities Education and Improvement Act

Reporting Category	Explanation
a. Did not improve functioning	Children who acquired no new skills or regressed during their time in the program.
b. Improved functioning, but not sufficient to move nearer to functioning comparable to same-age peers	Children who acquired new skills but did not improve their growth rate throughout their time in the program.
c. Improved functioning to a level nearer to same-age peers but did not reach it	Children who acquired new skills and accelerated their rate of growth during their time in the program. They were moving closer toward age-expected skills and behaviors but were still functioning below age expectations when they left the program.
d. Improved functioning to reach a level comparable to same-age peers	Children who were functioning below age expectations when they entered the program but were functioning at age expectations when they left.
e. Maintained functioning at a level comparable to same-age peers	Children who were functioning at age expectations when they entered the program and when they left the program.

Note. States report the percentages of children each year in each category. The percentages should add up to 100% of the children who exited the program during the year. This is done separately for each of the three child outcomes. For additional information, see: http://www.fpg.unc.edu/~eco/assets/pdfs/SummaryStatementDefinitions.pdf

The national accountability system for EI and ECSE employs two standards against which each child's progress in each of three outcome areas are compared. States report annually to the U.S. Department of Education on children's progress between program entry and exit for all children who have been in the EI or ECSE program for at least 6 months. For each of the three EI and ECSE outcomes, states report the percentage of children in each of five mutually exclusive and exhaustive progress categories (see Table 1). One standard involves determining whether or not children who entered below age expectations made greater than expected gains between program entry and exit. The other involves comparing the child's status at exit to age-expected development. The logic behind these standards is that if children are acquiring skills at an accelerated rate after program participation with some even catching up to age expectations, then these gains can be considered the "value added" to children's development based on program participation (Bagnato, Suen, Brickley, Smith-Jones, & Dettore, 2002; Early Childhood Outcomes Center, 2005; Wolery, 1983). Given the diversity of the population being served in EI and ECSE, there is no expectation that all program participants will show accelerated growth, but some should. The implication for selection of assessment tools for EI and ECSE accountability systems with respect to this third consideration is that the tools must be able to provide data about rate of growth and status relative to age-related expectations for each of the three outcomes.

Good Assessment is Good Assessment

The section above highlighted three considerations uniquely related to early childhood assessment when data are used to inform accountability decisions. The desirable features in an assessment tool that will provide valid information for accountability decisions are many of the same features that characterize good tools used for other purposes, such as eligibility determinations or instructional planning. Like Andrea's state in the example above, many states have developed their EI and ECSE accountability systems to make use of assessment information that teachers and service providers are collecting and using for other purposes. The features of good early childhood assessment instruments have been reviewed extensively elsewhere (McLean, Wolery, & Bailey, 2004; Neisworth & Bagnato, 2005). We provide only a brief summary here with additional commentary related to the use of assessment instruments for accountability decisions.

> *The desirable features in an assessment tool that will provide valid information for accountability decisions are many of the same features that characterize good tools used for other purposes such as eligibility determinations or instructional planning.*

Assessment instruments must produce valid and reliable scores. Validity refers to the degree to which evidence supports the proposed use of the information produced by an assessment (American Educational Research Association, American Psychological Association, & National Council on Measurement in Education, 1999; National Research Council, 2008). Of particular relevance to assessment and accountability is that validity applies to the *use* of the assessment results, not to the assessment itself. When an assessment is used for a purpose other than the purpose for which it was developed, the user has the responsibility to gather evidence supporting the validity of the information for the new use. Data must be collected to show that the assessment tool provides information that is adequate for the accountability decisions being made. Reliability, the consistency with which information is provided across different assessors or different versions of the assessment, is critical to interpreting information across accountability units. Because account-ability often means examining scores across programs and over time, it is important that assessment results are consistent regardless of who conducts the assessment or when the assessment is administered.

Assessment instruments used with young children need to accommo-date the unique needs of the young child, including children with delays and disabilities. The nature of the young child, especially a young child with a delay or disability, is a poor match for obtaining accurate informa-tion in a decontextualized, direct child assessment situation (McLean, 2004; Neisworth & Bagnato, 2004). Young children might not respond on demand, especially to requests from a stranger or in a novel situation. Some children might not be able to attend for long periods of time. Lack of famil-iarity with assessment materials might influence the skills that children demonstrate. Others, because of the nature of their disability, cannot see the materials, hear the examiner, or respond in the specific way that many standardized direct assessments requires. Given the myriad of challenges created by decontextualized, direct child assessment situations, many pro-

fessional organizations support gathering information about what young children know and can do by observing how they function in everyday contexts and situations (American Speech-Language-Hearing Association, 2008; Bagnato, Neisworth, & Pretti-Frontczak, 2010; National Association Early Childhood Specialists in State Departments of Education & National Association for the Education of Young Children, 2003; Neisworth & Bagnato, 2005). The use of multiple sources of information about performance is also encouraged to better understand children's skills in different environments and when interacting with a variety of individuals.

Assessing children by observing them in daily routines or activities or by using informants (such as parents, caregivers, and teachers) poses dilemmas for accountability in that the program providers who know children well and are in the best position to provide this information also have a vested interest in how their program is portrayed. Can observers be unbiased and accurate when they know the results will be used to evaluate their own program? Equally important is the question of whether policy makers and others will see outcome data that are used to inform decisions about program effectiveness as credible if it is produced by program personnel (Schultz & Kagan, 2007). This is not an insurmountable challenge, but it is an issue that must be addressed systematically when program staff completes assessments for accountability purposes (Bagnato, 2007).

For systems using assessments completed by program staff, the onus on the program leadership is twofold: (1) to ensure that all assessors are trained in the use of the tool, and (2) to collect information substantiating reliable administration across assessors. Direct child assessments have more scripted administration and scoring procedures than observation-based assessments or scales that require assessor judgment. These procedures might be expected to result in more consistent administration of the tools. However, direct assessments, as will be discussed in the next section, raise other kinds of issues for validity. Regardless of the type of assessment tool that is used, information that demonstrates validity and reliability of scores for use in accountability systems should be collected and reported.

Options and Challenges in Assessing for Accountability

The considerations related to assessment for accountability in particular, and early childhood assessment in general, offer important guidance for the design of early childhood accountability systems. System designers, however, must choose from among a finite set of assessment tools to measure whether program objectives, including the achievement of child outcomes, are being

Table 2

State Approaches to Measurement for Federal Accountability Reporting Requirements for Early Intervention and Early Childhood Special Education for Data Reported in February 2010

Approach	Early Intervention[a]		Early Childhood Special Education[b]	
	%	N	%	N
One tool statewide	13	7	15	9
Publishers' online analysis	5	3	10	6
Child Outcomes Summary Process	73	41	61	36
Other	9	5	12	7
Unknown	0	0	2	1

[a]Based on 56 states and jurisdictions.
[b]Based on 59 states and jurisdictions.

attained. The choice of an assessment tool is associated with benefits and drawbacks that must be considered when developing and implementing an accountability system (Early Childhood Outcomes Center, 2004). To date, state EI and ECSE programs have had to choose among limited options for measuring child outcomes as they have developed and implemented their accountability systems. Table 2 shows the approaches states are using to collect data on child outcomes for EI and ECSE accountability systems. Each approach carries with it one or more decisions that states had to make with regard to assessment tools. The decisions made by states and the implications for these approaches will be described in this section.

Use a Single Tool or Use Multiple Tools Statewide? Assessments for various kinds of decisions had been conducted in EI and ECSE programs for many years prior to the development of state accountability systems. In designing their accountability systems, states needed to address whether they would use a single tool statewide, which likely would mean requiring an additional assessment tool be administered for accountability purposes. As shown in Table 2, only a few states are using a single assessment tool statewide for federal reporting. Most state agencies, for a variety of reasons (e.g., did not believe that one tool could provide valid data for all types of children they serve; did not have the authority or funds needed to require one tool, etc.), did not opt to use a single tool statewide for federal reporting, even though a single tool simplifies reporting.

States that opted to make use of the information generated by different assessments being given around the state for accountability reporting faced the challenge of how to combine data across tools to provide the information required by the federal government (Table 1). To address this dilemma and also to address the need to combine information from multiple sources about an individual child, the Early Childhood Outcomes (ECO) Center developed the Child Outcomes Summary (COS) process. This process is used by the majority of states for federal outcomes reporting for EI and ECSE (Table 2). The COS allows programs to make use of information from assessments and other sources, such as parent report, to provide data in a common metric that can be aggregated across programs and the levels illustrated in Figure 1 to inform accountability decisions.

The COS is not an assessment tool, but a process for summarizing information from multiple sources, including assessment tools, in each of three outcome areas. The COS provides a structure to convert this information into a 7-point rating relative to age-expected behavior. The child's team members (e.g., teachers, parents, early interventionists, therapists) review the information that has been collected about the child's functioning across settings and situations and apply specific criteria to derive a single rating for each of the outcomes (Greenwood et al., 2008; Hebbeler, Barton, & Mallik, 2008). A comparison of a child's COS ratings at program entry and program exit provides the requisite information to summarize the pattern of the child's progress and compare aggregated information to the two standards embedded in the federal reporting requirement: children's status relative to typically developing peers at program exit and whether the children entering below age expectations made greater than expected progress while in the program.

Use an Existing Assessment Tool(s) or Design One? States obtaining information for accountability directly from an assessment tool instead of through a summary process like COS need to decide whether to use one or more existing instruments or to design a new tool. Existing assessment tools have a number of shortcomings that limit their utility for reaching decisions related to accountability. Some, but not all, existing early childhood assessment tools have undergone sufficient research to establish psychometric adequacy of using data for some purposes (Kelley & Surbeck, 2007). Many early childhood assessments, however, were developed years ago and do not reflect principles of universal design (Thompson, Johnstone, & Thurlow, 2002), nor do they include adaptations and accommodations. Most were not developed for use with populations of culturally and linguistically diverse young children. An added challenge for EI and ECSE programs is that many tools are organized around various developmental domain structures (e.g., motor, communication, cognitive, adaptive, social), but programs need to provide data on the three child outcomes required for federal reporting.

One way to address the shortcomings of current assessment tools for use in accountability systems is to design a new one. Few state agencies have the resources, time, or expertise required for this kind of an undertaking. Most states have opted to use one or more existing assessment tools to measure child outcomes either as the single source of information or as one of the sources of information in the COS process. As shown in Table 2, a few states are using online observation-based assessments to collect data on the three outcomes. These assessment tools are organized around domains. To convert the results from these assessments to the three federal outcomes, the assessment publishers used crosswalks to link items to the three outcomes. The publishers have developed algorithms to provide scores for the three outcomes in addition to scores by domains. For examples of how assessment content has been crosswalked to the three outcomes, see the Early Childhood Outcomes Center (2006). These crosswalks also are used by COS teams to assist team members in understanding how the content of the assessments they are using relate to the three outcomes.

The issue of measuring the three outcomes with domains-based assessment tools is being addressed differently in states that use a standardized, norm-referenced assessment for EI and ECSE reporting throughout the state. Because the domain structure in these tools should not be altered, states have adopted decision rules about which domain scores to use for which outcomes. One validity-related question for this approach is whether the domain score permits appropriate inferences about the child's functioning in an outcome area.

California is one of a few states that opted to develop its own early childhood assessment tools. The development of the Desired Results system began many years before federal reporting requirements for EI and ECSE, but the state is using data from several of these tools to report accountability data for the ECSE program, in addition to using the assessment information for other purposes. One of these tools, the Desired Results Developmental Profile *access,* was one of the first early childhood tools to incorporate principles of universal design and to include adaptations for children with disabilities. The state also has developed an extensive online library of materials for professional development to support the use of this assessment. For more information on Desired Results Developmental Profile *access*, see Desired Results *access* Project (2011a) and Desired Results for Children and Families (Center for Child and Family Studies, n.d.).

How to Collect Information About Children's Functioning?

Selecting a tool for accountability is a decision about administration protocols as well as content. Administration protocols include direct testing, interview, and observation among others. No matter the administration protocol, assessors need to be skilled in the procedures for collecting information and scoring, but different administration protocols require different kinds of skills.

At one end of the assessment administration continuum are tools that require an assessor to use highly scripted procedures and materials with precise criteria to score performance on each task. The assessor administering this kind of direct assessment tool might or might not be familiar to the child. Assessments involving this level of standardized administration are often norm-referenced, meaning that strict adherence to the administration procedures allows the child's score to be compared to a norm group to see how the child's performance compares to that of other children the same age. To make valid inferences from norm-referenced standardized assessments, all items should be administered exactly as directed. Examiners are rarely able to do this with young children, especially those children with special needs (Bagnato & Neisworth, 1995). Given variable functioning in child behavior and the need for accommodations, young children with disabilities are more likely than others to be among those whose administrations do not conform to standardized assessment protocols.

At the other end of the continuum are assessment tools that involve gathering information through observations of the child performing everyday tasks in everyday situations. An observer gathers information by watching the child and uses this information to score each item. The basis for the scoring is documented in a variety of ways including notes, work samples, and audio or video recording. Direct assessments administered by program staff might take staff away from working with other children, whereas program staff administering observation-based assessments can remain involved in ongoing activities while collecting the assessment information. Assessment tools that use observation have traditionally been used for instructional and intervention planning and often do not provide information on performance relative to same-age peers (although some provide information drawn from the literature about age-expected behaviors). Historically, for this instructional planning purpose, information about age-related relative performance has been considered unnecessary.

In between direct assessment and observation-based assessment are tools that use tasks or structured item administrations, but allow for adaptations to procedures as necessary. These are tools that rely primarily on observation, but include some items with structured item administration; tools that allow for input from others familiar with the child such as parents; and tools that rely entirely on the parent's report.

A major dilemma for states in designing their EI and ECSE accountability systems was the inability of currently available observation-based tools to provide data about rate of growth and child status relative to age-related expectations for each of the three outcomes, which is an accountability reporting requirement. Some states that wanted to make use of information from tools that do not routinely provide information on age expectations addressed this dilemma by using the Child Outcomes Summary process, or through the use of online tools that regroup items into the three outcomes. In applying the COS rating scale criteria, team members are expected to make use of their professional knowledge of what children are expected to know and do at different ages. The online observation-based tools use an algorithm developed by the publisher to convert the item level data to status and progress relative to age expectations.

Who Will Administer? Choosing an observation-based approach almost certainly means that the assessment will be administered by program staff. Although direct assessments can be administered by personnel external to the program, it is difficult to envision an accountability system that is so well resourced that it could retain a cadre of external assessors who administer assessments year after year. For federal reporting, most EI and ECSE state agencies have opted to use assessments that were being used for other purposes for accountability (e.g., eligibility or intervention/instructional planning). Using assessments for multiple purposes minimizes the burden on staff and increases the feasibility of implementation by controlling costs.

Who to Include in the Data Collection? An additional decision related to assessment and accountability is whether to collect data on every child. Sampling saves resources and some argue it provides protection against misuse of assessment data at local program and child levels (Meisels, 2007; Schultz & Kagan, 2007). When assessment data are collected on only a small sample of children in a local program or classroom (see Figure 1), the information could not be used to make inappropriate decisions at the child level. An example of an inappropriate child-level decision would be using information from the Peabody Picture Vocabulary Test, a tool commonly used in early childhood program evaluations, to plan activities for the child or to deny a child entry to kindergarten. Concerns regarding inappropriate use of assessment information have been based on an assumption that the information being collected would not be sufficient for child-level planning. This has less applicability to EI and ECSE accountability where many states are making use of the information being collected for child-level decisions to inform accountability decisions.

A major disadvantage of using sampling is the reduced utility of the data for program improvement at levels below the targeted sampling level. For example, programs or classrooms in need of technical support or assistance cannot be easily identified based on data gathered for only a few children. Very few EI and ECSE state agencies use sampling to collect and report data to address the federal accountability requirements.

A Vision for the Next Generation of Assessment Tools

The challenges and trade-offs encountered by state agencies and early childhood programs as they build meaningful assessment of child outcomes into their accountability systems underscore the need for a new generation of early childhood assessment tools. Although many assessment tools in current use were innovative in their time, the science of assessment and child development have advanced considerably since their development and the needs for assessment tools (e.g., for accountability) have evolved over time (National Research Council, 2008; National Research Council and Institute of Medicine, 2000). We close with a summary of suggested key design features for the next generation of early childhood assessment tools.

The challenges and trade-offs encountered by state agencies and early childhood programs as they build meaningful assessment of child outcomes into their accountability systems underscore the need for a new generation of early childhood assessment tools.

We are operating from several premises. First, for purposes of both instructional planning and accountability, programs need a single tool that can address multiple areas of development and learning and provide information about child progress over time. There will always be a need for specialized tools to provide in-depth information in a particular developmental domain (e.g., motor) or content area (e.g., literacy). A tool designed to gather information about multiple areas of development will not replace these specialized tools. On the other hand, it is not sensible to expect a teacher or service provider to administer many different tools with different structures to get a multidimensional picture of a child. Second, a well-conceptualized tool could be used for multiple purposes such as informing instructional planning deci-

Table 3

Suggested Key Features for Next Generation of Early Childhood Assessment Tools

• Measure children's everyday behaviors.
• Gather information by making use of observations of children's behavior in everyday tasks and situations.
• Allow multiple ways to demonstrate competencies.
• Allow for input from multiple adults, including family members, who see the child in different situations.
• Apply principles of universal design.
• Measure children's development and learning over the entire period from birth to age 8.
• Provide information to address functional outcomes that cross domains along with information for the more commonly used domains.
• Provide information about age-expected functioning.
• Provide sufficient item density to measure status and progress of children.
• Address reliability of scoring in multiple ways, such as through item construction, professional development, and certification.
• Incorporate multiple methods of documentation.
• Utilize technology for assessment activities such as recording, scoring, and reporting of results.

sions, measuring progress, and supporting accountability if it is designed with these purposes in mind, and if it captures accurate and meaningful information about children in an appropriate way. A final premise is that the latest knowledge in assessment development will be applied and that the assessments will be held to high psychometric standards (American Educational Research Association et al., 1999; Bagnato, 2007; Bagnato et al., 2010; National Research Council, 2008; Neisworth & Bagnato, 2005).

Working from these premises, we have compiled a list of desirable features for the next generation of comprehensive early childhood assessment tools. In Table 3 we list these features. In the text, we describe the features and their importance for making decisions related to assessment data. The proposed features were drawn from a variety of sources, including the Division for Early Childhood (DEC) Recommended Practices, and our experiences in working with states to design and implement accountability systems (Division for Early Childhood, 2007; National Association Early Childhood Specialists in State Departments of Education & National Association for the Education of Young Children, 2003; National

Association of School Psychologists, 2009; Neisworth & Bagnato, 2005). Assessment tools currently available incorporate some of the features described, but no tool incorporates all of them.

The next generation of comprehensive early childhood assessment tools should:

- **Measure children's everyday behaviors**. To provide useful information about young children's behavior and learning in their typical activities, assessment tools must gather information about child behavior or performance in the context of typically occurring activities or tasks. Previous approaches to assessment development often led to the inclusion of unusual or decontextualized tasks because the task did a good job of making distinctions among children of varying abilities (Bailey, 2004). Contemporary assessments will need to build on current knowledge about development and developmental progressions to capture how children move to higher levels of complexity and competency in behaviors that are useful and important in their everyday life.
- **Gather information by making use of observations of children's behavior in everyday tasks and situations**. Because many young children will not perform behaviors on demand for a stranger or even someone they know, another option for gathering valid information about what children know and are able to do is to observe them displaying their skills and behaviors in everyday tasks and situations. Observations provide information about how and where children use skills functionally to accomplish everyday tasks. Observing across situations also provides information about mastery of a behavior or skill across situations, not only in limited contexts.
- **Allow multiple ways to demonstrate competencies**. Related to the emphasis on naturally occurring everyday behaviors is the recognition that many tasks of childhood can be solved in multiple ways and that there are multiple ways a child can show what he or she knows or knows how to do. This is especially important for young children whose response options might be limited because of a disability. Rigid criteria for response options almost certainly bias the task against some groups of children. Allowing multiple ways to show skill acquisition and mastery keeps the focus clearly on the underlying skill or concept (for example, Does the child have a concept of "many?" versus Can the child point to the picture with many?), and keeps the scoring from being unecessarily impacted by irrelevant performance requirements (e.g., must see or hear).
- **Allow for input from multiple adults, including family members, who see the child in different situations**. Getting input

from the different adults who see children in different situations gives a more complete, and for many young children, accurate, picture than can be obtained from observing behavior in a single setting. A complete understanding of children's functioning requires understanding how well skills generalize and how easily they are performed across situations (e.g., at home, in a play group, with parents, with other adults, etc.). Thus, gathering and combining information from multiple reporters provides a description of mastery across situations highlighting conditions where a skill is performed with ease and where it is less likely to be performed.

- **Apply principles of universal design.** Applying principles of universal design allows for more meaningful assessment of all children including children with disabilities, children who are dual language learners, or children from diverse cultures. Assessment tools that require children respond to highly structured tasks in very specific ways will by design necessitate the development of a variety of accommodations for the children who cannot participate in these kinds of assessment tasks. On the other hand, assessment tools that take advantage of children's naturally occurring behaviors and allow for multiple ways to demonstrate competence provide all children more opportunities to show what they know and can do. Even with universal design, some adaptations and accommodations may be required and detailed guidance on their use needs to be part of the development of any new assessment tool.

- **Measure children's development and learning over the entire period from birth to age 8**. One of the major shortcomings of current assessment tools is that many measure a narrow age range within early childhood, such as 3 to 5 years of age. An instrument with a narrow age range does not lend itself to tracking how an individual child changes over time because he or she soon crosses out of the bounds of the assessment tool. A narrow age range also creates problems for using the assessment with children with delays who are participating in preschool classrooms with same age peers, but who do not have skills at the same levels as peers. In keeping with the increased recognition of the value of longitudinal data (Early Childhood Data Collaborative, 2010), new tools need to track children's growth across the entire early childhood age span. Such tools will need to address the fact that early learning progressions may involve behaviors and skills that emerge in preschoolers that have no earlier counterpart (e.g., phonemic awareness).

- **Provide information to address functional outcomes that cross domains along with information for the more commonly used**

domains. Many state agencies collecting data for the three EI and ECSE outcomes have faced the same problem of how to reorganize information being collected by existing assessment tools into the three functional outcomes required for federal accountability. Functional outcomes can cross domains. For example, having positive social relationships with one's peers involves understanding social expectations, regulating one's own behavior, and being able to communicate appropriately. Tools developed to assess directly the three required outcomes would be easier to use and would provide data that are more valid and reliable for informing decisions about EI and ECSE accountability than tools that are currently available. Because other early childhood programs might define their outcomes in a more traditional domains-based framework, it will be important that the resulting information also addresses commonly used domains so that assessments can be used across a variety of early childhood programs. This should not be difficult to do if built into the design of the tool because children's everyday activities provide evidence for both functional behaviors and domain-based skills.

- **Provide information about age-expected functioning**. A fundamental principle of child development is that most children acquire skills in somewhat predictable sequences and within somewhat predictable age ranges (Blackman, 1999; King & Glascoe, 2003). This principle is the basis for the developmental milestone charts hanging in pediatricians' offices and the foundation for many developmental screening tools. When a child's development falls substantially outside of what is expected for his or her age, we provide EI or ECSE services because extremely slow skill acquisition is recognized as a serious problem with current and future negative consequences for the child (Meisels & Shonkoff, 2000; Sameroff, Seifer, Baldwin, & Baldwin, 1993). A number of current tools used for instructional planning provide practitioners with information about developmental and learning sequences, but do not provide information about the ages at which children would be expected to acquire these skills. Providing this additional information allows teachers and other practitioners to identify children who might require more intensive interventions because of their status or progress relative to what would be expected of same-age peers. Information that age anchors developmental tasks can be provided through assessment tools without requiring the decontextualized item administration of many norm-referenced tools. Professional development around age-anchored tools will need to stress appropriate and inappropriate uses of age expectations.

- **Provide for sufficient item density to measure status and progress of children.** One of the DEC recommended practices for assessment (A26) addresses the importance of assessment tools having sufficient item density to capture small increments of change being made by children with significant disabilities or delays (Neisworth & Bagnato, 2005). Children who are progressing slowly need assessments with items that capture small amounts of change, but very small increments between items would be inappropriate for many children. With computer adaptive testing, there is no reason that every child has to be assessed on the same set of items. Assessments can be designed to use a small number of items to efficiently pinpoint where a child is in a developmental progression and how much item density is appropriate. For example, computer adaptive testing was used to streamline the administration of a motor assessment targeting self-care and mobility domains (Haley, Ni, Fragala-Pinkham, Skrinar, & Corzo, 2005). The revised assessment was able to capture accurately children's motor ability with no more than 13% to 16% of the items in the full-length test. More information about computer adaptive testing is available from Waller and Reise (1989).
- **Address reliability of scoring in multiple ways such as through item construction, professional development, and certification.** Scoring criteria for some early childhood assessments, especially

tools designed for instructional planning, vary in how well they are defined. Such lack of specificity can create problems for score reliability (e.g., consistency of scores across examiners and time). If a tool is being used for instructional planning by teachers, then that tool still must be completed consistently in order to obtain accurate information about children's knowledge and skills (National Research Council, 2008). Achieving high levels of reliability must be built into the design of any tool by including detailed behaviorally based scoring criteria for each item and guidance for high quality professional development related to administration and scoring.

- **Incorporate multiple methods of documentation.** Observation-based assessments need documentation to support the accuracy of the scoring. Documentation is especially important when results are being used for accountability so program administrators can verify that scores are applied appropriately and without bias. Multiple forms of documentation should be built into the assessment system including observation notes, child work samples, photographs, and audio and video recordings (Jablon, Dombro, & Dichtelmiller, 1999; Losardo & Notari-Syverson, 2001).

- **Utilize technology for assessment activities, such as recording, scoring, and reporting of results.** Several current early childhood assessments have online capabilities to support item recording and report generation. Effective use of technology for assessment also includes online modules for professional development related to administration (Desired Results *access* Project, 2011b) and for documentation of children's products through photographs and of children's skills through video (Colorado Department of Education, 2011). Technology also can be used to tailor sets of items administered to children based on skill level of the child through computer adaptive testing as described above. Technology is changing so quickly that it is difficult to imagine the myriad of ways in which it will support effective assessment of young children in future years, but undoubtedly it is a powerful tool for addressing some of the challenges identified in this article and elsewhere (U.S. Department of Education, 2010). Web-based assessments also provide practitioners and parents with immediate and ongoing access to information.

Concluding Comments

State early intervention and early childhood special education agencies have made great strides in designing and implementing accountability systems that include data on child outcomes. Other early childhood programs are under pressure to follow suit. Valid and meaningful information about how programs are helping children develop and learn requires assessment tools that can be used to inform accountability decisions. We need 21st century early childhood assessment tools that incorporate scientific information from up-to-date research about early childhood development and assessment and that use new technologies. We look forward to a day when programs will be choosing among many good assessment options rather than deciding which shortcomings they can tolerate. With improved assessment tools, childhood accountability systems will be better positioned to generate valid information for multiple purposes, including decisions about successes and needed improvements across program levels within the service delivery system.

Note

Kathleen Hebbeler, Center for Education and Human Services, SRI International. Lauren Barton, Center for Education and Human Services, SRI International. Cornelia Taylor, Center for Education and Human Services, SRI International. Donna Spiker, Center for Education and Human Services, SRI International.

The contents of this article were developed under a cooperative agreement (#H324L030002) to SRI International from the Office of Special Education Programs, U.S. Department of Education. However, the content does not necessarily represent the policy of the Department of Education, and the reader should not assume endorsement by the Federal Government.

Correspondence concerning this article should be addressed to Kathleen Hebbeler, 600 Mockingbird Place, Davis, CA 95616. E-mail: kathleen.hebbeler@sri.com

References

American Educational Research Association, American Psychological Association, & National Council on Measurement in Education. (1999). *Standards for educational and psychological testing.* Washington, DC: American Psychological Association.

American Speech-Language-Hearing Association. (2008). *Roles and responsibilities of speech-language pathologists in early intervention* (Technical Report). Retrieved September 20, 2011 from www.asha.org/policy

Bagnato, S. J. (2007). *Authentic assessment for early childhood intervention: Best practices.* New York, NY: Guilford Press.

Bagnato, S. J. & Neisworth, J. T. (1994). A national study of the social and treatment "invalidity" of intelligence testing in early intervention. *School Psychology Quarterly, 9,* 81-102.

Bagnato, S. J., Neisworth, J. T., & Pretti-Frontczak, K. (2010). *LINKing authentic assessment and early childhood intervention: Best measures for best practices* (2nd ed.). Baltimore, MD: Brookes.

Bagnato, S. J., Suen, H. K., Brickley, D., Smith-Jones, J., & Dettore, E. (2002). Child developmental impact of Pittsburgh's Early Childhood Initiative (ECI) in high-risk communities: First-phase authentic evaluation research. *Early Childhood Research Quarterly, 17*(4), 559-580.

Bailey, D. (2004). Tests and test development. In M. McLean, M. Wolery, & D. B. Bailey, Jr. (Eds.), *Assessing infants and preschoolers with special needs* (3rd ed., pp. 22-44). Upper Saddle River, NJ: Pearson.

Blackman, J. A. (1999). Developmental screening: Infants, toddlers, and preschoolers. In M. D. Levine, W. B. Carey, & A. C. Crocker (Eds.), *Developmental-behavioral pediatrics* (3rd ed.). Philadelphia, PA: Saunders.

Center for Child and Family Studies. (n.d.). *Desired results for children and families.* Retrieved September 20, 2011 from http://www.wested.org/desiredresults/training/

Colorado Department of Education. (2011). *Results Matter video series on early childhood assessment.* Retrieved September 20, 2011 from http://www.cde.state.co.us/resultsmatter/RMVideoSeries.htm

Desired Results *access* Project. (2011a). Retrieved September 20, 2011 from http://www.draccess.org/

Desired Results *access* Project. (2011b). *Professional development.* Retrieved September 20, 2011 from http://draccess.org/prodevelopment/

Division for Early Childhood (DEC). (2007). *Promoting positive outcomes for children with disabilities: Recommendations for curriculum, assessment, and program evaluation.* Missoula, MT: Author.

Early Childhood Data Collaborative. (2010). *Building and using coordinated state early care and education systems: A framework for state policymakers*: Author. Retrieved September 20, 2011 from http://www.ecedata.org/files/DQC%20ECDC%20WhitePaper-Nov8.pdf

Early Childhood Outcomes Center. (2004). *Considerations related to developing a system for measuring outcomes for young children with disabilities and their families*. Menlo Park, CA: Author. Retrieved September 20, 2011 from http://www.fpg.unc.edu/~eco/assets/pdfs/considerations.pdf

Early Childhood Outcomes Center. (2005). *Comments from the Early Childhood Outcomes Center on proposed indicators for child and family outcomes*. Retrieved September 20, 2011 from http://www.fpg.unc.edu/~eco/assets/pdfs/ECO_response_to_OSEP_5-9-05.pdf

Early Childhood Outcomes Center. (2006). *Introduction to the ECO "crosswalks" of birth-to-five assessment instruments to early childhood outcomes*: Author. Retrieved September 20, 2011 from http://www.fpg.unc.edu/~eco/assets/pdfs/Crosswalk_intro.pdf

Government Performance and Results Act of 1993, Pub. L. No 103-62, §20, 107 Stat. 285.

Greenwood, C., Walker, D., Hornback, M., Wells, M., Hebbeler, K., Spiker, D., et al. (2008). *Validating the Child Outcomes Summary Form (COSF) for use in accountability systems for programs serving young children with disabilities*. Paper presented at the Conference on Research Innovations in Early Intervention (CRIEI), San Diego, CA.

Haley, S. M., Ni, P., Fragala-Pinkham, M. A., Skrinar, A. M., & Corzo, D. (2005). A computer adaptive testing approach for assessing physical functioning in children and adolescents. *Developmental Medicine & Child Neurology, 47*(2), 113-120.

Harbin, G., Rous, B., & McLean, M. (2005). Issues in designing state accountability systems. *Journal of Early Intervention, 27*, 137-164.

Hebbeler, K., & Barton, L. (2007). The need for data on child and family outcomes at the federal and state levels. *Young Exceptional Children Monograph Series, 9*, 1-15.

Hebbeler, K., Barton, L., & Mallik, S. (2008). Assessment and accountability for programs serving young children with disabilities. *Exceptionality, 16*(1), 48-63.

Jablon, J. R., Dombro, A. L., & Dichtelmiller, M. L. (Eds.). (1999). *The power of observation*. Washington, DC: Teaching Strategies.

Kelley, M. F., & Surbeck, E. (2007). History of preschool assessment. In B. Bracken & R. Nagle (Eds.), *Psychoeducational assessment of preschool children* (4th ed., pp. 3-28). Mahwah, NJ: Erlbaum.

King, T. M. & Glascoe, F. B. (2003). Developmental surveillance of infants and young children in pediatric primary care. *Current Opinion in Pediatrics, 15*(6), 624-629.

Losardo, A. & Notari-Syverson, A. (2001). *Alternative approaches to assessing young children*. Baltimore, MD: Brookes.

McLean, M. (2004). Assessment and its importance in early intervention/early childhood special education. In M. McLean, M. Wolery, & D. B. Bailey, Jr. (Eds.), *Assessing infants and preschoolers with special needs* (3rd ed., pp. 1-21). Upper Saddle River, NJ: Pearson.

McLean, M., Wolery, M., & Bailey, D. B., Jr. (2004). *Assessing infants and preschoolers with special needs* (3rd ed.). Upper Saddle River, NJ: Prentice Hall.

Meisels, S. J. (2007). Accountability in early childhood: No easy answers. In R. C. Pianta, M. J. Cox, & K. L. Snow (Eds.), *School readiness and the transition to kindergarten in the era of accountability* (pp. 31-47). Baltimore, MD: Brookes.

Meisels, S. J. & Atkins-Burnett, S. (2004). The Head Start National Reporting System: A critique. *Young Children, 59*(1), 64-66.

Meisels, S. J. & Shonkoff, J. P. (2000). Early childhood intervention: A continuing evolution. In J. P. Shonkoff & S. J. Meisels (Eds.), *Handbook of early childhood intervention* (2nd ed., pp. 3-34). New York, NY: Cambridge University Press.

Mintrop, H. & Sunderman, G. L. (2009). Predictable failure of federal sanctions-driven accountability for school improvement—and why we may retain it anyway. *Educational Researcher, 38*(5), 353-364. doi: 10.3102/0013189x09339055

National Association Early Childhood Specialists in State Departments of Education (NAECS/SDE), & National Association for the Education of Young Children (NAEYC). (2003). *Early childhood curriculum, assessment, and program evaluation: Building an effective, accountable system in programs for children birth through age 8* (Position Statement with expanded resources): National Association Early Childhood Specialists in State Departments of Education (NAECS/SDE), National Association for the Education of Young Children. Retrieved September 20, 2011 from www.naeyc.org/resources/position_statements/pscape.pdf

National Association of School Psychologists. (2009). *Position statement on early childhood assessment*. Bethesda, MD: Author.

National Child Care Information and Technical Assistance Center. (n.d.). State early learning guidelines. Retrieved September 20, 2011 from http://nccic.acf.hhs.gov/resource/state-early-learning-guidelines

National Research Council. (2008). *Early childhood assessment: Why, what, and how?* Committee on Developmental Outcomes and Assessments for Young Children, C. E. Snow & S. B. Van Hemel (Eds.). Board on Children, Youth and Families, Board on Testing and Assessment, Division of Behavioral and Social Sciences and Education. Washington, DC: National Academies Press.

National Research Council and Institute of Medicine. (2000). *From neurons to neighborhoods: The science of early childhood development.* Committee on Integrating the Science of Early Childhood Development, J. P. Shonkoff, & D. A. Phillips (Eds.). Board on Children, Youth, and Families, National Research Council, and Institute of Medicine. Washington, DC: National Academies Press.

Neisworth, J. T. & Bagnato, S. J. (2004). The mismeasure of young children: The authentic assessment alternative. *Infants and Young Children, 17*(3), 198-212.

Neisworth, J. T. & Bagnato, S. J. (2005). DEC recommended practices: Assessment. In S. Sandall, M. L. Hernandez, B. J. Smith, & M. E. McLean (Eds.), *DEC recommended practices: A comprehensive guide for practical application in early intervention/early childhood special education* (pp. 45-70). Longmont, CO: Sopris West.

Sameroff, A. J., Seifer, R., Baldwin, A., & Baldwin, C. (1993). Stability of intelligence from preschool to adolescence: The influence of social and family risk factors. *Child Development, 64*, 80-97.

Schultz, T. & Kagan, S. L. (2007). *Taking stock: Assessing and improving early childhood learning and program quality.* Washington, DC: Pew Charitable Trusts. Retrieved September 20, 2011 from http://www.pewtrusts.org/uploadedFiles/wwwpewtrustsorg/Reports/Pre-k_education/task_force_report1.pdf

Scott-Little, C., Kagan, S. L., Stebbins Frelow, V., & Reid, J. (2009). Infant-toddler early learning guidelines: The content that states have addressed and implications for programs serving children with disabilities. *Infants and Young Children, 22*(2), 87-99. doi: 10.1097/IYC.1090b1013e3181a1002f1094b

Shepard, L., Kagan, S. L., & Wurtz, E. (1998). *Principles and recommendations for early childhood assessments.* Washington, DC: National Education Goals Panel.

Stecher, B. M., Camm, F., Damberg, C. L., Hamilton, L. S., Mullen, K. J., Nelson, C., et al. (2010). *Toward a culture of consequences. Performance-based accountability systems for public services.* Santa Monica, CA: RAND Corporation.

Thompson, S. J., Johnstone, C. J., & Thurlow, M. L. (2002). *Universal design applied to large-scale assessments* (Synthesis Report 44). Minneapolis, MN: University of Minnesota, National Center on Educational Outcomes. Retrieved September 20, 2011 from http://www.cehd.umn.edu/NCEO/OnlinePubs/Synth44.pdf

U.S. Department of Education, Office of Educational Technology. (2010). *Transforming American education: Learning powered by technology. Draft National Education Technology Plan 2010.* Washington, DC: Author.

U.S. Department of Health and Human Serivces. (2010). *The Head Start child development and early learning framework: Promoting positive outcomes in early childhood programs serving children 3-5 years old.* Washington, DC: Author.

Waller, N. G. & Reise, S. P. (1989). Computerized adaptive personality assessment: An illustration with the Absorption scale. *Journal of Personality and Social Psychology, 57*(6), 1051-1058. doi: 10.1037/0022-3514.57.6.1051

Wolery, M. (1983). Proportional change index: An alternative for comparing child change data. *Exceptional Children 50*(2), 167-170.

Zigler, E. & Styfco, S. J. (2004). Head Start's national reporting system: A work in progress. *Pediatrics, 114*, 858-859. doi: 10.1542/peds.2004-0707

Resources
Within Reason
Assessment

Camille Catlett, M.A.,
University of North Carolina-Chapel Hill

Here you'll find additional resources to support the effective gathering, sharing, and use of information about infants, toddlers, and young children and their families. Resources range in price. Many are within an individual's budget while others may be more suitable for purchase by an agency or school.

Position Statements/Recommended Practices

DEC Recommended Practices in Early Intervention/Early Childhood Special Education: A Comprehensive Guide for Practical Application
S. Sandall, M. L. Hemmeter, B. J. Smith, and M. E. McLean. (2005).

This document is a good source for information about recommended practices and strategies for using them. Chapter 3 (Recommended Practices in Assessment) by John T. Neisworth and Stephen J. Bagnato offers definitions of terms, delineation of quality features, and a checklist for personal or program assessment practices. Missoula, MT: Author. Cost: $35.00.

Early Childhood Assessment

This document is a position statement on early childhood assessment from the National Association of School Psychologists.

http://www.nasponline.org/about_nasp/pospaper_eca.aspx

Early Childhood Curriculum, Assessment and Program Evaluation: Building an Effective, Accountable System in Programs for Children Birth through Age 8

What should children be taught in the years from birth through age 8? How would we know if they are developing well and learning what we want them to learn? And how could we decide whether programs for children from infancy through primary grades are doing a good job? Answers to these questions—questions about early childhood curriculum, child assessment, and program evaluation—are the foundation of this position statement from the National Association for the Education of Young Children and the National Association of Early Childhood Specialists in State Departments of Education.

> http://www.naeyc.org/files/naeyc/file/positions/pscape.pdf
> A two-page introduction, *Where We Stand on Curriculum, Assessment and Program Evaluation*, is available at:
> http://www.naeyc.org/files/naeyc/file/positions/StandCurrAss.pdf
> Expanded resources are available at:
> http://www.naeyc.org/files/naeyc/file/positions/CAPEexpand.pdf
> A supplement on screening and assessment of young English language learners is available at:
> http://www.naeyc.org/files/naeyc/file/positions/ELL_SupplementLong.pdf

Identifying Infants and Young Children With Developmental Disorders in the Medical Home: An Algorithm for Developmental Surveillance and Screening

This statement from the American Academy of Pediatrics provides an algorithm as a strategy to support health care professionals in developing a pattern and practice for addressing developmental concerns in children from birth through 3 years of age.

> http://aappolicy.aappublications.org/cgi/content/full/pediatrics;118/1/405

Promoting Positive Outcomes for Children with Disabilities: Recommendations for Curriculum, Assessment and Program Evaluation

This paper focuses specifically on children with disabilities, and is meant to serve as a companion document to the 2003 joint position statement, *Early Childhood Curriculum, Assessment and Program Evaluation–Building an Effective, Accountable System in Programs for Children Birth through Age 8* (see above).

> http://www.dec-sped.org/uploads/docs/about_dec/position_concept_papers/Prmtg_Pos_
> Outcomes_Companion_Paper.pdf

Books

Alternative Approaches to Assessing Young Children
A. Losardo & A. Notari-Syverson. (2011). (2nd ed.)

Six alternative assessment methods for young children (naturalistic, focused, performance, portfolio, dynamic, curriculum-based language) are detailed in this book. Chapters offer thorough descriptions of each approach, along with summaries of advantages and limitations, guidelines for implementation, suggestions for use in inclusive environments and samples of data collection forms. A companion CD-ROM includes more than two dozen printable forms for data collection, observation, progress monitoring, and IEP/IFSP development. Baltimore: Paul Brookes. Cost: $39.95.

Assessing Young Children in Inclusive Settings:
The Blended Practices Approach
J. Grisham-Brown & K. Pretti-Frontczak. (2011).

Research and recommended practices addressed in this book include (1) conducting authentic assessments during children's natural routines and play activities, (2) using assessment to inform effective program planning both for individual children and groups, (3) involving family members as collaborative partners, and (4) selecting assessment instruments. Specific attention is paid to assessing children of culturally, linguistically, and ability-diverse backgrounds. Cost: $34.95.

LINKing Authentic Assessment and Early Childhood
Intervention Best Measures for Best Practices
S. J. Bagnato, J. T. Neisworth, & K. Pretti-Frontczak. (2010).
(2nd ed.)

This book offers professional ratings and reviews of 80 authentic, widely used assessment tools for children from birth to age 8. Chapters focus on current best practices in authentic assessment, alignment with developmentally appropriate practice, and future directions for responsible assessment and intervention practices. Baltimore: Paul Brookes. Cost: $49.95.

Transdisciplinary Play-Based Assessment
T. W. Linder. (2008).

Creative strategies for gathering information about young children ages birth to 6 using natural play interactions are offered in this monograph. The book includes step-by-step guidelines for conducting play sessions, involving parents, working as a team, determining eligibility, writing reports, and linking assessment to play-based intervention activities that foster children's development. Baltimore: Paul Brookes. Cost: $54.95.

Using IGDIs: Monitoring Progress and Improving Intervention for Infants and Young Children
J. Carta, C. Greenwood, D. Walker, & J. Buzhardt. (2010).

Here is a comprehensive guide to successful use of all five Infant and Toddler Indicators of Growth and Development for Infants and Toddlers (IGDI) measures and their related support tools to inform and support your use of IGDI measures for progress monitoring and intervention decision making. Baltimore: Paul Brookes. Cost: $34.95.

Videotapes

Authentic Assessment in Early Intervention

Physical therapist Megan Klish Fibbe describes and illustrates how authentic assessment practices enhance her early intervention work with children and their families, including the use of observation, conversations with families, and video.

http://www.cde.state.co.us/media/ResultsMatter/RMSeries/AuthenticAssessInEI_SA.asp

Downloadable Video Series on Early Childhood Assessment

The Colorado Department of Education's Results Matter Program has developed a collection of videos that helps providers better understand ways to use observation, documentation, and assessment to inform practice. Two styles of videos are provided: (1) practitioners discussing and illustrating their exemplary practices; and (2) clips for practicing observation, documentation and assessment skills, showing children participating in typical routines and activities. Videos may be watched online or downloaded for use in educational and professional development activities. Some clips focus on early intervention topics; others focus more broadly on early care and education content.

http://www.cde.state.co.us/resultsmatter/RMVideoSeries.htm

Web Resources

Asking the Right Questions in the Right Ways: Strategies for Ethnographic Interviewing

This classic article by Westby, Burda, and Mehta provides a succinct summary of how to use questions effectively in gathering information. What to ask and how to ask it are both covered, and three charts summarize examples for expanding a repertoire of open-ended options.

http://www.asha.org/Publications/leader/2003/030429/f030429b.htm

Assessment Considerations for Young English Language Learners (ELLs) Across Different Levels of Accountability
L. M. Espinosa & M. L. López. (2007).

This report begins with a discussion of the changing demographics of the population of young children, the nature of the linguistic diversity in early education settings, and the implications of this increased diversity for dual language and literacy development during the preschool years. This is followed by a discussion of the major assessment considerations and recommendations for young ELLs. The final sections describe challenges in assessing young ELLs, effective strategies, and offer recommendations for the development of more comprehensive and integrated systems of assessment for ELL children, across the different levels of accountability.

http://www.pewtrusts.org/uploadedFiles/wwwpewtrustsorg/Reports/Pre-k_education/
Assessment%20for%20Young%20ELLs-Pew%208-11-07-Final.pdf

Developmental Screening, Assessment, and Evaluation: Key Elements for Individualizing Curricula in Early Head Start Programs (Technical Assistance Paper No. 4)

This paper provides guidelines for each element of the developmental process and offers appropriate principles for screening, assessment and evaluation. To aid program staff, this guide also suggests practices to avoid and identifies individualized strategies most likely to lead to a child's fullest potential. The guide also stresses the importance of determining the appropriateness of informal, as well as formal, evaluation methods.

http://eclkc.ohs.acf.hhs.gov/hslc/resources/ECLKC_Bookstore/PDFs/FinalTAP%5B1%5D.pdf

Developmental Screening and Assessment Instruments with an Emphasis on Social and Emotional Development for Young Children Ages Birth Through 5

The National Early Childhood Technical Assistance Center has compiled comprehensive information about early childhood (birth through age 5) developmental screening and assessment instruments, with a focus on social and emotional development. Almost 40 instruments are categorized by whether they address multiple domains of development or whether they focus on social emotional development. Each instrument comes with a description and information about the age range for which it is appropriate, the time needed to administer the instrument, how scoring works, and who should conduct the screening.

http://www.nectac.org/~pdfs/pubs/screening.pdf

Early Childhood Assessment: Why, What, and How
C. E. Snow & S. B. Van Hemel. (2008).

The charge to the Committee on Developmental Outcomes and Assessments for Young Children, which orchestrated and edited this work, was the identification of important outcomes for children from birth to age 5 and the quality and purposes of different techniques and instruments for developmental assessments. In addition to thoroughly addressing the original charge, the summary presents guidelines for assessment related to four issues: purposes, domains and measures, implementation, and systems. Washington, DC: The National Academies Press. Cost: $59.95.

http://www.nap.edu/openbook.php?record_id=12446&page=R1

Early Identification of Culturally and Linguistically Diverse Children (Aged Birth Through 5)

When assessing young children for early intervention or special education services, appropriate procedures need to be in place to determine which language will be used to conduct assessments and to ensure that appropriate assessment/screening tools are being used. It is critical to obtain a non-biased picture of the child's abilities, in order to determine whether certain patterns of development and behavior are caused by a disability or are simply the result of cultural and linguistic differences. This webpage provides a selection of resources that address these issues.

http://www.nectac.org/topics/earlyid/diverse.asp

Early Identification of Specific Disabilities and Children At-Risk

The National Early Childhood Technical Assistance Center has compiled a variety of helpful and informative resources at this site. Information is organized by category (e.g., attention deficit/hyperactivity disorder, autism spectrum disorders, deaf/blind, developmental delay).

http://www.nectac.org/topics/earlyid/idspecpops.asp

ECO Resources: Instrument Crosswalks

In the process of working with states on outcome development and measurement approaches, the ECO Center cross-referenced the functional skills assessed by various published instruments with the three child outcomes required by OSEP for Part B/619 and Part C programs, to assess the degree to which these instruments measure the required outcomes. Crosswalks were generated for instruments based on the frequency of informal requests from states. Priority was also given to instruments that states identified for outcomes measurement. These crosswalks are presented as a service to the field with the understanding that the ECO Center does not endorse the use of any specific assessment instrument.

http://www.fpg.unc.edu/~eco/pages/crosswalks.cfm#Crosswalks

Get It Got It Go: Tools for Improving Children's Developmental Outcomes

This University of Minnesota site provides materials and assessment tools for measuring the developmental growth of young children. In addition, the site includes information about the background of the Get It Got It Go assessment model and assessment types.

http://ggg.umn.edu/

Indicators of Growth and Development for Infants and Toddlers (IGDI's)

IGDI's are a set of measures designed and validated for use by early childhood practitioners to monitor infant and toddler growth and progress. Unlike standardized tests that are administered infrequently, IGDI's are designed to be used repeatedly by practitioners to estimate each child's "rate of growth" over time. The benefit of this approach is that the information can be used to make data-based decisions about intervention design and implementation at reasonable levels of training, time, and cost.

http://www.igdi.ku.edu/

Preschool Assessment: A Guide to Developing a Balanced Approach

The National Institute for Early Education Research has used this issue of *Preschool Policy Facts* to summarize what is known about effective assessment, why it's important, and how to do it in ways that are reliable and valid.

http://nieer.org/resources/factsheets/12.pdf

Research Synthesis on Screening and Assessing Social-Emotional Competence

This synthesis provides information for early care and education providers on using evidence-based practices in screening and assessing the social-emotional competence of infants, toddlers, and young children. The synthesis is organized around common questions related to screening and assessing social-emotional competence. It begins with a discussion of what is meant by social-emotional competence, and then describes general issues and challenges around screening and assessment. The authors then discuss the roles of families, culture, and language in screening and assessing social-emotional competence, and end with a list of resources and some examples of social and emotional screening and assessment tools.

http://csefel.vanderbilt.edu/documents/rs_screening_assessment.pdf